Principles of Faith
(Rosh Amanah)

THE LITTMAN LIBRARY OF JEWISH CIVILIZATION

EDITORS

David Goldstein
Louis Jacobs
Vivian D. Lipman

This Library is dedicated to the memory of
JOSEPH AARON LITTMAN

Principles of Faith
(Rosh Amanah)

Isaac Abravanel

Translated with an Introduction and Notes
by *Menachem Marc Kellner*

Rutherford • Madison • Teaneck
Fairleigh Dickinson University Press
London and Toronto: Associated University Presses

Associated University Presses, Inc.
4 Cornwall Drive
East Brunswick, N. J. 08816

Associated University Presses Ltd
69 Fleet Street
London EC4Y 1EU, England

Associated University Presses
Toronto, Ontario, Canada M5E 1A7

Library of Congress Cataloging in Publication Data

Abravanel, Isaac, 1437–1508.
  Principles of faith—Rosh amanah.

  (Littman Library of Jewish civilization)
  Translation of Rosh amanah.
  Bibliography: p.
  1. Judaism—Works to 1900. 2. Thirteen articles
of faith (Judaism) I. Kellner, Menachem Marc,
1946–   II. Title. III. Title: Rosh amanah.
BM550.A19613   1981   296.3   80-67697
ISBN 0-8386-3080-4

Printed in the United States of America

To the Memory of My Parents,
Rabbi Abraham A. Kellner
and Rebbitzen Kay T. Kellner

Contents

List of Tables

Note on the Text and Translation

The *Rosh Amanah* was written by Don Isaac Abravanel (1437–1508) in 1494 in Naples, two years after its author had been expelled from Spain. It was the first of Abravanel's works to be printed, appearing in that form in Constantinople in 1505.[1] The book has been published in at least nine subsequent editions, making it one of Abravanel's most published works. After the Constantinople edition, the Rosh Amanah was next published in Venice, 1545; Cremona, 1557; Altona, 1750 and 1770; Tarnopol, 1813; Koenigsberg, 1861; Warsaw, 1881 and 1884; and Tel Aviv, 1958.[2] The Constantinople edition was reproduced in Don Isaac Abravanel, *Opera Minora* (London, 1972). There exists one complete manuscript of the *Rosh Amanah* (Ms. Munich Cod. Hebr. 92, fol, 161–205). The manuscript, however, postdates the *editio princeps* and is quite evidently based upon it.

The *editio princeps* serves as the basis for the present translation. I have also consulted the Cremona and Tel Aviv editions. The former corrects some of the obvious misprints of the first edition and provides sources for a few of the biblical and rabbinic citations. Aryeh Albert produced the Tel Aviv edition, basing it, as it appears, on the Cremona text. He introduced paragraphing and some punctuation, but often in an idiosyncratic manner.

The *Rosh Amanah* was translated in its entirety into Latin and French while the first five chapters only were translated into English. The Latin translation, by Guilielmum Vorstium, was published in Amsterdam in 1638 under the title *Liber de capite fidei*. It was published again in 1684. This translation contains several long notes by the translator. B. Mossé authored the French translation (based on the Cremona text)

11

and called it *Le principe de la foi* (Avignon, 1884). This was recently reproduced on microfiche by Inter Documentation Company (Zug, Switzerland, n.d.). Isaac Mayer Wise's very loose English translation of chapters one through five appeared in *The Israelite* (Cincinnati, 1862), 8: 212, 220–21, 228–29, 236–37, and 244–45. Wise called it *The Book on the Cardinal Points of Religion*.

The name *Rosh Amanah* was derived from a play on the words of Song of Songs 4:8.[3] There is no scholarly unanimity on how best to translate the title. Solomon Schechter, in his "Dogmas of Judaism," included in the first series of his *Studies in Judaism* (Philadelphia, 1905), p. 174, simply calls it *Top of Amanah*. Theodore Gaster, "Abravanel's Literary Work," in Trend and Loewe, eds., *Isaac Abravanel: Six Lectures* (Cambridge, 1937), p. 48, renders it as *The Essentials of Faith*. Jacob Minkin, *Abarbanel and the Expulsion of the Jews from Spain* (New York, 1938), p. 221, translates the title as *Foundation of Faith*. *Pinnacle of Faith* is the rendition adopted by Louis Jacobs in his *Principles of the Jewish Faith* (New York, 1964), p. 23. Benzion Netanyahu, *Don Isaac Abravanel: Statesman and Philosopher,* 3rd ed. (Philadelphia, 1972), p. 285, translates *Rosh Amanah* as *Principles of Faith*. Netanyahu cites the poetic dedication of Abravanel's son Don Judah to the *Rosh Amanah* and Abravanel's own introduction to the work in support of his translation of the title. Don Judah's poem, which is included in all the editions of the *Rosh Amanah*, ends with the words "And in it are the roots and principles {*rashei;* literally, "heads"} of beliefs; therefore did my father call it *Rosh Amanah.*" Abravanel's introduction is couched in what is called *lashon meshubeẓet;* it is a tour de force of biblical and rabbinic texts and citations strung together in a way which resists direct translation. There can be no doubt from Don Isaac's last line, however, that Netanyahu is correct and that Abravanel meant what we would call *Principles of Faith* by *Rosh Amanah*.

Abravanel's introduction is not translated in this edition. An actual translation would not be intelligible in English and a paraphrase would lose all of the flavor and much of the sense of the original. In this introduction he explains that he wrote the book for two reasons. First, because the Jewish people were becoming confused by the plethora of competing lists of principles put forward in his time and, second, in order to defend the honor of Maimonides in the face of the attacks of his critics, especially Crescas and Albo. In the introduction below I point out how faithful Abravanel was to his self-appointed task.

The text of the *Rosh Amanah* itself is highly eclectic. Abravanel works biblical verses and rabbinic dicta into his prose very liberally and in some places borrows so heavily from earlier writers that he opens himself to the charge of plagiarism. The book gives every indication of having been written hastily. It is repetitious, often poorly organized, and written in a Hebrew which is frequently graceless and sometimes downright ungrammatical. In a number of places biblical verses are quoted incorrectly. Sometimes this seems to be done purposefully, but there are several places where it is clearly a mistake, although whether it is Abravanel's fault or that of his printer I cannot say.

In the present translation I have sought to walk the fine line between faithfulness to the original text, on the one hand, and respect for the English language and the patience of my readers, on the other. I have introduced words and phrases that were not found in the original but which were clearly demanded by the plain sense of the Hebrew. I have placed in brackets all additions which were not clearly needed in this way but which I supplied to aid intelligibility. Punctuation and paragraphing is, of course, my own. Where I have significantly altered the reading on stylistic grounds I have given the literal translation in a note. Where I have adopted a translation which might reasonably be construed as idiosyncratic, or where I translate a technical term, I have supplied the Hebrew original (transliterated according to the system of the *Encyclopaedia Judaica*) in a note.

Wherever possible, I have used already published English translations of sources quoted by Abravanel. I have done this not only in order to make it easier for the non-Hebrew reader to locate these sources in their contexts, but also so that there would be some noticeable stylistic difference between Abravanel and those whom he quotes, just as there is in the original Hebrew. I have not hesitated to introduce minor emendations into these translations wherever I thought it necessary. Biblical quotations are from the original Jewish Publication Society translation. I have purposely not recast any of them: the archaic and somewhat stilted English of the JPS translation makes them stand out much as they do in the Hebrew of the *Rosh Amanah*. I have on occasion supplied in square brackets portions of verses omitted by Abravanel. Biblical material is everywhere italicized. Quotations from the Babylonian Talmud are taken from the Soncino edition.

In translating names I have omitted honorifics and prayers for the peace of the deceased. Thus, in place of Abravanel's "The Rabbi and Guide" and "Moses, our Master, peace upon him," I simply have "Maimonides" and "Moses." I have everywhere translated expressions denoting the Deity as "God."

Acknowledgments

It is a pleasure to acknowledge the assistance of friends and colleagues who have helped at various points in the preparation of this study. Although I am certainly grateful to my wife, Jolene S. Kellner, for all those things for which authors customarily thank their wives in contexts such as this, in the present case my indebtedness is actually much greater and more concrete. Not only did she help compile the list of biblical and rabbinic citations, but she actually read the Hebrew text of the *Rosh Amanah* to me twice; once when I established the text on the basis of which the present translation was made and once again when I checked the translation against the text. For this, and for simply being what she is, I am deeply grateful.

Three people have had more influence on me than anyone else. To two of them this book is dedicated. The third is Steven Schwarzschild, from whose sage counsel and guidance I have benefited at every stage of this work.

Whatever felicity of style is found in this book is due to the careful criticism of Mrs. Tyra Lieberman, who examined every line of it with patience and care. Rabbi Yisroel Kellner was unfailingly helpful in tracing obscure rabbinic citations and in suggesting translations for difficult passages. Other individuals who were kind enough to answer queries of mine on various points include Norbert Samuelson, Shalom Rosenberg, Avraham Nuriel, Michael Glatzer, and David Groner. I am grateful to them all and here record my thanks.

David Goldstein, editor of the Littman Library of Jewish Civilization, responded promptly and helpfully to my many questions and thereby made my work much easier. Mrs. Esther Toledano of the University of Haifa typed the manu-

15

script with care. My parents-in-love, Rabbi and Mrs. Abraham B. Shoulson, have been unfailingly helpful and supportive. To all these individuals I am very much indebted.

This book was completed, and these lines are being written, in the truly congenial surroundings of the Department of Jewish Thought at the University of Haifa. I am grateful to my colleagues in the department, especially Professor Sarah Heller Wilensky and Dr. Mordecai Pachter, for everything they have done to make my year among them so pleasant and rewarding an experience.

The manuscript of this book was typed with the generous assistance of the Research Authority of the University of Haifa and the Small Grants Committee of the University of Virginia.

Finally, I would like to thank my children, Avinoam David and Rivka Temima, for the gracious way in which they occasionally allowed me the use of my study.

Grateful acknowledgment is hereby made to the following publishers for allowing me to use previously published materials:

Journal of the American Academy of Religion for permission to use M. M. Kellner, "R. Isaac Abravanel on the Principles of Judaism," *JAAR* 45/4 Supplement (December 1977), pp. 1183–1200.

Tradition for permission to use M. M. Kellner, "R. Isaac Abravanel on Maimonides' Principles of Faith."

Jewish Quarterly Review for permission to use M. M. Kellner, "Maimonides, Crescas, and Abravanel on Exodus 20:2: A Medieval Jewish Exegetical Dispute," *J.Q.R.* 69 (January 1979), pp. 129–57.

The Jewish Publication Society of America for its courtesy in allowing me to reprint portions of its editions of *The Holy Scriptures* and Joseph Albo's *Sefer Ha-Ikkarim*, both copyrighted by the Jewish Publication Society of America.

The Soncino Press for its courtesy in allowing me to reprint portions of its editions of *The Babylonian Talmud, Midrash Rabbah*, and Maimonides' *Sefer Ha-Mitzvoth*, all copyrighted by the Soncino Press.

Introduction

Maimonides' formulation of thirteen principles of faith marked an important development in the history of Jewish theology.[1] His innovation, however, did not go unchallenged. Maimonides was attacked from two directions. Some critics accepted his claim that Judaism had principles of faith but disagreed with his formulation and enumeration of them. Others rejected the project of creed formulation altogether and attacked Maimonides for listing any dogmas or principles at all. They did not claim that Judaism had no beliefs (the "dogma of dogmalessness" was unknown in the medieval period) but, rather, that all the beliefs of Judaism were its foundations and that one could not single out any particular beliefs as "principles" of Judaism. The *locus classicus* for the enunciation of this position is R. Isaac Abravanel's *Rosh Amanah*. This dispute is of considerable significance: basically it involves two entirely different views of what Judaism is. Maimonides and those who followed him held that Judaism had some theological essence or basis which could be expressed in a series of fundamental principles. Those whom Abravanel represents denied this claim and maintained, in effect, that the heart of Judaism was its entire body.

The dispute between Maimonides and Abravanel on this issue also involves the wider question of the relationship between Judaism and philosophy. As I will discuss again below in greater detail, one of the unarticulated items on the agenda of many of those who sought to enumerate the principles of Judaism was to make possible philosophical speculation on religious beliefs. By establishing clear-cut criteria for religious orthodoxy, they were making it possible for the philosopher to engage in philosophical speculation on beliefs not included in the list of basic dogmas without fear of being accused of heresy. By establishing the minimal criteria of religious orthodoxy, then, Maimonides and his followers in effect made Jewish philosophy possible. Abravanel, however, denied that there are any minimal criteria of religious orthodoxy (since all beliefs are primary, and none are secondary) and thus sought to make Jewish philosophy impossible.

Maimonides' enumeration of the principles of Judaism is found in his commentary to the Mishnah. The *Siraj (Maor* or *Illumination),* as this Arabic work is called, was his first major literary production. It was written in Maimonides' youth, during a period of great personal dislocation, as he fled the Almohade persecutions in his native Cordova. The principles themselves are found in the introduction to his commentary to the first mishnah in the tenth chapter of Sanhedrin *(Perek Ḥelek).* The mishnah reads:

> All Israel have a share in the world to come, for it is written, *Thy people are all righteous; they shall inherit the land forever, the branch of my planting, the work of my hands, that I may be glorified* [Isaiah 60:22]. But the following have no portion therein: he who maintains that resurrection is not a biblical doctrine, the Torah was not divinely revealed, and an *apikoros.* [2]

Maimonides takes the opportunity provided by this mishnah to formulate his vision of the eschaton, describing the days of the Messiah in detail. To this description he appends a list of those beliefs which a Jew must hold in order to merit immortality. In summary form they are (1) that God exists; (2) that God is one; (3) that God is incorporeal; (4) that God is eternal; (5) that God alone may be worshipped; (6) that prophecy exists; (7) that the prophecy of Moses is superior to all other prophecy; (8) that the Torah was divinely revealed; (9) that the Torah is immutable; (10) that God knows the deeds of men; (11) that God rewards the righteous and punishes the wicked; (12) that the Messiah will come; (13) that the dead will be resurrected. [3]

The holding of these principles not only defines a Jew—an innovation in and of itself because Maimonides was the first

Jewish thinker to make being Jewish dependent upon belief—but it is also a necessary condition for a person to attain immortality. Maimonides says:

> When a man believes in all these fundamental principles, and his faith is thus clarified, he is then part of that "Israel" whom we are to love, pity, and treat, as God commanded, with love and fellowship. Even if a Jew should commit every possible sin, out of lust or mastery by his lower nature, he will be punished for his sins but will still have a share in the world to come. He is one of the "sinners in Israel." But if a man gives up any of these fundamental principles, he has removed himself from the Jewish community. He is an atheist, a heretic, an unbeliever who "cuts among the plantings." We are commanded to hate him and destroy him. Of him it is said: *Shall I not hate those who hate You, O Lord?* [Psalms 139:21].[4]

This claim about the saving character of the principles elevated them to the status of dogma in the strict sense. It was a radical move, one for which Maimonides had very little precedent.

Abravanel's approach to this issue was complex. Although he was a vociferous critic of the Jewish Aristotelians,[5] he had profound respect for Maimonides. This tension is evident in the *Rosh Amanah*. The book was written, Abravanel informs the reader, to defend Maimonides against those who rejected his formulation and enumeration of the principles, particularly Don Ḥasdai Crescas (1340–1410) and the latter's pupil, Joseph Albo (fifteenth century).[6] The first twenty-two chapters of the *Rosh Amanah* are devoted to an extended and subtle defense of Maimonides. Abravanel's discussion here has been called "the most thorough analytic study of the 'thirteen principles' " available.[7] In chapter twenty-three, however, Abravanel performs a notorious about-face and attacks the very possibility of creed formulation in Judaism, insisting that Judaism has no dogmas or principles and that every single one of its precepts and beliefs is as important as every other one.

The book follows a strictly logical order of development. It begins with a citation of the thirteen principles themselves, in an otherwise unknown Hebrew translation.[8] Abravanel then summarizes the opinions of Crescas and Albo before devoting four chapters (3 through 6) to a listing of twenty-eight objections to Maimonides' principles, twenty of which he culled primarily from the writings of Crescas and Albo and eight of which he raised himself. This procedure is Abravanel's standard practice in almost all of his philosophical and exegetical works. First he raises a series of questions and then he proceeds to answer them. In the next six chapters Abravanel discusses nine propositions which he presents as being necessary for his argument. Having established the ground rules for his discussion, Abravanel proceeds to take up the objections seriatim, disposing of each in turn in chapters 12 through 21. In chapter 22 he criticizes the creedal formulations of Crescas and Albo. He also notes that, if he had to choose principles for the Jewish faith, he would put forward only one, creation. Chapter 23 contains his arguments against Jewish credalism while chapter 24 is occupied with a defense of his claim that Judaism has no dogmas in the light of the fact that the Mishnah itself (Sanhedrin, X.1) seems to posit dogmas for Judaism.

Several commentators have sought to explain Abravanel's apparent self-contradiction in the *Rosh Amanah*. David Neumark maintains that Abravanel only attacked the project of creed formulation in order to demonstrate his orthodoxy and that it did not represent his true opinions.[9] But, as Benzion Netanyahu urges, given the overall antiphilosophic thrust of Abravanel's writings there seems to be little justification for this interpretation.[10] In another location I suggested that Abravanel defended Maimonides because of the great respect in which he held him and because he felt that, if there had to be creed formulations, there ought not to be a proliferation of them since that would breed doubt and confusion.[11] In this I followed the suggestions of Joseph Sarachek[12] and Eugene Mihaly.[13] But a close examination of Abravanel's arguments in the *Rosh Amanah* suggests a different explanation altogether, one which sheds new light on the book and Abravanel's aims in it and which illuminates the respective positions of Maimonides, Crescas, and Albo.

A proper understanding of Abravanel's own position in the *Rosh Amanah* depends upon a close analysis of the term "principle" *(ikkar)* as he uses it. There are at least three different ways in which the term is used in the context of the medieval debate on the principles of Judaism. It is impossible to understand what Abravanel is trying to accomplish in the *Rosh Amanah* without distinguishing these three senses of the term. Once they are distinguished, however, Abravanel's intent is discerned without difficulty and his otherwise surprising about-face in chapter 23 is easily understood.

Maimonides, as is evident from his statement at the end of his principles, quoted above, maintained that the principles were dogmas in the strict sense of the word: holding them is a prerequisite for salvation. The point is emphasized in his *"Hilkhot Teshuvah."* There he says:

> The following have no portion in the world to come, but are cut off and perish, and for their great wickedness and sinfulness are condemned for ever and ever: Sectarians and *apikorsim;* those who deny the Torah, the resurrection of the dead or the coming of the Redeemer. . . . Five classes are termed heretics: he who says that there is no God and the world has no ruler; he who says that there is a ruling power but that it is vested in two or more persons; he who says that there is one ruler, but that He is a body and has form; he who denies that He alone is the First Cause and Rock of the Universe; likewise, he who renders worship to any one beside Him, to serve as a mediator between the human being and the Lord of the Universe. Whoever belongs to any of these five classes is termed a heretic.
>
> Three classes are called *apikorsim:* he who denies the reality of prophecy and maintains that there is no knowledge which emanates from the Creator and directly reaches the human mind; he who denies the prophecy of Moses, our teacher; and he who asserts that the Creator has no cognizance of the deeds of the children of men. Each of these classes consists of *apikorsim.* [14]

The importance of all this in the present context is that Maimonides contends here that, if someone makes a doctrinal mistake, he loses his portion in the world to come.

Maimonides' strict opinions concerning doctrinal orthodoxy are reiterated at the very end of the *Guide of the*

Perplexed. His position apparently remained consistent throughout his life and found expression in the great works of his youth, maturity, and age. Interpreting the famous parable of the palace, he says:

> Those who are within the city, but have turned their backs upon the ruler's habitation, are people who have opinions and are engaged in speculation, but who have adopted incorrect opinions either because of some great error that befell them in the course of their speculation or because of their following the traditional authority of one who had fallen into error. Accordingly, because of these opinions, the more these people walk, the greater is their distance from the ruler's habitation. And they are far worse than the first. They are those concerning whom necessity at certain times impels killing them and blotting out the traces of their opinions lest they should lead astray the ways of others.[15]

In the parable the "ruler's habitation" represents human perfection, which, for Maimonides, means intellectual perfection. Thus, doctrinal error carries one further from human perfection and from the reward for that perfection, immortality.

Maimonides' position on this issue formed the basis for an extended discussion of the nature and definition of dogma in medieval Jewish philosophical theology. Rabbi Abraham ben David of Posquières (c.1125–1198) is the first major figure to take issue with Maimonides on the matter of the relationship of doctrinal orthodoxy and salvation.[16] In his glosses on the *Mishneh Torah* he says, with respect to Maimonides' claim that a person who affirms the corporeality of God is a heretic:

> Why has he called such a person a heretic?
> There are many people greater than and superior to him who adhere to such a belief on the basis of what they have seen in verses of Scripture and even more in those *aggadot* which corrupt right opinion about religious matters.[17]

Rabad is not affirming the corporeality of God here. But he does insist that a person who is led to believe that God has a body by the literal sense of scripture or by the sayings of the rabbis is no heretic and is not condemned thereby to lose his portion in the world to come. Rabad seems to be reverting to the pre-Maimonidean position of classical Judaism, that it is willful disobedience, not doctrinal error, which cuts a person off from the world to come.

Rabad is cited as an authority by the next important figure to discuss this issue, R. Shimon ben Ẓemaḥ Duran (1361–1444), the renowned Talmudist who fled Spain for North Africa after the persecutions of 1391.[18] In his *Ohev Mishpat*, a commentary on Job, Duran writes, "Know this, O reader, that the great principle in all this is to believe what the Torah included in these matters. He who denies what was included in the Torah—knowing that it was the teaching of the Torah—is a heretic and is excluded from Israel."[19] Duran here modifies Maimonides' strict position with respect to heresy. One is not a heretic simply because one holds false beliefs. One must intentionally hold such beliefs. Duran makes this explicit a bit further on:

> You also ought to know that one who has properly accepted the roots of the Torah but who was moved to deviate from them by the depth of his speculation and who thereby believed concerning one of the branches of the faith the opposite of what has been accepted as what one ought to believe and tries to explain the verses of Scripture according to his belief, even though he errs, he is no heretic. For he was not brought to this deviation by heresy at all and if he found a tradition from the Sages to the effect that he ought to turn from the position he had adopted, he would do so. He only holds that belief because he thinks that it is the intention of the Torah. Therefore, even though he errs he is not a heretic according to what is agreed upon by our people since he accepted the roots of the Torah as he should.

Duran maintains, therefore, that unintentional heresy, at least with respect to derivative principles, is no heresy. But he does maintain that Judaism does have principles and that intentional heresy with respect to them is indeed heresy and excludes one from the category of Israelites and, by implication, from the category of those who have a share in the world to come.

Maimonides, Rabad, and Duran, despite their important disagreements, all understand the principles of Judaism in the same way, as dogmas which define religious orthodoxy and which, at least for Maimonides and Duran, must be held in order to merit salvation. They differ on which beliefs are principles, and on the question of unintentional heresy, but they use the term "principle" in the same way.

Ḥasdai Crescas introduces a new understanding of the term "principle." Crescas sees the *ikkarim* in a logical sense, as axioms of the religion. On this understanding the principles of Judaism are those beliefs upon which the whole structure of the faith depends and with the refutation of which it would collapse.

Discussing the "cornerstones" and "foundations" of faith, Crescas writes, "They all share [the characteristic] of being beliefs held by one who believes in God's Torah; denying them is like denying the whole Torah."[20] These are distinguished from "true opinions," which are such that "he who does not believe them is not called a heretic."[21] In his introduction to Treatise II of the *Or Ha-Shem* Crescas explains why one who denies the cornerstones of the Torah is likened to one who denies the whole Torah. He writes: "The second treatise deals with the cornerstones of Torah; that is, that they are the foundations and pillars upon which the House of the Lord stands. With their existence the existence of the Torah as commanded by God can be conceived. If the absence of one of them could be conceived, the entire Torah would collapse, God forbid."[22] The "cornerstones" of the Torah are, therefore, those beliefs without which belief in the Torah could not be held. Crescas reiterates this understanding of the principles of Judaism in his introduction to Treatise III, where he distinguishes the "cornerstones" from "true beliefs": "We did not see fit to place these [true beliefs] among the cornerstones of the Torah since, even though belief in them is obligatory and denying them is an act of such great rebelliousness that one who denies them is considered to be in the class of sectarians, the existence of the Torah can be conceived without them. We therefore did not consider them to be foundations or roots for it."[23]

Crescas's six cornerstones of faith (God's knowledge of existents, providence, God's power, prophecy, human choice, and that the Torah has a purpose) are all beliefs without which the Torah cannot be conceived and, as Warren Harvey points out, are all ideas which follow analytically from the claim that God revealed the Torah by an act of volition.[24]

Crescas's student, Joseph Albo, was strongly influenced by his master in the question of how to understand the principles of Judaism. He disassociates himself from the dogmatic interpretation of the principles as held by Maimonides and Duran and says:

> But a person who upholds the law of Moses and believes in its principles, but when he undertakes to investigate these matters with his reason and scrutinizes the texts, is misled by his speculation and interprets a given principle otherwise than it is taken to mean at first sight; or denies the principle because he thinks that it does not represent a sound theory which the Torah obliges us to believe; or erroneously denies that a given belief is a fundamental principle, which however he believes as he believes the other dogmas of the Torah which are not fundamental principles; or entertains a certain notion in relation to one of the miracles of the Torah because he thinks that he is not thereby denying any of the doctrines which it is obligatory upon us to believe by the authority of the Torah,—a person of this sort is not an unbeliever. He is classed with the sages and pious men of Israel, though he holds erroneous theories. His sin is due to error and requires atonement.[25]

Albo reiterates this point in the same chapter and says:

> We say, therefore, that a person whose speculative ability is not sufficient to enable him to reach the true meaning of scriptural texts, with the result that he believes in the literal meaning and entertains absurd ideas because he thinks they represent the view of the Torah, is not thereby excluded from the community of those who believe in the Torah, Heaven forbid! Nor is it permitted to speak disrespectfully of him and accuse him of perverting the teaching of the Torah and class him among unbelievers and heretics.[26]

Albo further disassociates himself from the dogmatic or doctrinal understanding of the principles by quoting Rabad's criticism of Maimonides with approval.[27] Rejecting the doctrinal interpretation of the principles of Judaism, Albo adopts the logical or axiomatic understanding introduced by his teacher, Crescas. In the table of contents of his *Sefer ha-Ikkarim* Albo writes that the "purpose of this work is to explain what are the essential principles of divine law."[28] These principles, he says, are those "without which a divine law cannot exist."[29] He makes the logical character of the principles explicit in chapter 3 of book 1 where he discusses the term *ikkar* (principle):

> The word *ikkar* is a term applied to a thing upon which the existence and duration of another thing depends and without which it can not endure, as the root is a thing upon which the endurance of the tree depends, without which the tree can not exist or endure. The Rabbis of the Talmud use this term frequently. They speak, for example, of a thing which has an *ikkar* [basis] in the Torah or not. Hence the term may be used of the basic principles upon which the existence of religious law depends, like the existence of God. For it is clear from the nature of this doctrine that it is fundamental and belief in it is essential to a divine law, for a divine law can not be imagined without belief in the existence of God. For this reason we must investigate in order to know what beliefs are properly fundamental in divine law.[30]

Albo's entire work is given over to the investigation of what beliefs "are properly fundamental in divine law." Albo's criticisms of Maimonides' enumeration of the principles—summarized by Abravanel in *Rosh Amanah* 3 below—are also for the most part based on this understanding of the principles.

We have seen how Maimonides and Duran present what I have called a doctrinal or dogmatic interpretation of the principles of Judaism and how Crescas and Albo understand them in what may be called a logical or axiomatic sense. There is, however, a third understanding of the principles, one which sees them neither as doctrines which must be held in order to merit salvation nor as axioms from which the other beliefs of the religion follow. This third interpretation of the principles sees them as nothing more than pedagogical devices, designed to help the unlearned understand some important truths about their faith. This may be called the heuristic interpretation of the principles. It is on this basis that Abravanel approves of Maimonides' principles and defends them from the attacks of Crescas and Albo.

Abravanel rejects the doctrinal interpretation of the principles, at least as it is held by Maimonides and Duran, on the grounds that all of the beliefs of Judaism are doctrinally essential. Actually, Abravanel does not deny the claim that certain beliefs must be held in order to merit salvation. He simply elevates every belief of Judaism to the status of necessary dogma. He says: "There is no need to lay down principles for the Torah of God which ought to be believed by every Israelite in order to merit life in the world to come as Maimonides and those who follow after him wrote, for the entire Torah, and every single verse, word, and letter in it is a principle and root which ought to be believed."[31]

Abravanel rejects the axiomatic or logical interpretation of the principles on the grounds that, with one possible exception,[32] Judaism has no axioms such that the religion would collapse with their refutation. He further argues that the thinkers who adopted this understanding of the principles of Judaism did so because they were unduly influenced by the example of secular science. At the beginning of *Rosh Amanah* 23 Abravanel writes:

> They were brought to postulate principles in the divine Torah only because they were drawn after the custom of gentile scholars as described in their books. . . . Our scholars, having been dispersed among the nations and having studied their books and sciences, learned from their deeds and copied their ways and customs with respect to the divine Torah. They said: "How do these gentiles pursue their sciences? They do this by positing first principles and fundamentals upon which a science is based. I will do so also and postulate principles and foundations for the divine Torah."[33]

Judaism, according to Abravanel, thus has no principles in

the sense of dogmas (as Maimonides and Duran had thought) and it has no principles in the sense of logical axioms (as Crescas and Albo had thought). It does, however, have great, praiseworthy, and important beliefs which may be singled out for the edification and improvement of the masses. These beliefs may be called principles, but only in a heuristic sense. It is Abravanel's contention that Maimonides presented his principles, certainly as dogmas, but also as pedagogical guides for the unlearned. It is in that latter sense, and in that sense only, that he defends Maimonides' principles.

This point may be clarified by summarizing the ways in which Maimonides and Abravanel agree and disagree. They agree in rejecting the axiomatic or logical interpretation of the principles; they agree that adherence to dogma is a prerequisite for salvation; they agree that Maimonides' thirteen principles are great, praiseworthy, and important beliefs. They disagree, however, on one important point: Maimonides maintains that belief in the thirteen principles is sufficient for attaining salvation while Abravanel holds that belief in *all* of the teachings of Judaism is necessary for salvation.

Abravanel emphasizes this latter point in a number of places in the *Rosh Amanah*. In chapter 12 he rejects Rabad's position on the grounds that,

> according to it, [even] one who unintentionally denies every principle will acquire a portion in the world to come. . . . It would be possible, according to this, to find a man who does not believe in any one of the principles or beliefs of the Torah and yet who should not be called a sectarian or heretic if he were brought to this blind foolishness by his failure to understand the meaning of the Torah. These opinions are intolerable . . . for a false opinion about any one of the principles of faith turns the soul from its true felicity and will not bring [one] to life in the world to come, even if the opinion is held without intention to rebel.[34]

This difference of opinion between Maimonides and Abravanel is crucial. By specifying those basic dogmas which must be accepted by one who seeks to merit the world to come, Maimonides makes philosophical speculation on religious beliefs possible. The principles define what one must believe; all other beliefs are not on the level of principles and are the fit objects of philosophical inquiry and interpretation.

If there were as many fundamental principles as there are miracles and promises in the Torah, then intelligent people would not be permitted to "investigate the fundamental principles of religion and to interpret the biblical texts in accordance with the truth as it seems to [them]."[35]

But this is exactly what Abravanel wants. The idea which Albo rejects did indeed "occur" to him and he held it tenaciously. His is indeed an orthodox position in the strictest sense of the word. He simply rejects the possibility of any philosophical inquiry into any of the teachings of Judaism. This attitude is expressed in a number of places in the *Rosh Amanah*. In chapter 23 he writes,

> Therefore, I said, *this I recall to my mind* [Lamentations 3:21], that the divine Torah, with all its beliefs, is completely true. . . . We are not permitted to doubt even the smallest thing in it that it should be necessary to establish its truth with those principles and roots. For he who denies or doubts a belief or narrative of the Torah, be it small or great, is a sectarian and *apikoros*.[36]

Further on in the same chapter he says, "All of the commandments of the Torah, as well as the attributes and opinions taught therein, are divine. He who denies the smallest of them all, in that he uproots something from the Torah and denies it, is not worthy to be of the world to come."[37]

It may be that Abravanel rejected the legitimacy of philosophical discussion of religious beliefs because he saw in such discussions a source for the spiritual weakness which he attributed to fifteenth-century Iberian Jewry. It was to combat this weakness and confusion that he wrote the *Rosh Amanah*.[38]

With this background we may now see that contrary to what is ordinarily thought to be the case, there is no "about-face" in the *Rosh Amanah* on the issue of creed formulation. Abravanel does not defend Maimonides in twenty-two chapters only to attack him in the twenty-third. Throughout the book he defends Maimonides only to the extent that the latter adopts the heuristic interpretation of the principles.

He opens his defense of Maimonides in the first of his nine propositions (chapter 6) by pointing out that the term *ikkar* (principle) is not completely synonymous with the terms *shoresh* (root) and *yesod* (foundation). All three are terms used to denote principles of faith in discussions of Jewish credalism. While they all signify "a thing upon which the existence and duration of another thing depends and without which it cannot endure"[39] (i.e., principles in the axiomatic sense), the term *ikkar* often means only the most important thing in its class, even if nothing else depends upon it for its existence. Thus, according to Abravanel, Maimonides' thirteen principles ought not to be considered as the axioms of Judaism, but as "praiseworthy, essential, and fundamental beliefs of exalted degree."[40]

In chapter 9 Abravanel argues that Maimonides put forward his principles for the masses in order "to perfect men and women who were not perfected by speculative investigation,"[41] that is to say, for heuristic purposes. In chapter 21 Abravanel points out that Maimonides did not lay down "these principles of his for *the wise men who knew the times* [Esther 1:3] but *for all of the people from every quarter, both young and old* [after Genesis 19:4]."[42] Abravanel makes the argument at length in chapter 23:

> We may say in defense of Maimonides that he . . . did not choose principles among them [i.e., the beliefs of the Torah] in order to say that we are obliged to believe these principles but not others. His intention was, rather, correctly to guide those men who neither studied nor served their teachers enough. Since they could not comprehend or conceive of all the beliefs and opinions which are included in the divine Torah, Maimonides chose the thirteen most general beliefs to teach them briefly those matters which I discussed in the fifth proposition in such a way that all men, even the ignorant, could become perfected through their acceptance. From this point of view he called them principles and foundations, adapting [his language] to the thinking of the student, though it is not so according to the truth itself. . . . He postulated the principles for the masses, and for beginners in the

study of Mishnah, but not for those individuals who plumbed the knowledge of truth for whom he wrote the *Guide*. If this was his opinion, then his intentions were acceptable and his actions were for the sake of heaven.[43]

According to the standard interpretation of the *Rosh Amanah*, Abravanel defends Maimonides' formulation of the principles of Judaism in chapters 1 through 22 only to turn around in chapter 23 and attack the entire project of creed formulation (including Maimonides' attempt) altogether. I suggest that this is not Abravanel's intention at all. He is consistent throughout the book.

In chapters 1 through 22 Abravanel defends Maimonides' heuristic interpretation of the principles in the face of the attacks leveled by Crescas and Albo. In chapter 23 Abravanel goes on the offensive himself and attacks the axiomatic and doctrinal interpretations of the principles of Judaism. This simply furthers his defense of Maimonides. His attack on creed formulation is a continuation of his defense of Maimonides.

The interpretation of the *Rosh Amanah* offered here is supported by an analysis of chapter 23 of the book. It is in this chapter that Abravanel is supposed to turn around and attack Maimonides after having defended him in the rest of the book. Abravanel opens the chapter by saying that Maimonides, Crescas, and Albo were led to posit principles in the Torah by the example of secular sciences.[44] He then states and defends his own view that there are no principles of Judaism since its beliefs, narratives, and commandments are all equally true and precious. He then goes on to distinguish Maimonides from Crescas and Albo and thus to exculpate him. This is the passage quoted just above.

Maimonides, Abravanel informs us, had adapted his language to the needs of the uninformed masses. He faults Crescas and Albo for having taken Maimonides' words at face value. Maimonides had posited the principles for the uninitiated; Crescas and Albo, however, "took these things literally and put those beliefs at the level of roots and principles, like the first principles of the sciences, as I have discussed."[45] We see here that it is Crescas and Albo who are faulted with holding the axiomatic view of the principles, not Maimonides. Abravanel follows this with a critique of the axiomatic or logical view, insisting that Judaism is a seamless, entirely interdependent whole: "The divine Torah would collapse with the denial of any narrative, opinion, or belief in it."[46] All the beliefs of Judaism are its principles; there are no axioms which underlie the other beliefs, from which the latter may be derived and without which they could not endure. This is the attitude which Albo excoriated as making all philosophical investigation on religious questions impossible.

We see, therefore, that far from turning around to attack Maimonides here in chapter 23, Abravanel continues to defend him. He distinguishes Maimonides' position from that of Crescas and Albo. He rejects the latter, imputes the heuristic view of the principles of Maimonides and on those grounds he defends him: "If this was his opinion then his intentions were acceptable and his actions were for the sake of heaven."[47]

It is now clear that Abravanel is consistent throughout the *Rosh Amanah*. He did not defend Maimonides and the project of creed formulation only to turn around and attack them. He defends Maimonides' principles (as heuristic devices) throughout the book. He sets up his nine propositions so as to make this defense possible and constantly repeats that he is defending Maimonides' principles as praiseworthy beliefs, not as dogmas or axioms of Judaism. In chapter 23 his attack is directed, not at the principles as heuristic devices, but as axioms or dogmas the holding of which is necessary in order to merit life in the world to come.

It ought to be noted here that at this point the question might be raised as to whether—from Abravanel's perspective —there is any disagreement between Maimonides and himself at all. It is evident that they both agree on the salvific character of the principles; the point on which they appear to disagree is one of numbers. It may be argued that Maimonides did hold that acceptance of all the beliefs of Judaism was a prerequisite for salvation. Assuming, as Abravanel certainly did, that Maimonides accepted the entire Torah, may it not be said that he held that all the beliefs of Judaism are included in the thirteen principles, which latter he proposed merely as a summary of the entire list?

It is tempting to say that Abravanel did read Maimonides in this fashion because then it would be evident that, far from attacking him in *Rosh Amanah* 23, Abravanel is actually in complete agreement with Maimonides throughout. There is no doubt that some of the passages quoted above from *Rosh Amanah* 23 appear to be consistent with this reading of the situation.

Ultimately, however, I do not think that we can say that Abravanel read Maimonides in this fashion simply because he never makes it clear that he does. This in the face of the fact that he would have every reason to trumpet it from the rooftops since then he would be able to claim the prestige and support of Maimonides for his own position. Moreover, he did not lack opportunities to propose this interpretation of Maimonides (it would have been relevant in chapters 20 and 23, for example), yet he refrained from doing so.

I might note that, whether or not Abravanel interpreted Maimonides in this fashion, the interpretation itself is open to serious question and would have to be defended in the context of a broad-ranging study of Maimonides. This is so for a number of reasons. First, because it rejects the Strauss-Pines theory of Maimonides' true attitudes concerning philosophy and *halakha* (assuming as it does that he accepted the entire Torah without reservations).[48] Second, this interpretation of Maimonides can be accepted only if one can show that Maimonides ultimately meant the principles to be *believed* rather than *known* (since Maimonides could hardly expect the masses—for whom the principles were intended—to arrive at demonstrative knowledge of all the principles and beliefs of the Jewish religion).[49] Third, this interpretation of the principles involves the implicit rejection of the Guttmann/Hyman thesis concerning the metaphysical character of the principles, a thesis, however, which is strongly supported.[50]

A full understanding of Abravanel's position on the question of dogmatics in Judaism is complicated by the fact that he does not appear to be wholly consistent on the issue. In several places he asserts that Judaism has at least one belief which may be construed as an axiom of the faith in the same way, it seems, in which Crescas and Albo understood their principles of faith to function. This is belief in creation.

In *Rosh Amanah* 22 (p. 192) after reviewing various opinions on the creed, Abravanel writes:

> Were I to choose principles to posit for the divine Torah I would only lay down one, the creation of the world. It is the root and foundation around which the divine Torah, its cornerstones, and its beliefs revolve and includes the creation at the beginning, the narratives about the Patriarchs, and the miracles and wonders which cannot be believed without belief in creation. So, too with belief in God's knowledge and providence, and reward and punishment according to [one's observance of] the commandments, none of which one can perfectly believe without believing in the volitional creation of the whole world.

He is maintaining here that belief in creation makes possible belief in miracles and many of the other teachings of Judaism. This accords perfectly with the axiomatic definition of the term "principle" proffered by Crescas and Albo.

Abravanel reiterates this position in two other works which he wrote in the last years of his life, *Shamayim Hadashim* (1498) and *Mifalot Elohim* (1501). In the former he wrote, "Therefore, belief in the creation of the world is the cornerstone and foundation upon which the whole Torah depends."[51] He goes on to cite his argument from *Rosh Amanah* 8 to the effect that Maimonides implicitly included the doctrine of creation in his thirteen principles.

Abravanel devotes all of chapter 3 of Treatise I of the *Mifalot* to arguing that belief in creation is a fundamental principle. He writes:

> We ought to know the relative importance[52] of belief in the creation of the world as recounted by the Torah relative to the other narratives of the Torah. I say that the importance of belief in this divine narrative relative to the other narratives of the Torah and its commandments is like the importance of a foundation and root relative to what is founded and built upon it.[53]

Abravanel seems clearly to be contradicting himself here. Either the Jewish religion has axioms or it does not. We cannot say that he changed his position since the contradiction is found, not only between different works, but in two consecutive chapters in the *Rosh Amanah* (22 and 23).

The contradiction between chapters 22 and 23 of the *Rosh Amanah* may be explained more easily than the contradiction between Abravanel's position in *Rosh Amanah* 23, on the one hand, and his position in the *Mifalot* and *Shamayim Ḥadashim*. In chapter 22 Abravanel attacks the critics of Maimonides, criticizing their substantive positions. He ought to be understood as saying that, even if Crescas and Albo were correct in positing axioms for the Jewish faith, they still erred in their choice of axioms. Were one to choose axioms for Judaism, he says, the only belief which ought to be so chosen is belief in creation.

In *Shamayim Ḥadashim* and *Mifalot Elohim*, however, Abravanel flatly states that belief in creation is a foundation and cornerstone of Judaism. This clearly contradicts Abravanel's position in *Rosh Amanah* 23. *Shamayim Ḥadashim* and *Mifalot Elohim*, like almost everything else Abravanel wrote after the Expulsion, subserve a messianic end.[54] Following Maimonides in *Guide*, II.25, Abravanel had to establish the createdness of the world in order to make possible miracles in general and the miracle of redemption in particular. In asserting that creation is a foundation of faith, Abravanel might very well have been self-consciously contradicting the position presented in *Rosh Amanah*. He may have felt that the need of the hour (consoling and encouraging the battered victims of the Expulsion by reinforcing their belief in redemption) overrode the need for consistency. It is also possible that he meant that creation was a foundation of Judaism in a psychological as opposed to a theological sense: that without belief in the messiah, which, in turn, is based on belief in creation, the Jewish people would not have the strength to maintain their faith.

There is no doubt, then, that Abravanel contradicts himself. The position concerning the status of belief in creation enunciated in *Shamayim Ḥadashim* and *Mifalot Elohim* does contradict the position enunciated in *Rosh Amanah* 23. It seems likely that Abravanel was aware of the contradiction but nonetheless felt it important to ignore it.

I have been concerned, up to this point, with trying to present an interpretation of the *Rosh Amanah* which shows Abravanel's defense of Maimonides and his own rejection of all creedal formulations to be consistent. I distinguished three different senses of the term "principle": the dogmatic, the axiomatic, and the heuristic. I argued that Abravanel rejects the possibility of principles of Judaism in the first two senses of the term but accepts the possibility in the third sense and that it was for their heuristic value that he defended Maimonides' principles.

The *Rosh Amanah*, however, is important for more than its discussion of the place of dogma in Judaism and in the balance of this introduction I will discuss two other important and interesting issues raised in the book. The first relates to what may be Abravanel's most important contribution toward our better understanding of Maimonides' principles. It is also valuable for shedding light on Abravanel's cavalier use of his sources. The second relates to an important debate between Maimonides and Crescas. It is important in its own right; but Abravanel's discussion of it sheds further light on his relationship with Maimonides and his own position in the *Rosh Amanah*.

The fifth of Abravanel's nine preliminary propositions takes up the whole of chapter 10 in the *Rosh Amanah*. As Abravanel puts, it, the proposition states

> that the number of foundations and principles of faith as stated by Maimonides was neither accidental nor inadvertent; nor [did Maimonides choose the number thirteen] in order to match the thirteen attributes of God's mercy or the thirteen hermeneutical principles of Torah exegesis. Rather, with this number Maimonides intended to teach one or all of three lessons and great speculative teachings.[55]

The chapter itself is given over to a discussion of the three "lessons" taught by the order and interrelationship of the thirteen principles.

Abravanel was neither the first nor the last scholar to seek to explain the inner structure of Maimonides' thirteen principles. But, as shall be seen, he was one of the most innovative. Among the first was Rabbi Simeon ben Ẓemaḥ Duran. In the introduction to his *Ohev Mishpat* Duran distinguishes between fundamental principles (which, explicitly following the terminology of the Sabbath laws, he calls *avot*, "fathers") and the subprinciples implied by them (*toladot*, "consequences"). He maintains that Maimonides chose his thirteen principles because they were all explicitly taught by biblical verses and not because they are the thirteen most important principles of Judaism. He writes:

Were it not for the dependence upon the verses, the number [of principles] would be smaller or greater [than thirteen]; for, if we counted [only] the fundamental principles we would have only three principles, while if we counted the sub-principles there would be more than thirteen. However, the fundamental principles are three and no more. Belief in God and what follows [from that belief] is one principle. [Its sub-principles are]: existence, unity, eternity *a parte ante,* incorporeality, and that it is proper to worship only God and no other. These five sub-principles all follow from one fundamental principle. Belief in the Torah and necessary corollary beliefs is one principle which is that God through the intermediation of the separate intellects causes a divine overflow[56] to extend to those who cleave unto Him so that they become prophets of different ranks, seeking to direct human beings to the service of God. Included in this principle are four [derivative principles]: prophecy, the prophecy of Moses, revelation,[57] and that the Torah will never be changed for divine activity is perfect, enduring, and eternal. Belief in retribution and its necessary corollary beliefs is one principle which is that God knows the deeds of men and rewards and punishes them according to their deeds, either in this world or in the next world, and either with the days of the Messiah or with the resurrection of the dead. Included in this principle are four [derivative] principles: God's knowledge and retribution, the coming of the Messiah, and the resurrection of the dead.[58]

Duran thus reduces Maimonides' thirteen principles to three fundamental principles, which, he maintains, are necessary for human perfection.[59] Duran initiated what has become a standard element in almost all interpretations of the thirteen principles, namely that they fall naturally into three main groups. Duran was also the first explicitly to link the three main groups of principles to the mishnah in Sanhedrin. In his *Magen Avot* he writes:

> Divine revelation, reward and punishment, and the existence of God are foundations of the Torah. It is a foundation of faith to believe in God, in His existence, unity, priority, and that it is proper to worship [only] Him. This is included under [the heading] *apikoros*, as mentioned above. Next, [one should] believe in the prophecy of the prophets and in the prophecy of Moses, in the Torah and in its eternity. This is included under [the heading of] "divine revelation." Next, [one should] believe in reward and punishment and its offshoots. This is included under [the heading of] "resurrection."[60]

It is well known that Duran strongly influenced Joseph Albo.[61] This is evident in Albo's enumeration of the principles of Judaism (he writes: "It seems to me that the general and essential principles of divine law are three: existence of God, providence in reward and punishment, and divine revelation"),[62] and in the way in which he derives the rest of the Maimonidean principles from these three. On this subject he writes:

> It may be that Maimonides has the same idea concerning the number of fundamental principles as the one we have just indicated, and that his list consists of the three chief principles that we mentioned, plus the derivative dogmas issuing from them, all being called by him principles. Thus he lays down the existence of God, a fundamental doctrine, as the first principle. Then he enumerates along with it as principles four other dogmas which are derived from it, viz., unity, incorporeality, eternity, and exclusive worship. Then he lists as principles revelation, another fundamental doctrine, together with three other dogmas derived from it, viz., prophecy, superiority of Moses, and immutability

of the law. Then comes divine omniscience and providence in reward and punishment, the third fundamental doctrine, together with three other dogmas implied in it and derived therefrom, viz., spiritual retribution, Messiah, and resurrection.[63]

Duran's influence on Albo in this regard is further seen in *Ikkarim*, I.10, where Albo connects his three principles to mishnah Sanhedrin, X.1 much as Duran did in his *Magen Avot*.

Another of Abravanel's predecessors who wrote on the subject of the internal structure of the Maimonidean principles was Abraham ben Shem Tov Bibago.[64] There is little point in discussing Bibago's contribution at this point, however, since Abravanel borrowed it, in some places almost word for word, in *Rosh Amanah* 10. It is the third of the three "lessons" which Abravanel says Maimonides sought to teach by his ordering of the principles.[65]

In recent times the subject of the internal structure of the thirteen principles has been taken up by a number of scholars. Surprisingly, Schechter doesn't discuss it in his "Dogmas of Judaism" but David Neumark does, offering a novel interpretation. He divides the principles into two groups, those which can be verified by proof and those which can be neither proved nor disproved.[66] Meyer Waxman subjects Neumark's discussion to withering criticism and proposes that the principles be divided into the same three groups into which Duran divided them; he labels them God (principles 1–5), Torah (principles 6–9), and Man (principles 10–13).[67] In this, as we shall see, he follows a suggestion of Abravanel. More recently Yaakov Stieglitz[68] and Arthur Hyman[69] have reverted to the classic division of Duran and Albo. Hyman follows them as well in relating the three groupings to the different terms in mishnah Sanhedrin, X.1.

We thus see that of the scholars, both medieval and modern, who have interested themselves in the question of the internal structure of the Maimonidean principles, all but Neumark (and Bibago) follow the threefold division first proposed by Duran. It is to Abravanel's credit that, his dependence upon Bibago notwithstanding, he breaks new ground in this question and in so doing adds significantly to our understanding of the principles.

Abravanel sees the structure of the thirteen principles as teaching at least three separate "lessons." The first approach divides the principles as did Duran and Albo, but with a different emphasis, showing their interrelatedness. On this understanding the first five principles describe God, the Commander; the next four relate to the content of His commands, the Torah; the last four relate to those whom God commands, the Israelites. The emphasis here, however, is on how the principles lead to obedience to the Torah. We observe the Torah either because of the exalted nature and "perfect rank" of its Commander, because of its own perfection, or because of the "hope for reward and the fear of punishment"; the latter is the subject of the last four principles.

The second of the three lessons relates to the cognitive status of the principles. Here Abravanel seems to be breaking new ground entirely. He divides the principles into four groups. The first (principles 1–3) consists of those which are philosophically acceptable without reservation. These are principles which Maimonides, according to Abravanel, thought were rationally demonstrable. The next three principles, while not being entirely acceptable philosophically, are rationally demonstrable to one degree or another. The third group (principles 7–9) consists of principles about which Aristotelian philosophy must remain agnostic since they relate to claims (about the Torah) which may be true or false but which are not necessarily so, one way or the other. According to this analysis, the last four principles must be rejected by Aristotelian philosophy since they all deal with ramifications of God's knowledge of particulars, which Aristotle denies.

The last "lesson," the one derived from Bibago, divides the principles into two groups: those relating to God and those relating to His works. The first group is comprised of principles 1–4. The principles of unity, incorporeality, and eternity (priority) are shown to be related to Maimonides' doctrine of negative attributes. The second group, principles 4–13 (principle 4 falling into both groups) is itself divided into four parts. The first subdivision consists of principles relating to those actions of God which are general and occasional (creation, miracles, prophecy). The principles in the second subdivision relate to those of God's actions which are particular and transitory and which relate to the Jewish people specifically. In this group Abravanel (Bibago) includes the superiority of Mosaic prophecy, divine revelation, and the immutability of the Torah. The third subdivision consists of those principles which relate to the actions of God which are both general and permanent. This category includes God's knowledge and providence, and retribution. Those particular actions of God which will occur in the future (Messiah and resurrection) define the last of the four subdivisions. On this account, the thirteen principles are shown to follow Maimonides' discussion of divine attributes (*Guide*, I.51–60). They all express either attributes of negation or attributes of action. These are the only kind of attributes which, according to Maimonides, may be predicated of God.

While this last analysis, which Abravanel borrowed from Bibago, may appear to be somewhat strained, the first two "lessons" which he derives from the number and internal structure of Maimonides' principles of faith certainly add to our understanding of them and demonstrate the truth of Abravanel's claim that Maimonides' choice and ordering of his principles "was neither accidental nor inadvertent."

The *Rosh Amanah*, as I noted above, is important for reasons that transcend its argument concerning the place of dogma in Judaism and its analysis of the internal relationships and order of Maimonides' thirteen principles. Abravanel, among other things, makes an important contribution to one of the best-known Jewish exegetical and philosophical disputes of the Middle Ages, that between Maimonides and Crescas on the proper understanding of Exodus 20:2, the opening verse of the Decalogue. Abravanel's discussion takes up all of chapter 18 of the *Rosh Amanah*. It is interesting in its own right, for the light it sheds on the issues dividing

Maimonides and Crescas, and for the way in which it helps us further to understand Abravanel's relationship to Maimonides.

The questions raised in this dispute relate not only to the proper understanding of the verse in question, in particular to the question of whether or not it constitutes a commandment, but also to the enumeration of the biblical laws which Jewish tradition claims to number 613.[70]

In Tractate Makkot of the Babylonian Talmud (23b–24a) we read:

> R. Simlai when preaching said: Six hundred and thirteen precepts were communicated to Moses, three hundred and sixty-five negative precepts, corresponding to the number of solar days [in the year], and two hundred and forty-eight positive precepts, corresponding to the number of the members of man's body. Said R. Hamnuna: What is the [authentic] text for this? It is, *Moses commanded us Torah, an inheritance of the congregation of Jacob* [Deuteronomy 33:4]. "Torah" being in letter-value equal to six hundred and eleven,[71] *I am* [Exodus 20:2] and *Thou shalt have no* [Exodus 20:3] [not being reckoned, because] we heard [them] from the mouth of the Almighty.[72]

This idea that the Torah contained exactly 613 commandments became widely accepted in the Jewish tradition and gave rise to a whole genre of literature dedicated to identifying and enumerating the 613 commandments. One of the first books actually to contain such a list is the *Halakhot Gedolot,* attributed to Simeon Kayyara (ninth century).[73] Scores of liturgical poems, known as *Azharot,* were composed during the Middle Ages, all of them embodying enumerations of the 613 commandments.[74] These poems were meant to be recited on the holiday of Shavuot, traditionally accepted as the anniversary of the revelation at Sinai.

One of the most important attempts to enumerate the 613 commandments is that of Moses Maimonides. In his *Sefer ha-Miẓvot* he lists and explains all the commandments. He also provides a lengthy introduction in which he explains the principles which guided him in his choice of which precepts to include in his list.

Maimonides opens the *Sefer ha-Miẓvot* with positive commandment number 1:

> BELIEVING IN GOD. By this injunction we are commanded to believe in God; that is, to believe that there is a Supreme Cause who is the Creator of everything in existence. It is contained in His words (exalted be He): *I am the Lord thy God, who brought thee out of the land of Egypt,* etc. [Exodus 20:2].
>
> At the end of Tractate Makkot it is said: "Six hundred thirteen Commandments were declared unto Moses at Sinai, as the verse says, *Moses commanded us a law* [*Torah*] [Deuteronomy 33:4]"; that is, he commanded us to observe as many Commandments as are signified by the sum of the letter-numbers TORAH. To this it was objected that the letter-numbers of the word TORAH make only six hundred and eleven; to which the reply was: "The two Commandments, *I am the Lord thy God,* etc., and *Thou shalt have no other gods before Me,* we heard from the Almighty Himself."
>
> Thus it has been made clear to you that the verse, *I am the Lord thy God,* etc., is one of the 613 Commandments, and is that whereby we are commanded to believe in God, as we have explained.[75]

Maimonides reiterates this position at the very beginning of his great law code, the *Mishneh Torah:*

> The foundation of all foundations and the pillar of all sciences is to realize that there is a First Being who brought every existing thing into being. All existing things, whether celestial, terrestrial, or belonging to an intermediate class, exist only through His true existence. . . .
>
> To acknowledge the truth of this is an affirmative precept, as it is said *I am the Lord thy God.* And whoever permits the thought to enter his mind that there is another deity besides this God, violates a prohibition; as it is said, *Thou shalt have no other gods before me,* and denies the essence of Religion—this doctrine being the great principle on which everything depends.[76]

Maimonides makes the same claim, that "I am the Lord thy God" expresses a positive commandment, in his *Commentary on the Mishnah,* where he enumerates the basic principles of Judaism:

> *The First Fundamental Principle:* To believe in the existence of
> the Creator; that there is an Existent complete in all the senses of
> the word "existence." He is the cause of all existence. . . . This
> first fundamental principle is taught in the Biblical verse: *I am the
> Lord thy God.*[77]

These texts clearly demonstrate that Maimonides understood Exodus 20:2, "I am the Lord they God," to express a
commandment. It is, logically, the first positive commandment in the Torah and "the great principle on which everything depends."[78] Maimonides' position here can be explained in terms of a statement he makes in the *Guide of the
Perplexed* (II.33, p. 364):

> This is their dictum: "They heard *I am* and *Thou shalt have no*
> from the mouth of the Force." They mean that these words
> reached them just as they reached Moses our Master and that it
> was not Moses our Master who communicated them to them. For
> these two principles, I mean the existence of the deity and His
> being one, are knowable by human speculation alone. Now with
> regard to everything that can be known by demonstration, the
> status of the prophet and that of everyone who knows it are
> equal; there is no superiority of one over the other. Thus these
> two principles are not known through prophecy alone. The text
> of the Torah says: *Unto thee it was shown,* and so on
> [Deuteronomy 4:35]. As for the other commandments, they
> belong to the class of generally accepted opinions and those
> adopted in virtue of tradition, not to the class of the intellects.

It is Maimonides' claim, therefore, that God's existence
and unity are rationally demonstrable and that human beings
may, in principle, be commanded to accept their truth. This
reflects Maimonides' general position concerning the relationship between faith and reason. He sought to integrate
halakha (Jewish Law) and philosophy.[79] The first two statements of the Decalogue, the content of God's unmediated
revelation to the people of Israel, the first of which is the
foundation of all foundations of the Jewish faith, are presented as rationally demonstrable philosophic teachings.

This issue is the crux of the philosophic dispute between

Maimonides and Crescas. Crescas wanted to divorce religion from philosophy and to establish the former on purely dogmatic grounds. Indeed, in its overall structure, his *magnum opus,* the *Or ha-Shem,* is nothing other than a statement and explication of the basic dogmas of Judaism. Crescas therefore claims that *I am the Lord thy God* and *Thou shalt have no other gods before Me* are not commandments. *Halakha* (Jewish Law), in particular, and Jewish religion in general, he can be understood as saying, are not grounded in philosophy (rationally demonstrable statements about God's existence and unity).[80] This distinction, as Warren Harvey points out,[81] was symbolized in Crescas's projected two-part work, *Ner Elohim (Lamp of God),* of which the *Light of the Lord* was to have been the first part. The second part, *Ner Mizvah (Lamp of the Commandment)* was never written. It was meant to be a strictly *halakhic* work, one which its author hoped would supersede Maimonides' code, the *Mishneh Torah.*[82]

The argument between Maimonides and Crescas, therefore, is of far-reaching philosophico-theological significance and relates to a basic question concerning the very nature of Judaism. At the risk of oversimplification, the question may be stated as follows: Is Judaism ultimately a religion of reason or a religion of faith?

The dispute between Maimonides and Crescas, however, was not carried on in terms of the actual issues which divided them. Rather, as is so often the case in similar matters, it was expressed on another plane altogether; in this case, through their different understandings of Exodus 20:2 "I am the Lord thy God." Maimonides' understanding of this verse was subjected to strong criticism by Ḥasdai Crescas in the Preface *(Haẓa'a)* to his *Or ha-Shem.*[83] Crescas leveled three different arguments against Maimonides' position. The third of these relates directly to the question of the proper exegesis of Exodus 20:2.[84] He wrote:

> He who counted it a positive commandment to believe in the existence of God committed a notorious error. . . . [Maimonides was] brought to this, that is, to count this root as a commandment, by the dictum at the end of Talmud Makkot which says:

"Six hundred thirteen precepts were communicated to Moses at Sinai. What is the [authentic] text for this? It is, *Moses commanded us Torah* [Deuteronomy 33:4]." They asked: "But *Torah* in letter value is equal to six hundred eleven!" They answered: "*I am* [Exodus 20:2] and *Thou shalt have no* [Exodus 20:3] [are not reckoned because] we heard them from the mouth of the Almighty."[85] [Maimonides thought because of this dictum] that *I am* and *Thou shalt have no* were two commandments and therefore counted belief in the existence of God as a commandment. It is clear that this does not follow for what was intended there is that the God who is called thus is the Deity and Guide who brought us out of the land of Egypt.[86] Maimonides properly followed this understanding in his *Sefer ha-Miẓvot* in which he counted the first commandment as involving belief in divinity: "By this injunction we are commanded to believe in God: that is, to believe that there is a Supreme Cause who is the Creator of everything in existence. It is contained in His words (exalted be He): *I am the Lord thy God.*"[87] He thus explained God's divinity in terms of His having created all existent beings. Because of this God said, *Who brought thee out of the land of Egypt* [Exodus 20:2] by way of proving this belief: from it we come to understand God's power and that all existent beings are, when compared to Him, *as clay in the potter's hand* [Jeremiah 18:6].[88]

On this account the commandment relates to the belief that it was God who brought us out of the land of Egypt. But this way of understanding the verse is clearly false itself. This is so because the reference to *I am* and *Thou shalt have no* [in the passage from Makkot] may readily be seen to include all of the utterance which continues through . . . *of them that love Me and keep my commandments* [Exodus 20:6]. Since both these utterances are spoken in the first person, as it says: *I am the Lord . . . Who brought thee out* [Exodus 20:2], *before Me* [20:3], *for I the Lord thy God* [20:5], and *of them that love Me and keep My commandments* [20:6]; and since the rest of the utterances are spoken in the third person, as it says, *for the Lord will not hold him guiltless* [20:7], *for in six days the Lord made* [20:11], and *on the seventh day He ceased from work and rested,*[89] [therefore, the Sages] held that *I am* and *Thou shalt have no* [were heard] from the mouth of the Almighty.[90] All of the authors who enumerate *Azharot* saw fit to count *Thou shalt not make unto thee a graven image* [20:4] and *Thou shalt not bow down to them* [20:5] as two [separate] admonitions; this is the truth itself.

Were we to count *I am* as a commandment there would then be three commandments which we heard from the mouth of the Almighty[91] and [the total number of commandments] would then rise to six hundred fourteen.[92] If we consider *Thou shalt have no other gods* [20:3] as an admonition not "to believe in, or ascribe deity to, any but Him," as Maimonides wrote,[93] [then the number of commandments] would rise to six hundred fifteen.[94] It is therefore appropriate that we say that it was not the intention of those who said *"I am* and *Thou shalt have no* [other gods] we heard from the mouth of Almighty" that each [verse] be considered a commandment. Rather, they explained that we heard them from the mouth of the Almighty because both were spoken in the first person, as [said] above. It follows that the two admonitions we heard from the mouth of the Almighty in the utterance *Thou shalt have no* were *Thou shalt not make unto thee a graven image, nor any manner of likeness* [20:4] and *thou shalt not bow down unto them* [20:5]. These, with the six hundred eleven we heard from the mouth of Moses, add up to six hundred thirteen.

All that remains to be explained is why they[95] did not count *Thou shalt have no other gods before Me* as an admonition which would then make three admonitions in that utterance. This is easily explained. If will and choice did not apply to beliefs, then the term "admonition" could not be applied to them. But if, withal, the term "admonition" *is* applied to them then the explanation of *Thou shalt have no* would be that one should not accept any other thing as God.[96] [Indeed,] it has been established in [Tractate] Sanhedrin that one who does so is guilty of a capital offense.[97] But they did not see fit to consider *Thou shalt have no* and *Thou shalt not bow down unto them* as two [separate commandments] for the root of them both is one, viz., the acceptance of divinity. But *Thou shalt not make unto thee a graven image* [20:4] [applies] even if one did not worship [the image] or accept it as divine. They were therefore counted as two [separate commandments]. But it never occurred to them to consider *I am the Lord thy God* as a commandment since it is the root and presupposition of all the commandments, as [said] above.[98]

As noted above, Abravanel wrote the *Rosh Amanah* in order to defend Maimonides from the criticisms leveled at his enumeration of the principles of Judaism by Ḥasdai Crescas and Joseph Albo. Following the practice of most of his

philosophical and exegetical works, Abravanel lists all of the
objections he can find to Maimonides in the writings of
Crescas and Albo (and adds eight of his own) before turning
to the defense proper. He summarizes Crescas's argument,
therefore, in chapter 4 of the *Rosh Amanah,* paraphrasing it
very closely.[99] He does not, however, respond to the argument itself until he gets to chapter 18. In that context he
points out that Crescas's argument is strongly influenced by
an argument of Moses Naḥmanides' found in his glosses to
Maimonides' *Sefer ha-Miẓvot.* Naḥmanides introduces the
exegetical argument there in order to support the opinion of
the author of the *Halakhot Gedolot* who did not count *I am
the Lord thy God* as a commandment. But Naḥmanides
himself concludes (in his gloss to the first negative commandment): "But what is *good in my sight* (I Samuel 29:6) in
this matter is that we count *I am the Lord thy God* as a
commandment, in accordance with the opinion of
Maimonides." This accords with Naḥmanides' statement in
his commentary to Exodus 20:2, "This divine utterance constitutes a positive commandment."[101]

We may now turn to Abravanel's defense of Maimonides as
presented in chapter 18 of his *Rosh Amanah.* Abravanel
begins the chapter with a brief summary of Crescas's exegetical objection to Maimonides. He then opens his defense by
pointing out that there are many places where the Bible
presents Moses speaking in God's name. The fact that Exodus
20:3–6 are presented in the first person, therefore, does not
make it impossible that they were said by Moses.

Abravanel then proceeds to attack Crescas's position. He
points out that, even if we don't count *I am the Lord thy God*
and *Thou shalt have no other gods before Me* as commandments, there are still three commandments—and this is the
opinion of all who enumerate the commandments—in the
passage which Crescas says the Israelites heard directly from
God. But, adding these to the 611 taught by Moses, the total
would come to 614! Following this, Abravanel goes on to
adduce biblical and rabbinic support for Maimonides' interpretation of Exodus 20:2.

Having answered the criticisms of Crescas, Abravanel introduces a new critique of Maimonides, one raised by certain unidentified "contemporary scholars."[102] They claim to find support for the claim that Exodus 20:2 is not a commandment in two passages from rabbinic literature, one in the Midrash (Mekhilta) and one in the Talmud (Tractate Horayot). Abravanel responds by showing how each passage can be read so as to be consistent with the views of Maimonides. He also adduces interpretations of the passages (by Naḥmanides in the case of the Mekhilta passage and by Rashi in the case of the passage from Horayot) which understand them as he does, so that they are consistent with Maimonides' position.

Abravanel then goes on the offensive again himself, using the same weapon introduced by the "contemporary scholars": citations from rabbinic literature. He introduces two midrashim which support Maimonides' position. Abravanel concludes the chapter with a brief critique of the putative position of the author of the *Halakhot Gedolot*.

We must now point out something which, on the face of it, is really quite remarkable. Notwithstanding his extended defense of Maimonides' position concerning the status of Exodus 20:2 here in the *Rosh Amanah*, Abravanel in the end adopts Crescas's interpretation! In his commentary to the Decalogue Abravanel writes:

> I have already mentioned in the question[103] that R. Ḥasdai proved that the term "commandment" according to its [proper] definition does not apply to beliefs. His arguments are strong. Therefore, the words of the author of the *Halakhot Gedolot* are *best in my eyes* [after I Samuel 29:6] since he did not count *I am the Lord your God* as a commandment. It is his opinion that the six hundred thirteen commandments are all decrees of God in which He decreed how we should act or refrain from acting. But the belief in His existence He made known to us through signs and demonstrations[104] and the revelation of the Divine Presence. It is the principle and root from which the commandments are derived, but is not counted in their number.[105]

Abravanel himself drew attention to the blatant contradiction between his positions in the *Commentary* and in the *Rosh Amanah*. A bit further in the same passage he wrote:

I have already discussed this issue in the eighteenth chapter of the treatise *Rosh Amanah* which I wrote. There I defended the opinion of Maimonides while here I spoke *as it was in my heart* [Joshua 14:7]; there is no contradiction in this. [106]

There is no contradiction in this because, as Abravanel makes abundantly clear in the *Rosh Amanah* 23, while he wrote the book to defend Maimonides, he did not subscribe to the latter's views concerning the principles of Judaism. Once he had begun the job of defending Maimonides, he followed it through, subjugating his own views to the task at hand. It should not be surprising that in the dispute between Maimonides and Crescas on the status of Exodus 20:2 Abravanel should side with Crescas. It is Crescas, after all, who is defending the autonomy of religion from philosophy, a position that Abravanel certainly held. If anything is surprising here it is that Abravanel managed to subjugate his strongly held views in order to make his defense of Maimonides all the more powerful. But that, of course, is entirely within the task he set for himself in writing the *Rosh Amanah*.

Principles of Faith
(Rosh Amanah)

A List of the Chapters in This Treatise

are included in others of them and why each one of them is listed as an independent principle.

10. An explanation of the fifth proposition. There will be explained in it three lessons and great teachings which Maimonides intended through the number of his principles.

11. An explanation of four other propositions which we shall need. The first: in what kind of commandments can there be principles. The second: that the principles ought to be unique to the divine Torah. The third: that the principles are beliefs concerning God or His actions. Fourth: that beliefs come to a man [only] after the necessary preparations.

12. Solutions to the first three objections which were raised on the principles. There I explained whether one ought to be called a sectarian if he is drawn by the literal sense of Scripture to believe something other than the truth in the matter of the principles. I also explained there that it is forbidden to place intermediaries between man and his Creator.

13. A solution to the fourth objection, on the issue of the eternity of the Torah. I explained the objections which follow from the arguments brought by R. Ḥasdai and his disciples.

14. A solution to the fifth objection, on the principle of the coming of the Messiah. There I explained R. Hillel's dictum, "Israel has no Messiah."

15. A solution to the sixth objection, relating to the principle of the resurrection of the dead.

16. Solutions to eleven other objections. With them are completed the seventeen objections raised by the scholars on Maimonides' principles.

17. Solutions to the first and second objections raised by R. Ḥasdai with respect to the commandments which Maimonides counted among the principles.

18. A solution to the third objection raised by R. Ḥasdai on Maimonides in connection with R. Simlai's statement in [Tractate] Makkot on the commandment *I am* [Exodus 20:2] and on the endeavors of other scholars to support him in this.

19. Solutions to three other objections which I raised against Maimonides.

20.   Solutions to three more of those objections. There I explained part of the first chapter of the *Sefer ha-Madda* and commented on the passage [beginning] *Thus saith the Lord, learn not the ways of the nations* [Jeremiah 10:1].

21.   Solutions to two other objections which I raised on the principles. This completes the solution to the twenty-eight objections concerning Maimonides' words on the principles and commandments.

22.   An investigation into the opinions of other scholars on the principles [including] the opinion of R. Ḥasdai, the opinion of R. Joseph Albo, and other opinions which I discussed there.

23.   An explanation of what I consider to be the correct opinion in this matter.

24.   One objection which might occur with respect to that opinion and its solution. There I explained, with great thoroughness, the first mishnah in *Perek Ḥelek*, "All Israel have a share in the world to come."

1

On the Opinion of Maimonides[1] Concerning the Foundations[2] of the Torah and Its Principles[3]

The first [person] to begin positing principles and foundations of the divine Torah was Maimonides, in his commentary to *Perek Ḥelek* of Tractate Sanhedrin on the mishnah, "All Israel have a portion in the world to come."[4] You should know that Maimonides wrote his *Commentary on the Mishnah* in the Arabic language and that there are two [Hebrew] translations of this chapter extant.[5] Even though their meaning is the same there are some differences in wording between the two. However, in that one of the translations is by Rabbi Samuel [ibn] Tibbon,[6] it is proper that we rely upon it in the light of his great wisdom and his greatness as a translator.[7]

I will cite the foundations which Maimonides presented there in his own words:

> What will suffice for what has to be mentioned here—and this is an appropriate place for it—is to make clear that the principles of our Torah and its foundations are thirteen: The first foundation: the existence of the Creator. [This is the belief] that there is a perfectly existent Being Who is the cause of the existence of [all other] beings and from Whom they derive their continued existence. If His nonexistence were supposed, then the existence of all [other] beings would be impossible. [But], if the nonexistence of all other beings were supposed, He alone would still exist, and His existence would be neither destroyed nor diminished, for He does not depend [for His existence] upon the existence of anything else. But everything other than He, from the Separate Intellects[8] and the Spheres to what is beneath them depend for their existence upon Him. We learn this first foundation from the utterance,[9] *I am the Lord your God* [Exodus 20:2]. This is a positive commandment.
>
> The second foundation: God's unity. [This is the belief] that He is one, not like the one of a genus nor like the one of a

species. [He is further] not like the one composed of many units, nor like a simple body which is one in number but which is susceptible of infinite division. But, rather, God is one by virtue of a unique unity. We learn this second foundation of faith from the statement, *Hear, O Israel, the Lord our God, the Lord is One* [Deuteronomy 6:4]. This is a positive commandment.

The third foundation: [God's] incorporeality. [This is the belief] that this Unity is neither a body nor the power of a body and that nothing which occurs to bodies, such as motion and rest, can occur to Him, whether essentially or accidentally. Thus, [the Sages] denied that He is subject to composition or decomposition[10] and the prophet said, *To whom then will ye liken me, that I should be equal?* [Isaiah 40:25]. If God were a body He would be like [other] bodies. Wherever Scripture speaks in terms of God having the attributes of a body, such as sitting and standing, etc., it speaks in the language of mankind, as the Sages said, "The Torah speaks in the language of man."[11] The Sages of [each] generation have spoken at length on this issue. We learn this third foundation from *Ye saw no manner of form* [*on the day that the Lord spoke unto you in Horeb out of the midst of the fire*] [Deuteronomy 4:15] which is to say that you do not comprehend God by any image [of Him] you may have for, as we said, He is neither a body not the power of a body.

The fourth foundation is that this aforementioned One is truly eternal *a parte ante,* [12] and that everything other than He is not eternal when we compare them to Him. There are many proofs of this in Scripture. This fourth foundation we learn from *The Eternal God is a dwelling place and underneath are the everlasting arms* [Deuteronomy 33:27].

The fifth foundation is that God alone ought to be the object of worship, magnifying, extolling and of the uplifting of voices in exaltation. This should not be done to any existent Being other than He, whether it be any one of the angels, spheres, stars, or elements, or what is composed of the latter, for they are all appointed to their tasks.[13] They have neither sovereignty nor will, but only love of God. It behooves us not to establish them as intermediaries between man and God; rather, all thoughts should be directed to God and away from what is other than He.[14] We learn this fifth foundation from the commandment which we have been given prohibiting idolatry.[15] The majority of the Torah is taken up with this matter.[16]

The sixth foundation: prophecy. [This is the belief] that it should be known that there are in this human species [people possessing] many qualities and great perfection whose souls remain so pure that they receive the form of the intellect. Afterwards such human intellects are joined to the Agent [Intelligence][17] from which an exalted overflow emanates upon them. These are the prophets, this is prophecy, and this is its meaning. A complete explanation of this would be very long; it is not our intention here to provide a demonstration for each foundation and to explain its truth because that would involve every science. Rather, we will simply describe them. Many verses of the Torah give testimony about the prophets.

The seventh foundation is the prophecy of Moses.[18] This is that one is obliged to believe that he was the father of all the prophets, [both] those who preceded him and those who followed after him and that they were all beneath him in rank; that he alone was chosen by God from the whole human species and that he comprehended more of God than any other man who has existed or will exist. He is absolutely distinguished from other men so much that he [. . .].[19] The faculties of imagination, sense, and perception were removed from him so that he remained intellect only. It was therefore said that he spoke to God without the intermediation of an angel: *with him do I speak mouth to mouth* [Numbers 12:8].

I would have explained this wonderful matter except that I saw that these issues are very sensitive and [that such an explanation] would necessitate a very extended discussion, with many propositions and examples. It would [also] be necessary first to explain the existence of the angels and the difference of their degree from that of the Creator and [it would also be necessary] to explain the soul and its faculties; [it would be further necessary] to expand the explanation to include the forms which the prophets attribute to the Creator—and included in this discussion is the matter of the *Shiur Komah*[20] in all its particulars—so that the discussion, even were it composed in the briefest possible way, could not be completed in even a hundred pages. I will therefore leave it [for now] and will discuss it in its [proper] place, either in the book on Midrash which I plan, or in the book on prophecy which I have begun to write, or in a book devoted to these foundations which I shall write.

I return to this seventh foundation and say that the prophecy of Moses is distinguished in four ways from the prophecies of all the other prophets. First, they prophesied by virtue of an intermediary while Moses [did so] without an intermediary, as it says, *with him do I speak mouth to mouth* [Numbers 12:8]. Second, all the [other] prophets only received their prophetic inspiration while asleep, *In a dream, in a vision of the night* [Job 33:15], or, if during the daytime, only after a deep sleep had fallen on the prophet, so that his senses were nullified and it was as if he were asleep [at night]. This situation is called "vision" or "trance." But the word [of God] came to Moses in the daytime, while he stood between the two cherubs, as God had promised him: *And there I will meet with thee* [Exodus 25:22], and as God said, *If there be a prophet among you I the Lord [do make myself known unto him in a vision, I do speak with him in a dream.] My servant Moses is not so; [he is trusted in all My house;] with him do I speak mouth to mouth [even manifestly and not in dark speeches . . .]* [Numbers 12:6–8].

Third, when prophecy comes to one of the other prophets, even if only in a vision, his nature is weakened, the parts of his body tremble, and he is stricken with terror and comes close to the very gates of death, as it is said in Daniel, *. . . and there remained no strength in me; for my comeliness was turned in me into corruption . . . then was I fallen into a deep sleep* [Daniel 10:8, 9]. But Moses was not like this; when the word [of God] came to him, he did not tremble, as it said, *And the Lord spoke to Moses face to face [as a man speaketh unto his friend]* [Exodus 33:11]; that is, just as a man is not stricken with terror or fear at the words of his friend, so Moses was not stricken with terror or fear at the word [of God] since he was joined to the intelligence.

Fourth, prophecy did not come to any [other] prophet whenever he desired it, but only when God desired it. A prophet might remain many years without prophesying. Sometimes a prophet might petition God in prayer [to allow him] to prophesy, and after some days the prophecy comes, but it does not communicate to him what he sought. There were prophets who inclined themselves [toward prophecy], as did Elisha when he said, *But now bring me a minstrel. And it came to pass, when the minstrel played, [that the hand of the Lord came upon him]* [II Kings 3:15], even though they did not have the ability to prophesy whenever they wished. But Moses would prophesy at any time, according to his desire, as it said, *[And Moses said unto them;] Stay ye, that I might hear what the Lord will command . . .* [Numbers 9:8]. It says further: *Speak unto Aaron thy*

brother, that he come not at all times into the holy place . . .
[Leviticus 16:2]. "Aaron was included in this prohibition, but
Moses was not."[21]

The eighth foundation: revelation.[22] This is that one is obliged
to believe that the whole of the Torah found in our hands today is
the Torah which was given to Moses and that all of it is from the
mouth of the Almighty.[23] This is to say that Moses apprehended
it all from the mouth of God with a kind of apprehension which is
[metaphorically] called "speaking," like the transmission of
speech. No one knows what this apprehension is. Moses wrote
what was said to him, both the chronicles of events and the
matters of the Torah and its commandments, and it is for this
reason that he is called lawgiver.[24] There is no difference between
And the sons of Ham: Cush and Miẓraim [Genesis 10:6], *I am the
Lord your God* [Exodus 20:2], and *Hear, O Israel, the Lord our
God [the Lord is one]* [Deuteronomy 6:4]; it is all from the mouth
of the Almighty and it is all the Torah of God, perfect,[25] pure,
holy, and true. This is made a point of contention by every
heretic[26] since they think that [one can distinguish between]
kernel and husk in the Torah and that there are things in it which
confer no benefit [on anyone] which they attribute to Moses
[rather than God]. This falls under the category of [one who says]
"that the Torah was not divinely revealed."[27] The Sages said that
one who believes that the entire Torah came from the mouth of
the Almighty except for one verse which was not uttered by God
but by Moses himself is included in *Because he hath despised the
word of the Lord [and hath broken His commandment; that soul
shall utterly be cut off, his iniquity shall be upon him]* [Numbers
15:31],[28] may God be exalted above the words of heretics! But
every single word [of the Torah] contains wonders of wisdom for
him whom God has graciously given *learning and wisdom*
[Daniel 1:17]. Even with such [divine help] the limits of the
Torah's wisdom will not be reached: *the measure thereof is longer
than the earth* [Job 11:9]. Every man ought to seek to receive
from God what David, annointed of the God of Jacob, sought
from Him: *Open Thou mine eyes, that I may behold wondrous
things out of thy Torah* [Psalms 119:18]. The interpretation of the
Torah, the Talmud, is also from the mouth of the Almighty.
Those practices which we follow today, [such as] the shape of the
Sukkah and of the lulav, fringes, phylacteries, etc., are done
according to the same form which God described to Moses and
which Moses, faithful to his mission, described to us. You have

been taught this eighth foundation by the verse, *Hereby you shall know that the Lord hath sent me . . .* [Numbers 16:28].

The ninth foundation is the principle of [non-] abrogation. This [is the belief] that our Torah is the Torah of Moses and that it will never be abrogated or exchanged; that another Torah will never come from God and that nothing will be added to nor taken away from the written and oral Torah, as it said, *Thou shalt not add thereto, nor diminish from it* [Deuteronomy 13:1]. We have already explained what needs explanation in this foundation in the beginning of this composition.[29]

The tenth foundation is that God knows all the deeds of men and does not neglect them as was thought by those who said, *The Lord hath forsaken the land* [Ezekiel 8:12, 9:9]. Rather, [the truth accords] with the words of the prophet who said, *Great in counsel and mighty in work; Whose eyes are open [upon all the ways of the sons of man, to give every one according to his ways, and according to the fruit of his doings]* [Jeremiah 32:19]. The Torah says, *And the Lord saw that the wickedness of man was great in the earth* [Genesis 6:5], and [*The Lord said:*] *Verily the cry of Sodom and Gomorrah is great . . .* [Genesis 18:20]. All this teaches this tenth foundation.

The eleventh foundation: God will well reward those who observe His commandments and will punish those who violate them or fail to fulfill them; and that God's greatest reward is the world to come and His greatest punishment is cutting off [the sinner]. We have already explained this matter sufficiently in this chapter. The verse which teaches this foundation is *Yet now, if Thou wilt forgive their sin—; and if not, blot me, I pray Thee, out of the book which Thou has written* [Exodus 32:32], to which God responded, *Whosoever hath sinned against Me, him will I blot out of My book* [Exodus 32:33]. This is a proof of the reward of the righteous and of the punishment of the wicked.

The twelfth foundation: the days of the Messiah. This is that one must believe that *It will surely come, it will not delay, though it tarry, wait for it* [Habakkuk 2:3, reversed]. It is not proper to set a time for [the Messiah's coming] nor is it permitted to seek out Scriptural derivations in order to determine when he will come. It is for the reason that the Sages said, "Blasted be the bones of those who calculate the end!"[30] We must [constantly] recall the redemption and God's love and pray for it, in accordance with what was said by every prophet from Moses to Malachi. He who doubts this or makes light of it denies what the

Torah predicted in the story of Balaam[31] and in the weekly reading called *You are standing*.[32] Included in this principle is that a [legitimate] king of Israel must be descended from David through Solomon. Anyone who disputes the sovereignty of this family denies God and the words of His prophets.

The thirteenth principle[33] is resurrection of the dead, the meaning and secrets of which we have already explained.[34]

When all these principles are perfectly understood and believed in by a person he enters the community of Israel[35] and one is obligated to love and pity him and to act toward him in the ways in which the Creator has commanded that one should act towards his brother, with love and fraternity. Even were he to commit every transgression in the world, because of lust of the [evil] inclination, or because of the power of the baser elements in his nature, he is then one of the sinners in Israel and will be punished according to his sins, but he has a portion in the world to come.

But if a man does not believe all of these principles as he should, he leaves the community [of Israel], denies the fundamental,[36] and is called a sectarian,[37] *apikoros*,[38] and one who "cuts among the plantings."[39] One is required to hate him and it is proper to despise and destroy him. About such a person it was said, *Do I not hate them, O Lord, who hate Thee?* [Psalms 139:21].

But I have discussed these issues too much and have digressed from the intended aim of my composition. I did this, however, because of the great benefit it bestows with respect to the strengthening of faith. I have collected for you valuable things which are scattered in many important books. Therefore, acquire them and attain felicity thereby. Read these things many times and study them well. If your soul lead you astray so that you think that you understand them after one or [even] ten readings, know that you have [surely] been misled. Therefore, do not read it hastily,[40] because I did not compose it in a haphazard fashion. Only after extended study and examination of books and [only after] speculative investigation in order to distinguish true from false beliefs [did I determine which beliefs] were proper to study. [I did this] on the basis of clear arguments and proofs for every issue. I pray that God teach me the proper path.

You will further find that Maimonides recorded these principles in the *Sefer ha-Madda*, "*Hilkhot Yesodei ha-Torah*." Thus, in the first chapter he says that "the foundation of all foundations and the pillar of all sciences is to realize that there is a First Being, etc."[41] He said further:

> To acknowledge this truth is an affirmative precept, as it is said, *I am the Lord thy God* [Exodus 20:2]. And whoever permits the thought to enter his mind that there is another deity besides this God, violates a prohibition; as it is said, *Thou shalt have no other gods before Me* [Exodus 20:3].[42]

He also presented the principle of unity in that chapter, and said that it is a positive commandment.[43] [He also presented the principle of God's] incorporeality, but did not say that it was a commandment.[44] In the other chapters he presented some of these principles, but did not say that they were commandments.[45]

We also find that Maimonides himself in the book enumerating the commandments which he wrote presented [belief in] the existence of God as the first commandment and [belief in] His unity as the second.[46] He proved that *I am the Lord thy God* is a commandment from the dictum of the Sages in Tractate Makkot. "Six hundred thirteen precepts were communicated to Moses . . . what is the authentic text for this? *Moses commanded us Torah* [Deuteronomy 33:4]." They asked, "[But] Torah has a letter-value of [only] six hundred and eleven!" They answered, "*I am* and *Thou Shalt have no* [not being reckoned because] we heard them from the mouth of the Almighty."[47] This is consistent with what Maimonides wrote in the *Sefer ha-Madda*.

This is a statement of the opinions of Maimonides concerning these principles [as they are presented] in his *Commentary on the Mishnah, Sefer ha-Madda,* and *Sefer ha-Miẓvot.*

2

On the Opinions of Post-Maimonidean Scholars Concerning the Principles

Rabbi Ḥasdai [Crescas], in his *Or ha-Shem* puts forward the principles and foundations differently [than did Maimonides]. For he wrote that there are Torah beliefs, cornerstones which are the foundations and presuppositions of the commandments, and of all the beliefs [of Judaism]. These are the existence of God joined with two further beliefs, [God's] unity and incorporeality.[1] There are also cornerstones of Torah [according to R. Ḥasdai] which are foundations of the religion which "would collapse in its entirety if it could be imagined that one of them were missing."[2] These are six: God's knowledge of existent beings, His providence over them, His infinite power, prophecy, [human] choice, and purpose [of the Torah].

There are further [according to R. Ḥasdai] true beliefs which we ought to believe and which are independent of any particular commandments. A person who denies any one of them is called a sectarian. These are eight: creation, survival of the soul [after death], reward and punishment, resurrection of the dead, eternity of the Torah, the superiority of Mosaic prophecy, that the Priest is answered through the *Urim* and *Tummim*,[3] and Messiah.[4] There are additionally [according to R. Ḥasdai] true beliefs which we ought to believe which are dependent upon particular commandments. A person who denies any one of them is [also] called a sectarian. These are three: prayer and the priestly blessing,[5] the efficacy of repentance, and *Rosh ha-Shanah*[6] and the four divisions of the year.[7]

Rabbi Joseph Albo, however, in his *Sefer ha-Ikkarim*, extensively investigated these principles and determined that there were three. These are, according to his opinion, supergenera[8] which include all the other beliefs. These are [first], God's existence, under which are subsumed [His] unity and incorporeality. The second is divine revelation, under which are subsumed prophecy and the superiority of the prophecy of Moses. The third is reward and punishment, under which are subsumed [God's] knowledge and providence, Messiah, and resurrection of the dead.[9]

These men, *peaceable as they are with us* [Genesis 34:21], diverged in their opinions from[10] the position of Maimonides on the principles [of Judaism] because of the objections[11] which they saw. As it appears to me from their words, their objections to the position of Maimonides number twenty. Some of them they raised explicitly, and some of them are [only] implied in their words. I will state them *one after another to find out the account* [Ecclesiastes 7:27]. First [I] will state their objections to the principles [generally] and then their objections to the principles which Maimonides enumerated among the commandments. I will not record in detail which [objections] I gleaned from the words of R. Ḥasdai and which from the words of the author of the *Sefer ha-Ikkarim*. I will [then] add to these [objections] other objections [of my own] to the words of Maimonides on this issue which were not raised by the above-mentioned scholars.

3

On the Objections Raised Against the Principles

They said that insofar as [the word] *ikkar*[1] "is a term applied to a thing upon which the existence and duration of another thing depends and without which it cannot endure,"[2] like a tree whose existence is dependent upon its roots, it is difficult [to understand] why Maimonides posited all thirteen of the beliefs he listed as principles and cornerstones upon which the whole Torah depends. For, while this is justified with respect to the first foundation, that of God's existence, and with prophecy and revelation [as well as] with [God's] knowledge and providence, the others which he listed are not principles and foundations of the Torah such that it would be destroyed with their refutation.[3] This is particularly evident in the second principle, that of [God's] unity and in the third principle, that of [God's] incorporeality, for even though they are true beliefs, the Torah in its entirety would not be destroyed and the observance of the commandments would not be nullified if we believed differently.[4] It is therefore very difficult [to understand] why Maimonides recorded these two beliefs among the principles. This is the first objection.

The second objection relates to the fifth principle which Maimonides listed, that one ought to worship God.[5] This principle is a particular commandment, as it said, *And you shall serve the Lord your God* [Exodus 22:35]. It further said, *And you shall serve Him with all your hearts* [Deuteronomy 11:13]. Our Sages said, "What is the service of the heart? You must needs say, prayer."[6] Therefore Maimonides said in this principle that one ought to lift one's voice in praise and exaltation of God. It is difficult to number this among the principles for one ought not to count as a principle or root any particular commandment of the Torah. Were such not the case, the number of principles would be equal to the number of commandments.[7]

The third objection also relates to the fifth principle, in which Maimonides posited that God alone ought to be worshipped, that nothing else be worshipped,[8] and that we may not place intermediaries between man and his Creator. This is difficult [to understand] for if a person believes that God and His Torah are true, but he prays to the angels Gabriel or Raphael [asking that they] commend him to God, how would that cause the Torah to be destroyed in its entirety? Why should the prohibition of intermediaries be a principle and foundation?[9]

The fourth objection relates to the ninth principle, that the Torah of Moses will neither be uprooted nor exchanged for another. Nor will the Creator give another Torah aside from it, nor will there ever be any addition to or subtraction from it, as it is said, *You shall not add to it nor subtract from it* [Deuteronomy 13:1]. Maimonides explained the point of this principle in the *Guide*.[10] He said that the divine Torah is absolutely perfect, as it is written, *The Torah of the Lord is perfect* [Psalms 19:8]; a perfect thing cannot be the subject of any additions or deletions. Therefore it is impossible for it ever to change.

This [position of Maimonides'] is subject to a not insignificant objection: given that the Torah will never change in terms of the Giver and will never change in terms of itself in accordance with its perfection,[11] it is [still] possible that there might be a change in it in terms of the recipient.[12] I mean to say that God might add to, subtract from, or change the Torah at some time, either in its totality or in part, in accordance with what is best for its recipients. Have we not seen that He gave Adam special commandments and did not permit him to eat meat, while He gave Noah other commandments and permitted him [to eat] meat? He gave the commandment of circumcision to Abraham and added many other commandments to Moses since divine laws[13] change according to the [needs of the] time and in accordance to what is best for their recipients.[14] Just as an expert physician might prescribe a light regimen to a sick person at the beginning of his illness, while afterwards, when the illness subsides, "the mouth that forbade is the same mouth that permits."[15] This is no deficiency in the physician *qua* physician,[16] but, rather, great wisdom.[17] So it is in the case of the laws and commandments of the Torah. It is not impossible that they might change in accordance with [the needs of] their recipients and the needs of the time.

The evidence adduced by Maimonides to establish this principle, [namely] the verse, *You shall not add to it nor detract from it* [Deuteronomy 13:1] [is not conclusive since the verse] does not come to admonish us concerning the eternity of the commandments, but, rather, concerning the manner of performing them. [The verse admonishes us] not to learn from the idolators how they worship their gods and [in that way] add to or subtract from the commandments of the Torah, as the simple meaning of the passage indicates.[18]

If the [truth of the] matter accorded with Maimonides' words, how could the Sages have said that a court can abrogate something from the Torah in the case of abstaining from the performance of an action?[19] There is no doubt that they were not violating the prohibition of *You shall not . . . detract from it.* Similarly, they said that "Solomon ordained the laws of *eruv*[20] and [the washing of] hands."[21] Should we say that Solomon violated the prohibition of *You shall not add?* In Leviticus Rabbah they said that all the holidays are destined to be abolished with the exception of Purim and the Day of Atonement.[22] They also said, "why is [the pig] called 'swine' *(ḥazir)?* Because in the future God will return it [*ha-ḥaziro*] to Israel."[23] In the days of Ezra they changed the names of the months from what they had been called in the Torah, First, Second, Third, and so with all of them, and called them *Nisan, Iyar,* etc. This abolishes a commandment.[24]

Even if we accept Maimonides' interpretation of *You shall not add to it nor detract from it,* it still does not constitute a proof for the eternity of the Torah for [in this verse] Scripture only admonishes *us*[25] not to add to or detract from the commandments on our own authority. But what is to stop God from adding to or detracting from them? The author of the *Ikkarim* commented on this extensively in Treatise III, chapters 13, 14, 16, and 20. Look there.

The fifth objection relates to the twelfth of the principles counted by Maimonides, that of the coming of the Messiah. Even though this is a true belief, it is not a foundation such that the Torah would collapse with its refutation. We find in *Perek Ḥelek:* "R. Hillel said: There shall be no Messiah for Israel, because they have already enjoyed him in the days of Hezekiah."[26] We ought not to say that R. Hillel was excluded from the community of the Jewish religion and was a denier of the Torah, since the Talmud called him "Rabbi" and quoted a teaching in his name. This teaches that [belief in the Messiah] is not a principle.[27]

The sixth objection relates to the last principle, that of resurrection of the dead. Even though this is a true belief according to [both] the tradition and the Torah, it should not be posited as a principle of the Torah. Why should the Torah collapse in its entirety and its commandments be refuted if one believes that divine retribution occurs [both] in this world and in the world to come, but that there is no bodily resurrection after death?[28]

The seventh objection: If it was the opinion of Maimonides that it is a true principle that the Torah will not change at any time, neither in whole nor in part, not even in the days of the Messiah, then how could he count the coming of the Messiah and the resurrection of the dead among the principles? These are events which will occur in the future; after they actually take place they will of necessity no longer be principles. These two principles will thus necessarily change; with their change the Torah will change in the area of which they are a part. But it has already been posited that the Torah will not change! This is an insoluble dilemma.[29]

The eighth objection arises if we say that Maimonides did not count things as principles according to the definition of the word "principle" but, rather, counted as principles true and praiseworthy beliefs. If this is the case, it is difficult [to understand] "Why he did not include the doctrine that the *Shekhina*[30] dwells in Israel through the medium of the Torah?"[31] This is the greatest felicity which Israel merited.

The ninth objection: Why did not [Maimonides] count among the principles belief in the creation of the world? This is a belief which every Israelite ought to hold, as Maimonides [himself] established in the *Guide*, II. 25.[32] Just as he counted God's eternity *a parte ante* as a principle, he ought also to have counted the creation of the world as a principle.[33]

The tenth objection: "Why did he not include the dogma that we must believe in the miracles of the Torah in their literal sense?"[34] This is a great foundation and principle upon which everything depends. So also with "the other particular doctrines which everyone professing the Torah of Moses is obliged to believe,"[35] especially the Sinaitic experience.

The eleventh objection: "Why does [Maimonides] not include the principle that one should follow ancestral tradition? For it is a general principle of all divine laws, which cannot be conceived without it."[36]

The twelfth objection: Why did not Maimonides count [free] choice [as a principle]? It is a great principle, without which no religion could be conceived. Maimonides himself called it a principle in the *Sefer ha-Madda*, "Hilkhot Teshuvah" V.[37]

The thirteenth objection: Why did not Maimonides record[38] among the principles that God acts by will, since this belief is [logically] prior to the belief in the existence of signs and demonstrations?[39] This [belief] is a great pillar upon which the narratives of the Torah, its commandments, reward and punishment, and all the cornerstones of faith are built and upon which they depend. For if, Heaven forfend, we posit that God does not act by will, there would be no room for all this; [nor would there be room for] prophecy, the superiority of Moses' prophecy, revelation, the coming of the Redeemer, or the resurrection of the dead. But since God does act by will all these principles should be believed. This objection was not raised by these scholars,[40] but by a recent scholar.[41]

The fourteenth objection: Why did not [Maimonides] count among the principles that God lives, is eternal, is wise, is powerful, and other things among the attributes which we ought to believe?[42] Further, why are the principles thirteen in number? Was it [to make them] accord with the number of God's attributes[43] or with the thirteen hermeneutical principles by which the Torah is expounded?[44] In truth, Maimonides' principles bear no relation or similarity to these lists.[45]

The fifteenth objection: Why did [Maimonides] not record among the principles the matter of the end of man and belief in the survival of the soul[46] as did R. Ḥasdai? [R. Ḥasdai] included the purpose [of the Torah] among the cornerstones of the Torah and the foundations of the religion which are such that if we conceived the lack of one of them, [the religion] would be destroyed in its entirety.[47] [R. Ḥasdai] included the survival of the soul among the true beliefs which are such that if one denies them he is called a sectarian.[48]

The sixteenth objection: Why did [Maimonides] not record the response of the *Urim* and *Tummim* among the principles as did R. Ḥasdai? Among the true beliefs which we are obliged to believe and which are such that if one denies them he is called a sectarian, he included [the belief] that the priest is answered by the *Urim* and *Tummim*.[49]

The seventeenth objection: Why did not [Maimonides] count prayer, the priestly blessing, the efficacy of repentance, *Rosh ha-Shanah*, the Day of Atonement, and the four divisions of the year among the principles as R. Ḥasdai did? He included them in the class of true beliefs in which we must believe and which are such that if one denies them he is called a sectarian and which depend upon specific commands.[50]

These are the seventeen objections which I culled from the words of the scholars who criticized Maimonides' principles.

4

On Three Objections Which R. Ḥasdai Raised Against Maimonides with Respect to the Principles Which the Latter Enumerated from Among the Commandments

R. Ḥasdai also raised three other objections against Maimonides with respect to his having counted the first and second principles as commandments.[1]

The first objection: He wrote at the beginning of his book[2]—and there is no doubt that he was referring to Maimonides even though he didn't mention him by name—that he who counted *I am the Lord thy God* [Exodus 20:2] as a commandment was absolutely mistaken, for commandments are relational and none can be imagined without a known God Who commands. Thus, if we posit belief in the existence of God as a commandment, we must posit belief in the existence of God prior to belief in the existence of God, and so it will go ad infinitum. A thing would thus be its own cause. All this is absolutely false and shameful.

The second objection: It is apparent that the term "commandment" according to its [proper] definition only applies to matters with respect to which will and choice obtain. Inasmuch as this scholar proved in Treatise II, principle v,[3] chapter 5 of his work that choice and will do not obtain with respect to beliefs and opinions since they are nothing but the [consequence of] imagining that an intelligible [exists] outside of the soul as it is [pictured by] the soul. A person who believes something must feel necessity or coercion to believe it, either on the basis of rational argument or on the basis of miracles and wonders. It follows from this necessarily that the term "commandment" according to its [proper] definition cannot apply to beliefs and opinions. Thus, he erred who thought that [belief in] the existence of God and His unity are positive commandments.

The third objection relates to the proof adduced by
Maimonides that the utterance, *I am the Lord thy God* is a
commandment. [This proof depends upon] the words of
R. Simlai in the Talmud Makkot, as mentioned in the first
chapter.[4] R. Ḥasdai wrote that Maimonides was incorrect
because, even because [Leviticus 26:43] the reference [of the
Sages in Makkot] to *I am* and *Thou shalt have no* is best
understood as including the entire utterance which continues
through . . . *of them that love Me and keep My commandments* [Exodus 20:6]. [This is so] because both of these
utterances are said in the first person: *I am the Lord thy God;
before Me;* and . . . *of them that love Me and keep My
commandments.* The rest of the Decalogue, however, is said
in the third person: *for the Lord will not hold him guiltless*
[Exodus 20:7]; *for in six days the Lord made* [20:11]; and *On
the seventh day He ceased from work and rested.*[5] Therefore,
they concluded, "*I am* and *Thou shalt have no* were heard
from the mouth of the Almighty." Since those writers who
enumerated the commandments[6] counted *Thou shalt not
make unto thee a graven image* [Exodus 20:4] and *Thou shalt
not bow down unto them* [20:5] as two admonitions, then if
we counted *I am* as a commandment, there would be three
commandments "which they heard from the mouth of the
Almighty" and the number of commandments would come to
614. Were we to count *Thou shalt have no other gods* [20:3] as
an admonition against conferring divinity on anything but
God, as Maimonides wrote,[7] [the number of commandments]
would come to 615. It necessarily follows from this that when
R. Simlai said, "*I am* and *Thou shalt have no* we heard from
the mouth of the Almighty," he did not mean that each
utterance was a commandment but that the two commandments were in the utterance of *Thou shalt have no,* namely,
Thou shalt not make unto thee a graven image and *Thou shalt
not bow down unto them. Thou shalt have no* is not counted
among the commandments in that it is a belief with which will
and choice do not obtain. The utterance *I am* is, on this
account, the root and presupposition of all the commandments, but not a commandment itself.[8]

5

On Eight Other Objections Against Maimonides Which I Raised Myself

Aside from these objections[1] I have myself seen fit to raise other objections against Maimonides which were not considered by my predecessors.[2] These concern what he wrote in the *Sefer ha-Madda* and in his *Commentary on the Mishnah* concerning these principles and commandments

The first objection: Why did Maimonides present [only] some of the foundations listed in the *Commentary on the Mishnah*, in the "*Hilkhot Yesodei ha-Torah*" in the *Sefer ha-Madda* while omitting others? In the first chapter he discussed God's existence, His unity, and His incorporeality which are the first three princples.[3] In chapter 7 he discussed prophecy, the superiority of Mosaic prophecy, and revelation, which are three other principles.[4] In the ninth chapter[5] and in other chapters[6] he discussed the eternity of the Torah. Thus, of the thirteen principles listed in the *Commentary on the Mishnah* you have seven discussed in the *Sefer ha-Madda*. There remain six additional principles not mentioned in the laws contained in the *Sefer ha-Madda*. These are that God alone is eternal, that it is proper to worship Him, God's knowledge, reward and punishment, the coming of the Messiah, and resurrection of the dead. Maimonides included these among the principles which he presented in the *Commentary on the Mishnah* but did not mention in the "*Hilkhot Yesodei ha-Torah*" in the *Sefer ha-Madda*.[7] This is very strange in that the foundations of the Torah and its principles are one and the same.[8]

The second objection relates to the fact that in the *Sefer ha-Madda*, "*Hilkhot Yesodei ha-Torah*," Maimonides discusses other issues, such as love of God, fear of God,[9] [the obligation] to walk in God's ways,[10] [the obligation] to venerate the Temple,[11] and many matters from the sciences of physics and metaphysics. We cannot but assert that either these matters are not [to be counted] among the foundations of the Torah and its principles and for this reason Maimonides did not include them among the principles in the *Commentary on the Mishnah* or that everything mentioned by Maimonides in those laws in the *Sefer ha-Madda* is a foundation of the Torah. It must be asked with respect to the former case, why did Maimonides present them in the *Sefer ha-Madda,* interspersed among the foundations? Other commandments are not listed here. It must be asked with respect to the latter case, why did he not include them among the principles in the *Commentary on the Mishnah?* [On this latter view] also, the principles of religion would number twenty or thirty, corresponding to the number of those commandments and ideas[12] and not thirteen, as Maimonides had written.[13]

The third objection: Why is it that among all the thirteen principles and foundations of the Torah discussed by Maimonides, he only counted the first two of them—God's existence and unity—as commandments? About each of them he wrote: "To acknowledge the truth of this is an affirmative precept."[14] He also counted them as commandments in his *Sefer ha-Miẓvot.*[15] But he did not count the rest of the principles as commandments, whether positive or negative. It is very strange, for if they are all principles and foundations of the Torah which we are obliged to believe, how can we say that God did not command their belief? But if belief in them is not a commandment, it is not obligatory. This contradicts our statement to the effect that they are principles which we are obliged to believe!

We cannot say that he did not count them as commandments because they are beliefs—and the term commandment according to its [proper] definition cannot be applied to them, as is the opinion of R. Ḥasdai[16]—for the existence of God and His unity are beliefs, and Maimonides wrote that they are commandments. If we are to say that the principles were not counted as commandments since there are no verses in the

Torah commanding them, what do we do with[17] the third
principle, that of God's incorporeality, which is taught by a
complete verse? Maimonides adduced the verse as evidence of
God's incorporeality. [It is:] *Take ye therefore good heed
unto yourselves that ye saw no manner of form . . .*
[Deuteronomy 4:15]. According to the tradition of the Sages
[the words] *take heed, lest,* and *don't* all introduce negative
commandments.[18] Why, then, did Maimonides not count this
principle as a commandment? Similarly, the principle of
God's eternity, "and that everything other than He is not
eternal when we compare them to Him,"[19] which includes
the cornerstone of the creation of the world, as I shall
explain,[20] is stated explicitly in the verse, *For in six days the
Lord made the Heavens,* etc. [Exodus 20:11]. Similarly, the
principle that one ought to worship [only] God is found in
the verses, *And ye shall serve the Lord your God* [Exodus
23:25], and *And Him shalt thou*[21] *serve* [Deuteronomy 6:13].
Further, Maimonides proved the [truth of the] principle of
the eternity of the Torah from the verse, *Thou shalt not add
thereto, nor diminish from it* [Deuteronomy 13:1]. On the
basis of what argument, therefore, did Maimonides not count
these principles among the commandments in accordance
with the verses in which they are found, since he counted
other [things as] commandments on the authority of verses
much weaker[22] than these?

The fourth objection: Why in the *Sefer ha-Madda* did
Maimonides write of the first principle that it was "the
foundation of all foundations and the pillar of the sciences,"[23]
when he should have said, "one of the foundations," not "the
foundation of foundations"? Of what concern is it of ours
whether or not this foundation is the pillar of gentile sciences,
which are not of the children of Israel [I Kings 9:20]? He
doesn't call it this in his *Commentary on the Mishnah* or in his
book enumerating the commandments. There is a further
difficulty with what he said there following the statement of
the foundation: "Therefore His truth is not like the truth of
any one of them."[24] There is no need for this assertion and
the verses which Maimonides cites in this connection do not
teach what he intended. For, how does the *The Lord God is*

t̲ u̲th [Jeremiah 10:10] negate the truth of every other existent being as Maimonides wanted to prove from it? Further, the verse, *There is none other beside Him* [Deuteronomy 4:35], which Maimonides cites[25] does not mention truth at all.

The fifth objection relates to Maimonides' statement in chapter 1, paragraph three,[26] "This being is the God of the universe, the Lord of all the earth. And He it is Who controls the Sphere, etc." This opinion, viz., that the First Cause moves the highest sphere, is not of the essence of necessary existence. There are many opinions concerning this among the philosophers.[27] One [even] finds contradictory statements about this in what Maimonides wrote in the *Guide,* as I wrote in my treatise, *Ateret Zekenim,* which I composed in my youth.[28] Why then did Maimonides posit this disputed opinion [here] in explaining this first principle and foundation but did not write in the same vein in the *Commentary on the Mishnah* and the *Sefer ha-Miẓvot?* Even though Maimonides' proof of God's existence assumed as a premise the constant motion of the sphere, that is an opinion built upon the eternity *a parte ante* of the world[29]—God forbid that Maimonides should believe it! It must be asked, therefore, how what Maimonides wrote here in the *Sefer ha-Madda* differs from what he wrote in other places, either because there is no need for it, or because it deviates from the roots of religion.[30]

The sixth objection relates to the difficulties in Maimonides' explanation in the *"Hilkhot Yesodei ha-Torah"* of the principle of divine unity. He explained it in terms of God's incorporeality and also proved it from the motion of the sphere which is the very proof which he used for the principle of God's existence. It may be further asked why he did not adduce the verse, *There is none else beside Him* [Deuteronomy 4:35], as proof of God's unity instead of adducing it as proof of God's existence? There is no doubt that the verse is more relevant to the issue of God's unity than that of His existence. A question may also be raised in connection with what is written there in the *Sefer ha-Madda* in the discussion of the first foundation: "And whoever permits the thought to enter his mind that there is another deity besides this God, violates a prohibition; as it is said, *Thou shalt have no other gods before Me* [Exodus 20:3]."[31] This prohibition actually correlates to the positive commandment of God's unity and Maimonides should have cited it after the discussion of the commandment of God's unity,[32] not in the discussion of the first principle, that of God's existence. For, if the first principle is a positive commandment, viz., that we believe that God exists, then its correlative prohibition would be that we not believe *what the fool said in his heart: "There is no God"* [Psalms 14:1 and 53:2], not that [we refrain from believing] that there is another god aside from this One. This latter is without a doubt the prohibition corresponding to the [commandment of] God's unity.

The seventh objection relates to Maimonides' listing the first principle, that God exists necessarily, the second principle, that He is one, the third principle, that He is incorporeal, and the fourth principle, that He alone is eternal *a parte ante.* It is established by the science of metaphysics that from the very essence of a necessary existent it follows that [such an existent] is one, not a body nor the power of a body, and that it is eternal *a parte ante* and *a parte post.* Otherwise, it may not be said that it exists necessarily.[33] It follows from this that the first principle, that God exists necessarily, includes the three principles that follow it, these being God's unity, eternity, and incorporeality. Why, then, did Maimonides count them as separate principles, since they are included in the first principle and follow necessarily from it, when he did not include in the principles the rest of those things which follow from them?

The eighth objection relates to belief in the resurrection of the dead which Maimonides included among his principles in the *Commentary on the Mishnah.* Maimonides took this from the mishnah wherein it is written, "The following have no portion in the world to come: He who maintains that resurrection is not a Biblical doctrine."[34] According to the Mishnah, the principle is not just belief in the resurrection of the dead, but rather that such belief is taught by the Torah. Therefore the Sages of the Talmud sought to prove the doctrine of resurrection from verses in Scripture, as is clearly seen there in *Ḥelek*. It must be asked, therefore, of Maimonides how he could write that the principle is belief in the resurrection of the dead simply when he should have said that the principle is to believe that the resurrection of the dead is taught by the Torah, in accordance with the words of the Mishnah.

These, then, are all the objections which are raised in connection with this issue; in number they come to twenty-eight, symbolized by *He hath declared to His people the power of His works* [Psalms 111:6].[35] In order to answer the above-listed objections, and in order to explain the words of Maimonides, I have seen fit to preface [this work with certain] propositions which will direct us perfectly to understand Maimonides' intention and wisdom in the principles which he posited.

6

On the First Proposition Necessary for This Enquiry

The first proposition: The term "principle" [*ikkar*] does not signify only what the terms "root" [*shoresh*] and "foundation" [*yesod*] signify. For the term "root" signifies the first part of a plant and the beginning of its existence, upon which the branches of a tree [for example] depend and rest, as it says, *For he shall be as a tree planted by the waters, and that spreadeth out its roots by the river* [Jeremiah 17:8] and *His roots shall dry up beneath* [Job 18:16]. Similarly, the term "foundation" signifies the foundation upon which a building stands, as it says, *Raze it, raze it, even to the foundation thereof* [Psalms 137:7]. It says, *The foundations of the world were laid bare* [II Samuel 22:16]; this signifies the middle point which is the true center of the sphere [composed] of the element earth. Thus, the verse speaks in terms of "laying bare" since that point is covered by the rest of the parts of the earth in its entirety. It says, *The foundations of heaven did tremble* [II Samuel 22:8], which refers to the globe of the earth in its entirety. It calls that point "the foundation of heaven" for, as it has been established in the *Physics*, [1] there can be no revolving motion without a stationary point about which it [2] revolves. Thus, the terms "root" and "foundation" only signify "a thing upon which the existence and duration of another thing depends and without which it cannot endure." [3]

The term "principle" [*ikkar*], however, is [only] sometimes used in this sense, as when [Scripture] says, *Nevertheless leave the stump [ikkar] of its roots in the earth* [Daniel 4:12], or as the Sages said, "Throw a stick into the air and it will fall back to its place of origin [*ikkar*]."[4] They speak "of a thing which has its basis [*ikkar*] in the Torah or not."[5] Aside from using it in this sense the Sages also used the word to signify the most important and essential[6] thing in its class even if "the existence and duration of another thing" does not depend upon it. You will find this in their oft-repeated usage of the phrase "This is the essential [*ikkar*] thing."[7] The word is not used here to signify something which is a root for something else. [Thus] they said, "A Benediction is said over the principal [*ikkar*] kind [of food] and this serves for the subsidiary [foods]."[8] That is to say, [one makes a benediction over that] which one had intended to make the principal part [*ikkar*] of one's meal. In chapter "*Keẓad Mevarkhin*"[9] they said, with reference to the fruits of Ginnosar, "salted food is the principal [*ikkar*] item."[10] They said this because it[11] is more praiseworthy. In the first chapter of Berakhot they said,

> This does not mean that the mention of the Exodus from Egypt shall be obliterated, but that the deliverance from subjection to the other kingdoms shall take the first place [*ikkar*] and the Exodus from Egypt shall become secondary. Similarly you read: *Thy name shall not be called anymore Jacob, but Israel shall be thy name* [Gen. 35:10]. This does not mean that the name Jacob shall be obliterated, but that Israel shall be the principal name [*ikkar*] and Jacob a secondary one.[12]

Thus, *Behold with thine eyes* [Ezekiel 40:4] that the term "principle" [*ikkar*] is often used to signify a praiseworthy thing even if it is not a root for something else. In this vein the Sages said, "Study is not the essential thing [*ikkar*], but action."[13]

It is amazing, therefore, that the scholar Rabbi Joseph Albo in Treatise I, chapter 3 [of the *Sefer ha-Ikkarim*] wrote: "The word *ikkar* is a term applied to a thing upon which the existence and duration of another thing depends and without which it cannot endure."[14] On this basis he multiplied questions and objections against Maimonides to the effect that the principles he enumerated in the *Commentary on the Mishnah* cannot properly be called "principles" nor can they be included under its definition. In Treatise III of his book he himself is faced with the difficulty of explaining why he taught that revelation is a principle, and prophecy a derivation from it, when [the truth of] the matter is just the opposite: prophecy is the principle and revelation is derived from it.[15] His answer was that he considered[16] revelation a principle and prophecy a derivation from it, and he considered reward and punishment a principle and providence a derivation from it since the existence and duration of prophecy depend upon revelation and [the existence and duration] of providence [depend upon] reward and punishment. They are called "principles" only because revelation is the purpose of prophecy and reward and punishment are the purpose of providence; because of the exalted nature of these beliefs he counted them as principles.[17] But when this scholar raised objections against Maimonides, he said that the term "principle" may be used only with respect to matter and form while in answering objections to his own position he said that the word "principle" may be used with respect to the purpose of a thing.[18]

The clear truth is that the term "principle" [ikkar] may be used with respect to all three: a thing's matter, its form, and its purpose, which [last] is the most perfect part of it. When you know this you will understand the words which Maimonides wrote in his Commentary on the Mishnah at the beginning of the principles: "It ought to be made clear that the principles of our Torah and its foundations are thirteen."[19] With this he made clear that among the thirteen beliefs he was going to record there were foundations and essential roots[20] such as God's existence, revelation, God's knowledge, and reward and punishment. [There were also among them beliefs] which, while not[21] at the level of foundations, were principles, that is, praiseworthy, essential and fundamental beliefs of exalted degree. These are the other principles he recorded. After specifying in his introduction that some of them were principles and some were foundations Maimonides did not hesitate to call each one of them a foundation or a principle since the Commentary on the

Mishnah was not the proper place for investigating which of them were principles and which foundations. For it was his intention there only to instill true beliefs in the hearts of students and nothing else.[22] It sufficed him to posit and explain at the beginning of his statement that some of them[23] were principles and some foundations in order to turn aside the *murmurings of the Children of Israel* [Exodus 16:12; Numbers 14:27, 17:20].

But thou shalt again see [Ezekiel 8:6] that those principles and foundations put forth by Maimonides are neither principles of faith nor religion simply.[24] Rather, Maimonides intended them to be principles of Judaism such that he who believed in them would be included in that "Israel" about which the Mishnah said, "All Israel have a share in the world to come." It is as if he said that these principles are the foundations upon which *you will build and establish* [Numbers 21:27] your inheritance in the spiritual world to come which is for all *who bear the name, "Israel"* [after Isaiah 44:5]. By believing in them—even if one commits some sins, for which one will be punished in accordance with one's rebelliousness—one will still have a portion in the world to come. But without these beliefs and principles one cannot inherit the world to come.

See what Maimonides wrote at the end of the principles:

> When all these principles are perfectly understood and believed in by a person, he enters the community of Israel and one is obligated to love and pity him and to act towards him in the ways in which the Creator has commanded that one should act towards his brother, with love and fraternity. Even were he to commit every transgression in the world, because of lust or the [evil] inclination, or because of the power of the baser elements in his nature, he is then one of the sinners in Israel and will be punished according to his sins, but he has a portion in the world to come.
>
> But if a man does not believe all of these principles as he should, he leaves the community [of Israel], denies the fundamental, and is called a sectarian, *apikoros,* and one who "cuts among the plantings." One is required to hate him and it is proper to despise and destroy him. About such a person it is said, *Do I not hate them, O Lord, who hate Thee?* [Psalms 139:21].[25]

Maimonides reveals with this statement that he did not present these principles and foundations because the Torah would collapse with the refutation of any one of them. Rather, it was his intention to explain the Mishnah which says, "All Israel have a portion in the world to come,"[26] and to establish a sign and definition whereby we might recognize and know *who is he and where is he* [Esther 7:5] *who bears the name, "Israel"* [Isaiah 44:5], *the righteous one living by his faith* [Habakkuk 2:4], whom the Mishnah intended. Maimonides said that by believing these thirteen principles a person will be called an Israelite and will be destined for the world to come. Even if one knows nothing else of all the Torah, belief in these principles is sufficient to acquire spiritual perfection. Therefore, when any man of Israel and *the stranger that sojourneth among them* [Numbers 15:26, 29; 19:10; Joshua 20:9] who comes to find shelter "under the wings of the *Shekhina*"[27] should say, "Teach me Torah so that I will be destined for the world to come," it is only necessary to teach him these thirteen principles. With them, *Behold his reward is with him* [Isaiah 40:10; 62:11]; without them he will not be called by the name Israel and will not merit the life of the world to come.

Why Maimonides chose these beliefs, however, and not others, will be explained below.

7

An Explanation of the Second Proposition Necessary for This Enquiry

The second proposition involves an explanation of the first of Maimonides' principles. The first of the principles which he laid down he derived from the verse, *I am the Lord thy God* [Exodus 20:2]. This is also the first commandment which he included in his book enumerating the commandments: "to believe in God."[1] It was presented in a similar fashion by the scholars who followed him. There is great disagreement, however, among [these] scholars on how best to understand this principle. The author of the *Sefer Miẓvot Gadol*[2] wrote:

> It is a positive commandment to believe that He Who gave us the Torah on Mt. Sinai through Moses is He Who brought us out of Egypt. Thus it says, *I am the Lord thy God Who brought thee out [of the land of Egypt]*.[3]

The force of this commandment, propounded in this way, is that of the eighth foundation, which affirms revelation.

The author of the *Amudei Golah*[4] wrote:

> The first commandment is to know that He Who created heaven and earth is the only Ruler, above and below, and in the four corners of the earth,[5] as it says, *I am the Lord thy God*. It is written, *Know this day and lay it to thy heart, that the Lord, He is God in heaven above and upon the earth beneath; there is none else* [Deuteronomy 4:39]. [This includes] even the air, to refute the view of the philosophers who say that the world rules itself through the signs of the Zodiac.[6] In truth, however, God rules the whole world *by the breath of His mouth* [Psalms 33:6; Job

15:30]. He brought us out of Egypt and "no man bruises his finger here on earth unless it was decreed against him in heaven, for it is written, *It is of the Lord that a man's goings are established* [Psalms 37:23]."[7]

Thus, according to his opinion, the force of this principle is that we should believe in God's providence. This is the tenth principle, as I shall explain.[8]

Rabbi Abraham ibn Ezra[9] explained *I am the Lord thy God* [to mean] that one should know God, love Him with all one's heart, cleave to Him uninterruptedly, and never cease holding Him in awe.[10] This is another way, according to which the force of this principle would be the belief of the fifth principle, that one ought to worship and praise God.

Naḥmanides,[11] in his *Commentary on the Torah*[12] and in his glosses on Maimonides,[13] explains *I am the Lord Thy God* in a way which combines all three opinions which I have discussed. He said:

> [This Divine utterance constitutes a positive commandment. He said, *I am the Lord,* thus teaching and] commanding them that they should know and believe that the Lord exists and that He is God to them. That is to say, there exists an Eternal Being through Whom everything has come into existence by His will and power, and He is God to them, who are obligated to worship Him. He said, *Who brought thee out of the land of Egypt,* because His taking them out from there was the evidence establishing the existence and will of God, for it was with His knowledge and providence that we came out from there. The exodus is also evidence for the creation of the world, for, assuming the eternity of the universe, it would follow that nothing could be changed from its nature. And it is also evidence for God's infinite power, and His infinite power is an indication of the Unity.[14]

He thus combined in this utterance[15] most of the principles of faith, even though the verse does not point to them. Gersonides[16] wrote in a similar fashion.[17]

Rabbi ben Ḥasdai[18] wrote at the beginning of his book[19] that the point of [*I am*] *the Lord thy God* is that "the God who is called this is the Deity, and ruler Who brought us out of the land of Egypt." He thus considered the principle to involve belief in providence and nothing else.

With respect to this issue our master, Rabbi Nissim[20] and the author of the *Sefer ha-Ikkarim*[21] followed the litigants[22] I have discussed even though they did not cite these matters in the names of their authors,[23] but attributed their opinions to themselves. For Rabbi Nissim explained the verse as Rabbi Moses of Coucy, as commanding belief in revelation, while the author of the *Sefer ha-Ikkarim* interpreted it as belief in providence, following the opinion of the *Amudei Golah* and Rabbi Ḥasdai.[24]

I have caused thee to see with thine eyes [Deuteronomy 34:4] the diversity of their opinions, how each *turned his own way* [after Isaiah 53:6] in explaining Scripture and the intent of the commandment. There also exists diversity of opinion concerning Maimonides' intention in this principle. Rabbi Ḥasdai, at the beginning of his book, wrote: "He who counted it a positive commandment to believe in the existence of God committed a notorious error."[25] There is no doubt that he was referring to Maimonides. This shows that he understood Maimonides to hold in the *Sefer ha-Madda*[26] that the first commandment is belief in God's existence; i.e., that He alone exists and that His contrary does not exist. He may also have been brought to this opinion by what Maimonides wrote in the *Guide,* Part two, chapter 33, in the matter of the gathering at Mt. Sinai[27] with respect to the rabbinic dictum, "*I am* and *Thou shalt have no* we heard from the mouth of the Almighty."[28] He said: "For these two principles, I mean the existence of the deity and His being one, are knowable by human speculation alone."[29] Rabbi Ḥasdai thought that Maimonides understood the commandment differently in his book enumerating the commandments. Thus, he wrote:

> Maimonides properly followed this understanding in his *Sefer ha-Miẓvot* in which he counted the first commandment as involving belief in divinity: "By this injunction we are commanded to believe in God: That is, to believe that there is a Supreme Cause who is the Creator of everything in existence. It is con-

tained in His words (exalted be He): *I am the Lord thy God.*"[30]
He thus explained God's divinity in terms of His having created
all existent beings. Because of this God said, *Who brought thee
out of the land of Egypt* [Exodus 20:2] by way of proving this
belief: from it we come to understand God's power and that all
existent beings are, when compared to Him, *as clay in the potter's
hand* [Jeremiah 18:6].[31]

This scholar thus thought that Maimonides' statements in
these two places, i.e., the *Sefer ha-Madda* and the book
enumerating the commandments were not in agreement. He
thought that in the *Sefer ha-Madda* [Maimonides held] that
the first commandment is simply that God exists while he
thought that in the book enumerating the commandments
[Maimonides held] that the first commandment is to believe
that God is the efficient cause and creator of the world. But
good and right [Deuteronomy 12:28, etc.] study will show
that this is not so, neither with respect to what he thought
Maimonides wrote in the *Sefer ha-Madda*—that the first
commandment is to believe that God exists—nor with respect
to what he thought [that Maimonides intended] in the *Sefer
ha-Miẓvot,* that the first commandment is [to believe] that
God created and caused the world.

But it is Maimonides' intention in all of his writings and in
all of his books [to teach] that the first principle and commandment is that we believe that the deity whom we already
know exists does so in a more primary and perfect fashion
than does any other existent, and that His existence is not
contingent with respect to Himself,[32] like other beings, but
that He is necessarily existent with respect to Himself. It has
been established in metaphysics that it is of the nature of
necessary existence that if it could be thought not to exist, all
other beings would not exist, but if it could be thought that
there are no other beings existing, it alone would exist and its
existence would not thereby be negated—far from it! For His
existence does not depend on anything else while everything
else is dependent upon Him for its existence for He exists
necessarily by His very nature and gives existence and duration to all existents and receives nothing at all from them.

Maimonides made clear that this was what he meant by what he wrote with respect to the first principle in his *Commentary on the Mishnah*. He said:

> The first foundation: the existence of the Creator. [This is the belief] that there is a perfectly existent Being Who is the cause of the existence of [all other] beings and from Whom they derive their continued existence. If His nonexistence were supposed, then the existence of all [other] beings would be impossible. [But], if the nonexistence of all other beings were supposed, He alone would still exist, and His existence would be neither destroyed nor diminished, for He does not depend [for His existence] upon the existence of anything else. But all things other than He . . . depend for their existence upon Him. We learn this first foundation from the utterance: *I am the Lord thy God.*[33]

Thus, Maimonides did not say that the first principle was only that God exists, but, rather, that we should believe with respect to His existence that it is the most perfect possible existence and that He exists necessarily, not contingently. This is exactly what He meant in the *Sefer ha-Madda* when he said,

> The foundation of all foundations and the pillar of all sciences is to know that there is a First Being Who brought every existent thing into being. All existing things, whether celestial, terrestrial, or belonging to an intermediate class, exist only through His existence.[34]

You thus see that he did not say, "to know that God exists," but, "to know that there is a First and Perfect Being," with respect to the [different] degrees of existence. In saying that He "brought every existent thing into being," Maimonides teaches the continuance of His existence. Thus he said, "if it could be thought that He does not exist, then nothing else could exist,"[35] for this is the definition of necessary existence and its meaning.

This is also what he wrote in his book enumerating the commandments:

The first commandment which we were commanded is believing in God. By this injunction we are commanded to believe in
God; that is, to believe that there is a Supreme Cause Who is the
Creator of everything in existence. It is contained in His words
[exalted be He]: *I am the Lord thy God.* [36]

In this statement he meant [exactly] what he himself said in
the other places I mentioned that belief in God means that we
should believe that His existence is absolutely perfect and
necessary, and not contingent.

Part of the meaning of "necessary existence" is that it is the
form of the world, its efficient cause and end as Maimonides
wrote in the *Guide*. [37] Twelve things have been established in
Divine Science[38] which are true of necessary existence and
which cannot be denied of it. [39] One of them is that everything
but it is dependent upon it while it is dependent upon nothing
beyond itself. On this dependence, which is part of the nature
and meaning of necessary existence, Maimonides wrote in the
same book enumerating the commandments, "that there is a
[God, a] Supreme Cause Who is the Creator of everything in
existence."[40]

Maimonides, however, did not say a word in the first
principle or in the first commandment[41] about whether this
dependence upon God of [all other] existents —He being
their efficient cause—is constant and never interrupted as
Aristotle[42] maintains, or was created at some time, after
absolute nothingness[43] as the divine Torah has instilled in us.
For how could the first principle deal with creation, and the
second with God's unity, and the third with incorporeality
and the fourth in eternity *a parte ante* when it is known that
God's unity, incorporeality, and eternity *a parte ante* are said
of Him with respect to His essence and that knowledge of
them should precede knowledge of His actions, namely the
creation of the world? If Maimonides enumerated among the
principles of religion God's unity, incorporeality, and eternity, which are attributes of the First Cause and things
essential to it, how can one think that Maimonides would not
postulate the principle of God's perfect and necessary existence, which is the principle upon which everything depends?

But this is all a mistake. It is clear that the first principle and the first commandment is belief in God; i.e., that He is an absolutely perfect Being, existing necessarily with respect to His essence. This is what Maimonides meant in the *Guide,* in the aforementioned thirty-third chapter of part two, that *I am* and *Thou shalt have no* are two foundations.[44] He means to say God's existence and His unity. In saying "God's existence," Maimonides does not simply mean that He exists, but that we should believe concerning His existence that it is necessary, not contingent, and that God is the most perfect possible Existence.

This being the case with respect to this foundation, he said in the *Sefer ha-Madda,* that it is "the foundation of all foundations and the pillar of all the sciences."[45] This indicates that this foundation, that God exists necessarily, is not on a level equal to that of the other foundations but is rather the foundation and root of them all for they rest upon it and it does not rest upon them. Therefore did he call it "the foundation of all foundations" as I will explain below.[46]

All this establishes the truth of the first commandment and foundation, which is that we believe that God is an absolutely perfect Being, existing necessarily. This is the second proposition.

8

An Explanation of the Third Proposition Necessary for This Enquiry

The third proposition. There were included in the first principle two teachings,[1] the first being that God's existence is the most perfect possible.[2]

The second [principle includes] two other teachings. The first is that God has no partner or second in divinity. The second is that God has no composition or multiplicity at all.

Similarly, there are also included in the third foundation, that of incorporeality, two teachings. The first is that God is not a body, neither complex nor simple. The second is that God is not the power in a body, neither with respect to accidental nor natural forms.

Similarly, there are also two teachings in the fourth foundation. The first is that God is eternal *a parte ante*,[3] that is, that He has no beginning. The second is that everything other than He, when compared to Him, is not eternal *a parte ante;* that is that all other things are created and we cannot say of any one of them that it is eternal *a parte ante*. On this basis it is established that the opinion of Aristotle, that the world is eternal *a parte ante*,[4] and also the opinion of Plato,[5] are not true opinions. This principle denies them and instills [in us the belief] that God alone is eternal *a parte ante* and that everything other than Him is not eternal *a parte ante*, but created, as I shall make clear below.[6]

There are also two beliefs included in the fifth foundation. The first is that one ought to worship God and raise one's voice in praise of Him. This is so because God has infinite power and acts with choice and will. Worship and praise are therefore appropriate to Him but not to the spheres, stars, or heavenly princes whose power is finite, limited and ordered and who have neither sovereignty nor desire and will. Prayer to them is therefore of no effect for they can do neither ill nor good. Despite the opinion of the scholars that the Separate Intellects act with volition[7] and will, and that the heavenly bodies are living, cognizing beings who are moved by desire, there is no doubt that they cannot choose to act in any but the way in which they are caused to act for their activities are ordered and they cannot act in any other way. The second [belief included in the fifth foundation] is that one may not posit intermediaries between man and his Creator. This is so because He is the true Ruler of our nation [and] *Jacob is the lot of His inheritance* [Deuteronomy 32:9]. Thus, the entire prohibition of idolatry derives from this principle.

Similarly, there are two teachings in the sixth principle, which deals with prophecy, as Maimonides explained in the *Guide.*[8] The first is the need for natural and speculative preparation as conditions for the occurrence of prophecy. The second [teaching] is that [prophecy will not occur] if the divine will should withhold it. In this connection, Maimonides said in his explanation of this foundation: "Afterwards, such human intellects are joined to the Agent Intelligence from which an exalted overflow emanates upon them."[9] This emanation will not occur if it is withheld by the Divine will.[10]

Similarly, the seventh foundation, which deals with the prophecy of Moses, also includes two beliefs. The first is that he was more perfect in his temperament and intellect than any other member of the [human] race. The second is that in the degree of his prophecy he was exalted over all the prophets, so much so that Maimonides wrote in the *Guide* that the term "prophecy" is only applied to Moses and the other prophets ambiguously.[11] From this follow the four differences between the prophecy of Moses and that of the other prophets which Maimonides recorded.[12] I see no point to explaining them here since I discussed them at length in my *Maḥaze Shaddai.*[13]

Similarly, two other beliefs are brought in the eighth

foundation, which deals with revelation. The first is that all of
the written Torah found in our hands today is the Torah that
was given to Moses "from the mouth of the Almighty,"[14] that
is to say that Moses apprehended it all from God's mouth
with that type of apprehension called "speech." The second is
that the traditional commentary on the Torah, the Talmud,
also comes "from the mouth of the Almighty," and that
Moses received it at Sinai and taught it to the Israelites orally.
It is therefore called the Oral Torah.

Similarly, two other teachings are brought in the ninth
principle, which deals with the eternity of the Torah. The first
is that this Torah will never be uprooted nor exchanged by our
people at all; that is, that the Jews will never exchange it on
their own account. The second is that the Creator will never
give another Torah, neither in its entirety nor by adding or
subtracting some part to or from it.

Similarly, the tenth principle, which deals with divine
knowledge, also includes two beliefs. The first is that God
knows all the actions of men; that is, their particular actions.
Maimonides explained the second belief by saying, "[God]
does not neglect them";[15] that is to say, God does not ignore
them but, rather, extends His providence over them. The
proof which he presents [for this principle] includes these two
teachings. By saying, *Great in counsel, and mighty in work,
Whose eyes are open upon all the ways of the sons of men . . .*
[Jeremiah 32:19] the issue of divine knowledge is established;
his saying further, *. . . to give everyone according to his ways
and according to the fruit of his doing* [Jeremiah 32:19] refers
to the matter of God's providence and justice. So also the
other verses which Maimonides cited in elucidating this principle teach both these things; i.e., God's knowledge and
providence.

Similarly, there are two teachings brought in the eleventh
foundation. The first is that God will repay those who
observe His commandments with a goodly reward and will
punish those who transgress them or don't fulfill them. The
second is that the greatest reward is life in the world to come
and the greatest punishment is the cutting off of the soul. The
meaning of this principle is that *all of the ways of God are just*

[after Deuteronomy 32:4]; [He is] *a God of faithfulness and without iniquity, just and right is He* [Deuteronomy 32:4]. What this world to come and what this cutting off of the soul are will be explained in the treatise *Ẕedek Olamim* which I am composing about them.[16]

Similarly, there were also two teachings included in the twelfth foundation. The first is that we ought to believe that the King Messiah, about whom the prophets promised, *will surely come* [Habakkuk 2:3] without doubt, and that *though he tarry, wait for him* [Habakkuk 2:3]. The second is that in that time only a king from the house of David and the seed of Solomon will rule over Israel and that all who dispute the sovereignty of this family deny God and the words of the prophets. This is so because all of the prophets prophesied about him, as when it says, *and David My servant shall be their prince forever* [Ezekiel 37:25, transposed].

Similarly with the thirteenth and last foundation, which is about resurrection of the dead. Maimonides did not explain it at all in his *Commentary on the Mishnah* [17] but relied on what he wrote in the beginning of the Mishnah in the introduction to *Perek Ḥelek* and in his *Treatise on Resurrection*,[18] as he said, ". . . the meaning and secrets of which [i.e., the thirteenth principle] we have already explained."[19] [It can be seen] from what he wrote in that Treatise that there are also many teachings in this principle. I will mention two of them. The first is that the dead will live [again] in body and soul. The second is that the resurrection will be for the righteous only and that they will use their senses and live and die as we do today, as I will discuss below.[20]

I have thus explained Maimonides' intention with regard to these foundations, to the effect that there is no foundation or principle among them in which there are not at least two teachings. In some of them there are more than two but there are without a doubt no fewer than two teachings in each principle.

This is the third proposition.

9

An Explanation of the Fourth Proposition Necessary for This Enquiry

The fourth proposition. There is no doubt that if one investigates these foundations and principles according to correct methods of inquiry and with an honest mind,[1] it will truly be found that some of them are included in others. Thus other principles are included in the first foundation, that of God's necessary existence. These are that He is one, eternal *a parte ante* and incorporeal, for all of these follow from the essence of necessary existence, as has been established in metaphysics.

Similarly, incorporeality is included in the principle of unity, as Maimonides made clear in the first part of the *Sefer ha-Madda*.[2] In the same way, you will find that in the foundation of revelation other principles are included. These are prophecy, which is the root of the Torah, the superiority of the prophecy of Moses, since the Torah was given through him, and the eternity of the Torah, since it was given from heaven in that great public assembly by the master of all the prophets. You will also find that other principles are included in the foundation of reward and punishment. These are divine knowledge and providence, the coming of the Messiah, and the resurrection of the dead. All of these are forms of recompense for the servants [of God] and of punishment to those who *have forfeited their lives* [after Habakkuk 2:10].

Even though some of these principles are included in others, Maimonides saw fit to make them all principles and stated each of them as a separate principle since he wasn't propounding these principles of his for scholars who know the sciences, but for *all the people from every quarter, both young and old* [Genesis 19:4, transposed]. All the more so did he follow what was necessary for him in explaining the Mishnah. He therefore detailed every single praiseworthy belief, and posited each as a separate principle since he intended to perfect men and women who were not perfected by speculative investigation. Maimonides also found certain lessons[3] in the number of these principles, as I shall relate.[4]

This is the fourth proposition.

An Explanation of the Fifth Proposition Necessary for This Enquiry

The fifth proposition is that the number of the foundations and principles of faith as stated by Maimonides was neither accidental nor inadvertent;[1] nor did [Maimonides choose the number thirteen] in order to match the thirteen attributes of God's mercy[2] or the thirteen hermeneutical principles of Torah exegesis.[3] Rather, with this number Maimonides intended to teach one or all of three lessons[4] and great speculative teachings.

The first lesson which Maimonides meant to teach with these roots is that the true servant of God cannot escape placing as the goal of his service [one of three things. The first is] the exalted and perfect character of God. From this perspective Maimonides presented the first five principles. They are [first], that God is the most perfect possible Existent and that He exists necessarily, in and of Himself and that because of the perfect character of His existence we ought to serve Him. Second, that God is One; because of this also we ought to love Him and cleave to Him, since aside from Him there is no God. Thus Moses after communicating [the fact of] God's unity in the verse, *Hear, O Israel, the Lord our God, the Lord is One* [Deuteronomy 6:4] immediately said, *And thou shalt love the Lord thy God* [Deuteronomy 6:5]. That is to say, since God is One and has no second, every heart and soul ought perfectly to love and cleave unto Him. The third principle, that of incorporeality, also teaches God's perfection, for spiritual things are more exalted and perfect than physical things. The fourth principle, that God is eternal *a parte ante*, and that everything else is created also teaches the [exalted] degree of His existence since "before any being created,"[5] *the Lord was one and His name was one* [after Zechariah 14:9]. [This fourth principle also teaches] that God created the world and endowed every created being with existence and goodness. The fifth principle, that God is the only proper object of worship, teaches three beliefs. These are that He is omnipotent, that He acts by will and volition, and that He rules our people without an intermediary. These five principles are presented from the perspective of God's perfect rank.

The second perspective [from which the principles are presented] is that of the commandment, that is to say, the Torah itself. With respect to this Maimonides presented [the next] four principles. They are, [first], the existence of prophecy among prophets in general; [second], its existence in an exalted degree in Moses—which indicated the exalted degree of the Torah given through him; [third], that the Torah which is in our hands today, together with its division into verses and the interpretation received by tradition,[6] was all given from Heaven. To prevent us from thinking that the Torah was given for a limited time [only] which has passed and ended, Maimonides presented the principle of the eternity of the Torah which teaches that it will neither be altered nor exchanged for another. These four principles all relate to the Torah itself.

The third aspect—that involving those who receive the command—relates to retribution: the hope for reward or the fear of punishment, for many people observe the Torah in order to receive the reward,[7] and not for its own sake. It was with respect to this aspect that Maimonides presented the principles of divine knowledge and providence and of reward and punishment because these all teach that God is just and does good *unto the good and to them that are upright in their hearts* [Psalms 125:4] both in this world and in the next while *the wicked shall be cut off from the land* [Proverbs 2:22]. But since there is room to doubt this because of the evils that overtake the righteous and the goodness and happiness enjoyed by the wicked, Maimonides, by way of solving the problem, presented the twelfth principle, about the coming of our Messiah, and the thirteenth principle, about the resurrection of the dead, for then there will be true reward for God's servants, *the children of Jacob, His chosen ones* [Psalms 105:106], and terrible punishment for idolators; *some to everlasting life, and some to reproaches and everlasting abhorrence* [Daniel 12:2]. From this it is clear that that the last two principles, those relating to the coming of the Messiah and to resurrection, are types and branches of the eleventh principle since they are particular types of reward and punishment in general. They were only included among the principles in order to anticipate and solve a problem as I said above[8] and will clarify further below.[9] I have thus explained the numbering of these thirteen principles to you as well as the first lesson which Maimonides sought to teach through their number.

The second lesson which Maimonides intended to teach through the [specific] number of these principles [relates to their philosophic status]. Aristotle[10] would admit to the truth of the first three principles in all their parts and roots. These are: the first principle, that of God's perfect and necessary existence; the second principle, that of God's unity—that there is no partner or second in divinity [with God] nor any composition or multiplicity in Him; and the third principle, that God is neither a body nor the force of a body. Aristotle would admit the truth of these three principles in all their parts, for they are matters [the truth of which] has been apprehended by rational demonstration.

Aristotle would admit [to the truth of] the next three principles, however, [only] from one point of view and would deny them from another point of view. Aristotle would accept our assertion in the fourth principle that God is eternal *a parte ante* and has no beginning. But he would deny our assertion that everything other than God is not eternal *a parte ante* but, rather, created. Similarly, Aristotle would admit to our assertion, in the fifth principle, that only God ought to be worshipped since He is omnipotent. But Aristotle would deny our claim that God rules and extends providence to our people without any intermediary. So also, Aristotle would accept our assertion, in the sixth principle, that prophecy depends upon perfection of character and knowledge and the purity of the soul [of the prophet]. But he would deny our claim that prophecy can be withheld by the divine will. These are the foundations which Aristotle would accept in part and would deny in part.

Next, Maimonides presents three principles which Aristotle would neither accept nor deny, since they cannot be treated within [the scope of] his [methods of] inquiry and since he would not consider them impossible. These are: the seventh foundation, that Moses was elevated above all other prophets by the purity of his character and the degree of his prophetic attainment; the eighth foundation, that the Torah as we have it today is divinely ordered and [was] apprehended through prophecy; and the ninth foundation, that the Torah will never change nor be replaced. The truth of these three beliefs can be neither proved nor refuted by rational inquiry or human speculation.

After this Maimonides presented the last four principles which Aristotle, according to the methods of his inquiry, would deny in all their parts. These are: [the tenth principle], that God knows particulars and extends His providence to them; [the eleventh principle], that God repays the righteous with a goodly reward in accord with the commandments they have fulfilled and repays the wicked with great punishment for not keeping and observing the commandments of the Torah; [the twelfth principle], that the Messiah will come in order to establish that reward and punishment; and [the thirteenth principle], that in the end of days [*many of*] *them that sleep in the dust of the earth shall awake . . .* [Daniel 12:2]. Aristotle would deny and refuse to accept these four beliefs because they involve particular divine reward, given according to the commandments and related to them.

Maimonides has thus taught us belief in these thirteen principles, of which the first three are perfectly established in all their parts by rational inquiry. Three others are partially established by speculative inquiry. [Another] three of them are possibly [true] according to [rational] inquiry, being neither necessarily [true] nor necessarily false. The last four principles are necessarily false according to philosophical speculation in the way I described. In that they are all correct beliefs, however, according to the Torah and in truth, belief in them is proper and necessary. It was because of their great importance that they were put forward as principles of faith.[11]

The third lesson which Maimonides sought to teach with this number of principles relates to the fact that a believer's faith in the divine Torah cannot but involve faith in God or in His works, for nothing else exists.[12] Now, that which we ought to believe about God is that He exists necessarily and is absolutely perfect. We have no way of imagining or comprehending His perfection except by way of negation; [we can] not do it positively. For, as Maimonides established in the *Guide*,[13] no positive attribute can be predicated of God. Solomon admonished [us] with respect to this in Ecclesiastes where he said, *Be not rash with thy mouth, and let not thy heart be hasty to utter a word before God; for God is in Heaven, and thou upon the earth; therefore, let thy words be few* [Ecclesiastes 5:1]. By this he means to say that one should not be eager, whether in one's words or inquiry, to predicate positive attributes of God for He *is in Heaven,* that is, absolutely beyond our ken.[14] His existence is absolutely different from ours, as different as the heavens are from the earth. Thus, His attributes are not like ours but are, [rather], absolutely different. Therefore, the only way in which it is possible for us to describe Him is with negative attributes. This is the meaning of the verse, *therefore let thy words be few,* that, is exclusionary[15] and negative.[16]

Maimonides, therefore, presented three principles, the second, third, and fourth, the meanings, and implications of which are negative. These·are that God is one, incorporeal, and eternal. The sense of the three of them is that God can be neither included in anything nor can He be limited. Limitation may occur in one of three ways. First, as in the case of a numerical attribute, encompassed by and included within number insofar as it is an attribute. Second, limitation by place, as in the case of bodies enclosed by their place. Third, limitation by time, as in the case of things which are subject to generation and corruption; time being greater than they at both their [temporal] extremities. It is [well] known that a thing limited in any of these three ways is deficient. Thus, after Maimonides presented the first principle, that of God's divinity, which is the foundation of all foundations,[17] he removed from God these three types of limitation. In asserting the second principle, that God is one, Maimonides established that God does not fall under [the category of] number since he made clear that God is not like the one of counting, nor of genus, nor of species. In asserting that God is not a body, he established that God is not defined by place, for what is not a body is not in any place. In asserting that God is eternal, Maimonides established that God does not fall under [the category of] time and is not limited by it. It is for this reason that He is called *eternal God* [Deuteronomy 33:27]. From this it may be seen that God is not deficient, for deficiency only results from the aspect of limitation. These first four principles thus establish beliefs which we ought to believe concerning God and His infinite perfection.[18]

With respect to God's actions, however, in that same fourth principle [Maimonides] made clear that God's first, all-embracing act was the creation of the world. In the fifth principle [Maimonides] established that God's power is infinite and that He acts by volition and will, not by nature, as is the case with other, created beings. These two propositions should be held by anyone who affirms creation *ex nihilo*.[19]

God's actions may be divided four ways. They are either general and occasional: [such as] the creation of the world, implied in the fourth principle; [such as] miraculous activity, which is hinted at in the fifth principle; [such as] the existence of prophecy, which is presented in the sixth principle. [The second category of God's actions is] actions which are particular and occasional, and which relate only to the generality of our nation. In this category [Maimonides] counted the seventh foundation, [the superiority of] the prophecy of Moses over [the prophecies] of all the other prophets; the eighth foundation, revelation; and the ninth foundation, the eternity of the Torah—that by its nature and essence it was given for eternity, never to change. [The third category] is of general and permanent actions. In this category [Maimonides] presented God's knowledge and providence in the tenth foundation, and reward and punishment in the eleventh foundation. The matters include all men and operate at all times. [The fourth category] is of particular actions which will occur in the future, such as the coming of the Messiah, presented in the twelfth principle, and resurrection of the dead presented in the thirteenth principle. This is called the principle of particular resurrection according to the opinion of Maimonides who wrote at the beginning of his commentary to the mishnah[20] that the resurrection of the dead will be restricted to the righteous. This follows the statement of the Sages who said that the [great] power of rain is for the righteous and wicked [alike] while the resurrection of the dead is restricted to the righteous.[21]

All this being so, [we find] that the number of the principles has been arrived at in a correct fashion. Some relate to God Himself and some relate to His actions; among [these actions] are [first] the general and occasional, [second] the particular and occasional—which are more closely related to the Torah, [third] the general and permanent, and [fourth] the particular actions which will occur in the future. Thus [we have] clarified this lesson which Maimonides [sought to teach] by the number of these roots.

We find in Tractate Ta'anit that, when R. Eliezer ben Pedat asked what was set aside for him in the world to come, he was told from Heaven: "thirteen rivers of balsam oil [as clear as the Euphrates and the Tigris] which you will be able to enjoy."[22] They hinted by this that he will live eternally in great pleasure because of the thirteen principles of faith in which he believed.[23]

Similarly, when R. Joshua ben Levi entered paradise,

Elijah heralded him, proclaiming, "Make room for the son of Levi, make room for the son of Levi!" As he proceeded on his way, he found R. Simeon b. Yoḥai[24] reclining on thirteen heaping sacks of gold.[25] "Are you," the latter asked him, "the son of Levi?"

"Yes," he replied.

"Has a rainbow ever appeared in your lifetime?"

"Yes," he replied.

"If that is so, you are not *the* son of Levi."[26]

The fact, however, is that there was no such thing[27] but he thought, "I must take no credit for myself."

This is found in chapter *ha-Maddir* of Tractate Ketubot.[28] There is no doubt that the thirteen heaping sacks of gold upon which R. Simeon was reclining are the thirteen principles of faith in which he believed during his lifetime, as they were posited by Maimonides. Because he believed in them, *his reward is with him and his recompense is before him* [Isaiah 40:10 and 62:11]. This is not the proper place to explain the other parts of the passage.

This is the fifth proposition.

11
An Explanation of Four Other Propositions Necessary for This Enquiry

The sixth proposition is that the divine Torah is divided into practical commandments,[1] which correspond to matter, and commandments of faith and knowledge, which correspond to form. Among these latter are beliefs which deal with the end,[2] such as the coming of the Messiah and the resurrection of the dead. Principles of faith ought not to be taken from practical commandments, whether general or specific, for "a person who violates a commandment [of the Torah] is called a transgressor and is liable to the penalty prescribed in the Torah for that commandment. But he is not excluded from the religion[3] and is not regarded as a denier [of the Torah] who has no share in the world to come; unless [his violation of the commandment is due to the fact that] he is in doubt whether it is a command of God [given to Moses on Sinai, or not]. If this is his attitude he falls into the class of those who deny the divine origin of the Torah [as the Rabbis of the Talmud explain in chapter '*Ḥelek*'].[4] All the commandments of the Torah are alike in this respect. [The command to send away the mother bird[5] is as important as any other. If we should count specific commandments as dogmas by reason of the last consideration], we should have as many principles as there are commandments."[6]

The principles, however, should be taken from the beliefs for, as has been scientifically established,[7] while matter and form may each be called "substance," the term is more appropriately used with respect to form than with respect to matter, for a thing truly exists through its form. The principles are therefore taken from the commandments of belief which deal with the end for a thing's perfection is its end and many times the end is included in a definition by virtue of its exalted degree. Therefore, love of God is not a principle, nor love of neighbor, about which it is written, *thou shalt love thy neighbor as thyself* [Leviticus 19:18]. Nor are *And thou shalt do that which is right and good* [Deuteronomy 6:18] and *Thou shalt not hate thy brother in thy heart* [Leviticus 29:17] and others similar to them [included among the principles]. For, while they are general commandments, they are also practical ones. Whether the [commanded] action be in the heart or other limbs, insofar as it is an action it ought not to be counted as a principle. Rather, only the beliefs which are the pillars and foundations of the divine Torah [ought to be so counted]. Thus, none of the commandments included in the laws of idolatry[8] are principles, even though they are included in the first principle since they are both specific and practical commandments.

This proposition was cited by the author of the *Sefer ha-Ikkarim* in Treatise I, chapter 14.[9] On this basis, he thought that Maimonides had erred in counting among the principles that God ought to be worshipped since there is a specific commandment to serve the Lord.[10] Similarly, as [Albo] says after this, "for the same reason, tradition is not regarded as a principle . . . since it is a specific commandment."[11] We therefore ought not to say [Albo maintained][12] that any of the principles is included in the Decalogue since it is composed of specific commandments and the principles are not specific commandments. This is the sixth proposition.

The seventh proposition is that the principles of the divine Torah ought to be unique to it insofar as it is divine. They should not be shared by another law,[13] whether natural or conventional,[14] for the principles are the differentia which distinguish the species. Faith in the divine Torah is therefore perfected through belief in the principles. Were they not unique to it, faith in the divine Torah would not follow necessarily from belief in them since they would not be unique to it insofar as it is the divine Torah. It was from this perspective that the author of the *Sefer ha-Ikkarim* rejected the foun-

dations propounded by R. Ḥasdai. Some of them—even
though they are general principles of divine religion the
existence of which cannot be conceived without them—are
not such that the existence of the Torah follows necessarily
from their existence. "We can make this clearer by the
following analogy. If one were to say that given nutrient and
sentient we have man [because if you have man you have
nutrient and sentient], he would [no doubt] be wrong."[15]
Given man, we have nutrient and sentient; but the matter
cannot be turned around—such that given only nutrient and
sentient we would have man—unless we add to them the
rational faculty[16] and say that given a nutrient, sentient and
rational[17] body we have man; this is correct. This is the
seventh proposition.

The eighth proposition is that these principles which
Maimonides used to lay the foundation of the House of the
Lord and its Torah are all beliefs in God or in His actions.
Other scientific statements about the nature of existence, true
and correct though they may be, ought not to be included
among the principles. They are propositions of natural science[18] but not principles unique to divine religion. Thus,
Maimonides did not count as principles that man has a soul,
that the soul is a form distinct from the body, that it survives
death eternally and is not destroyed with the destruction of
the body, and that the spheres live and cognize and move in
worship of God. For, notwithstanding that these and similar
beliefs are true, they are speculative propositions which accord with the truth but are not principles of the divine Torah.
Its principles and foundations are those things which we
ought to believe about God and His willful activities, and
nothing else. This is the eighth proposition.

The ninth proposition is that beliefs are actualized in a
man's heart and soul in the same way in which natural forms[19]
are actualized and fixed in their subject. Natural generation
necessarily depends upon prior preparation—either with respect to the quantity of things or with respect to their
quality—relevant to the form which is being actualized. There
is an analogy to this. For water to receive the form of air it
must be heated and must expand. In this way its matter is

prepared for receiving the form of air. The heat cannot but continue to grow on the form[20] of water, which latter remains until its strength is exhausted. The form of water will disappear and it[21] will receive the form of air. That form, however, will only be actualized in the moment after the completion of the preparation.

It is the same way with beliefs. It is necessary that they be preceded by knowledge of and inquiry into the things which support them. These may be miracles and wonders which cause the beliefs [to be accepted by] the soul or [they may be] the study of arguments and speculative demonstrations which bring one to them. Thus, knowledge and study, the pursuit of experience and its investigation, and the use of the senses with respect to those things which bring one to belief, are the dispositions and propaedeutics which bring a person to faith.[22] There is no doubt that seeking these dispositions is a matter of will and choice and that they can be acquired over time. After these dispositions, however, which the soul acquires over time, are acquired, the form of the belief which follows from them is fixed in the heart and soul of the man. For he will necessarily believe in the consequence which follows from that inquiry, knowledge, examination, and experience. That belief will occur suddenly, without choice or will, even though the acquiring of the dispositions and the matters which precede that belief are [themselves] a matter of choice and will, which occur in the soul over time.

It is thus established that in the matter of belief generally there is an element of will and choice which can be acquired over time. This is the pursuit of experience and knowledge, which are the dispositions for and propaedeutics of belief. There is also an element of necessity which comes in an instant, without time. This is the form of the belief and its end which occurs in the soul as a consequence of the knowledge and examinations which precede it. It is with respect to this aspect of willful choice which comes over time that commandments relating to beliefs obtain. Reward and punishment relate to beliefs, not from the aspect of the form of the belief, which comes at the very end, but from the aspect of the knowledge, inquiry, and other things which are propaedeutics to it and which a man does to acquire the disposition.[23] This is as I have explained in my book, *Maḥazeh Shaddai*, which I am writing.[24]

Forasmuch as God hath shown thee [Genesis 41:39] all these propositions, *Lo, I come unto thee in the cloud of my speculation* [Exodus 19:9] to respond to the twenty-eight objections which I have raised with respect to Maimonides' principles and foundations and the commandments he counted among them. For all these objections will be solved with these nine propositions[25] which I have laid down, as I shall say.

12
Solutions to the First Three Objections

With respect to the first objection, which asks why Maimonides counted God's unity and incorporeality as principles even though the Torah in its entirety would not be refuted if we believed the opposite, I respond and say that it has been established in the first proposition that the term "principle" [*ikkar*] is not used in the same way as are the terms "root" [*shoresh*] and "foundation" [*yesod*].[1] These [latter] refer to things upon which the existence and duration of other things depend absolutely. But [the term] "principle" may also be used of the most praiseworthy thing in its class. So, in the matter of beliefs, Maimonides enumerated among the principles the most exalted and perfect beliefs, these being the most praiseworthy in their class. It is from this perspective that God's unity and incorporeality are principles since they are beliefs which are very necessary for reaching perfection. Aristotle said that the little we know of divine matters is greater in degree and measure than the great deal we know about sublunar matters.[2] This is even truer when that knowledge deals with God's essence, as in the case of [His] unity and incorporeality, about [the former of] which Moses publicly admonished, *Hear, O Israel, the Lord, our God, the Lord is one* [Deuteronomy 6:4]. This denies belief in idolatry altogether. Similarly with [God's] incorporeality: *Take ye therefore good heed unto yourselves —for ye saw no manner of form* [*on the day that the Lord spoke unto you in Horeb out of the midst of the fire*] [Deuteronomy 4:15] is an emphatic admonishment about this matter. I have already stated in the fifth proposition above that the point of these two principles is that God is neither grasped nor limited, neither by place nor by number.[3]

Rabbi Abraham ben David[4] wrote in his glosses on Maimonides that he who says that God has a body because he followed the plain sense of Scripture is no sectarian:

> Abraham said: Even though the essence of the belief is like this,[5] one who believes that God has a body because he understood the language of Scripture literally ought not to be called a heretic. This [view] is strengthened by what was said of Elisha ben Abuyah:[6] *"Return ye rebellious children* [Jeremiah 3:22] except Elisha Aḥer[7] who knows his Master[8] and deliberately rebels against Him."[9] They thus indicate clearly that that man alone who knows the truth and deliberately denies it, belongs to the class of the wicked whose repentance is rejected. But the man whose intention is not to rebel, nor to depart from the truth, nor to deny what is in the Torah, nor to reject tradition, but who in his simplicity follows the simple sense of Scripture,[10] though he interprets it erroneously, is neither a heretic nor an unbeliever.[11]

But upon examination this position may be seen to be clearly false, for according to it, [even] one who unintentionally denies every principle will acquire [a portion in] the world to come. Thus, the belief of the Christians[12]—who took the words of Torah and prophecy literally, and believed their meaning to be as they understood it—would not deprive them of the true felicity[13] and we may not say that they are heretics and sectarians. It would be possible, according to this, to find a man who does not believe in any one of the principles or beliefs of Torah and yet who should not be called a sectarian or heretic if he were brought to this blind foolishness by his failure to understand the meaning of the Torah. These opinions are intolerable, according to both the faith of Torah and correct reason. For a false opinion about any one of the principles of faith turns the soul from its true felicity and will not bring [one] to life in the world to come, even if the opinion is held without intention to rebel. It is like poison which consumes the spirit of him who eats it, *and his spirit will be gathered to God* [Job 34:14], even if he ate it thinking that it was good and healthy food. Similarly, heresy and false beliefs in the matter of the principles of religion will expel the soul of man and without a doubt make it impossible for him to inherit the world to come.[14]

With respect to what they said about Elisha ben Abuyah, that "he knows his Master and deliberately rebels against him," [I say] that this man's heresy was more despicable than any other. This is so because of the evil nature of his temperament and, because of his having sunk himself in material lusts, he sought false arguments which differed from the truth found[15] among us; his heresy was, therefore, very great. But he who believes false opinions about the nature[16] of the Torah, to which [false beliefs] he was brought by his own study, or which he accepted from an erring teacher, is doubtless a heretic and sectarian, since his beliefs contradict the principles of the religion. But, withal, he has a better excuse than did Elisha ben Abuyah, who willfully pursued falsehood.[17]

With respect to its cause there are two kinds of heresy. The first kind is caused by stupidity and the lack of true understanding brought about either because one followed the plain sense of Scripture or for some other reason. About these [heretics] it is said, *Return, ye backsliding and heretical children* [after Jeremiah 3:22]. If they do repent, however, with corrected opinions and [with belief] in the truth of prophecy, *they will keep back their soul from the pit* [after Job 33:18]. The second kind of heresy is brought about by premediated rebelliousness, as was the case with Elisha Aḥer, whose heresy was rebellious and treacherous *and who was occupied in deeds of wickedness* [after Psalms 141:14] to dispute the truth and to deny it. Because of this the gates of repentance were sealed before him. Thus, they said, "except Elisha Aḥer, who knows his Master and deliberately rebels against him."

The common element between "backsliding children" who are heretics because of their stupidity, and Elisha Aḥer, who was a rebellious heretic, is that so long as they hold their false and mistaken beliefs they are sectarians and heretics and have no share in the world to come. However, if the "backsliding children" change because their ignorance is removed, because they perfect themselves by Torah speculation according to the truth, and because they are prepared *to make straight that which they have made crooked* [after Ecclesiastes 7:13] through repentance [then their repentance is accepted].[18] Elisha, however, did not have this hope and disposition since he was rooted in heresy by knowledge and rational thought.[19] Maimonides' writings on the principles ought to be understood in this way. He thus insisted, at the end of his treatise, that his words should be studied with great care, for they are not easy to understand, and that he chose these principles and their number after long and deep inquiry. One ought not, therefore, contradict them flippantly nor should one dispute them according to the prevailing thought of the moment.[20]

With respect to the second objection, which asked why Maimonides posited among the principles the fifth, [which teaches] that one ought not to place intermediaries between man and God,[21] we respond and say, as I stated in the third proposition,[22] that this principle encompasses [several] true and exalted beliefs. The first is that God acts by will and is not like the other existents—the angels, the spheres, the stars, and the substances and what are compounded from them—all of which are assigned their task and have neither control over their [own] actions nor desire to act as they do.[23] But God acts according to will and desire and therefore worship, song, exaltation, and praise are due Him.

The second belief is that God is omnipotent. Thus, he said, "for they are all appointed to their tasks,";[24] that is, their activities and power are defined and ordered,[25] their power is finite, and they cannot act but in the way in which they have been ordered. God, however, *doeth whatsoever pleaseth Him* [Ecclesiastes 8:3], as the Psalmist says, *Whatever the Lord pleased, that hath He done in heaven and in earth* [Psalms 135:6]. Worship is thus due Him because everything is in His hand *as the clay in the potter's hand* [Jeremiah 18:6] *and who may say unto Him, "What doest Thou?"* [Ecclesiastes 8:4].

The third belief is that each nation and tongue is distinguished by the care of a superior being which rules over it—as it says, *the prince [of the kingdom] of Greece* [Daniel 10:20][26] and *the prince of the kingdom of Persia* [Daniel 10:13]—with the exception of the Israelite nation which is not distinguished by the care of a star or prince[27] but by God alone, as Moses said:

> And lest thou lift up thine eyes unto heaven, and when thou seest the sun and the moon and the stars, even all the host of heaven, thou be drawn away and worship them, and serve them, which the Lord thy God hath allotted unto all the peoples under the whole heaven. But you hath the Lord taken and brought forth out of the iron furnace, out of Egypt, to be unto Him a people of inheritance, as ye are this day [Deuteronomy 4:19–20].

Rabbi Abraham ben Ezra wrote: "It is established by experience that every nation and city has its star and constellation but God greatly distinguished Israel for He is their Guide. They have no star, for Israel is the inheritance of the Lord."[28] On this it is said in the *Pirke de Rabbi Eliezer* that seventy princes drew lots on seventy nations and the lot of each prince fell upon one nation but that God's lot fell upon Israel, as it is said, *For the portion of the Lord is His people, Jacob the lot of His inheritance* [Deuteronomy 32:9].[29] By this they meant to say that the relationship which obtains between each prince and his people, namely, that he rules it without the intermediation of any other prince, is the same relationship which obtains between God and the nation of Israel, in that God rules Israel without the intermediation of any prince, star, or constellation. It is from this that the exclusion of all idolatry follows. That which was said about Israel, *Michael, your prince* [Daniel 10:21] does not mean that he was appointed over them, but that he interceded on their behalf before God. He was, therefore, not called "prince of Israel" as was the case with *the prince* [*of the kingdom*] *of Greece* and *the prince of the kingdom of Persia.* All this is as I wrote in my book, *Ateret Zekenim.*[30]

Therefore, Maimonides wrote in this principle that "one ought not place them as intermediaries between man and God; rather, all thoughts should be directed to God and away from what is other than He."[31] Maimonides did not say that this principle forbade intermediaries, for that is a practical commandment; i.e., a particular, negative commandment.

Maimonides said, rather, that the commandment follows from the principle. It is as if he said, "Because of this principle a man ought not to place intermediaries between himself and his Creator." As the prophet said, *If thou wilt return, O Israel, saith the Lord, yea return unto Me* [Jeremiah 4:1], not to any intermediary. The Sages expounded the verse, *as the Lord our God is whensoever we call upon Him* [Deuteronomy 4:7], "to Him ought you to cry out, not to Michael or Gabriel."[32]

One ought not raise an objection [to this] from Jacob's prayer, *the angel who hath redeemed me* [*from all evil, bless the lads . . .*] [Genesis 48:16], for the prayer was to God, as he said, *the God before Whom my fathers* [*Abraham and Isaac*] *did walk, the God Who hath been my shepherd* [*all my long life unto this day*] [Genesis 48:15]. The angel was God's agent of providence to save him. Therefore he said, *the angel who hath redeemed me from all evil,* for God's actions on sensible objects must necessarily be done through intermediaries, notwithstanding the fact that it is God Who is the Agent of individual providence through that other agent, as I explained in my treatise, *Ateret Zekenim.*[33] Abraham's statement, *The Lord, the God of Heaven, Who took me from my father's house. . . . He will send His angel before thee* [Genesis 24:7] supports this. In every place where we find a prayer to an angel the meaning of it is that it is a prayer to God to send His angel, the agent of His providence, to do the [sought after] work. Our Sages, in their wisdom, explained this very point. On the passage, *Behold I send an angel before thee,* [*to keep thee by the way, and to bring thee into the place which I have prepared. Take heed of him, and hearken unto his voice; be not rebellious against him; for he will not pardon your transgressions; for my name is in him*] [Exodus 23:20–21], they said: "*Be not rebellious against him;* i.e., exchange Me not for him."[34] That is to say, do not worship him, for only God may be worshipped, and no other being.

Joshua's bowing down before an angel[35] may be explained [either] as bowing to God Who *remembered His mercy and faithfulness towards the house of Israel* [Psalms 98:3] by sending that angel before them to [cause them to] inherit the land, or [in terms of Joshua's] submitting himself before the angel to do his bidding as is the custom of an inferior who submits himself before his superior.

The statements of the Sages and our own custom today of prostrating ourselves on the graves of the dead, that they might seek mercy for us, in accordance with what the prophet says, *Rachel weeping for her children* [Jeremiah 31:15][36] may be explained in one of two ways. We do it either to cause our souls to submit themselves before God, likening ourselves before Him as the dead. This is the opinion of the scholar who, in his responsum to an inquiry concerning why we go to the cemetery in times of trouble, said that we do it to show that we are like the dead, and as a sign of submission. This is similar to the reason why we wear sackcloth, which is to show that we are like animals. Or, we do it by way of praying that God will remember the merit and righteousness of the deceased, *which endures forever* [Psalms 119:10, etc.]. The sayings of the Sages ought to be understood in this and similar ways. It is not the case, heaven forfend, that they introduce intermediaries in their prayers, since they admonish us against it and forbid us to do it.

In Tractate Menaḥot [we find]:

R. Abba b. Isaac said in the name of R. Ḥisda [—others say, Rab Judah said in the name of Rab], "from Tyre to Carthage the nations know Israel and their Father Who is in heaven; but from Tyre westwards and from Carthage eastwards the nations know neither Israel nor their Father Who is in heaven." R. Shimi [b. Ḥiyya] raised the following objection [against Rab]: "Is it not written, *For from the rising of the sun even unto the going down of the same My name is great among the nations; and in every place offerings are burnt and presented unto My name, even pure oblations* [Malachi 1:11]?"—He replied, "You, Shimi! They call Him the God of Gods."[37]

In this passage the Sages make clear that part of the inhabited world recognizes God and knows His faith because they know Israel, the faithful, through whom they know their Father in heaven. In other places, however, where they do not know Israel, they do not know God. R. Shimi objected to this on the basis of the verse, *For from the rising of the sun even unto the going down of the same* which he thought showed that God's divinity is recognized in every place and by every nation. The Sages answered that [by those who do not recognize God is meant] those who introduce intermediaries and pray to them [beseeching] that they intercede on their behalf before the exalted God. This is what they meant by "God of Gods." There is no doubt that this is one of the branches of idolatry. They attribute such sublimity to God that they must pray to intermediaries. This opinion is still found among people; even today it is commonly known to be part of the Christian faith.[38] We do not believe that, but pray to the Lord our God, *whenever we call upon Him* [Deuteronomy 4:7].

With respect to the third objection—why did Maimonides count as a principle that we ought to worship God, since this is a particular commandment, as it says, *And you shall serve the Lord your God* [Exodus 23:25]?—we reply and say that the author of the *Sefer ha-Ikkarim,* who raised this objection, did not understand what Maimonides meant by this principle. Maimonides did not say that the principle was to worship God, for such worship is a practical commandment. If he intended that worship which we call prayer—in accordance with the rabbinic dictum, ". . . *and serve Him with all your heart* [Deuteronomy 11:13]. What is the service of the heart? You must needs say, prayer"[39]—then he intended a particular practical commandment and it has been made clear in the sixth proposition[40] that we ought not enumerate as a principle any particular commandment among the commandments of the Torah for the principles are all taken from the commandments of faith, not the practical commandments, as was brought forth in that proposition. But Maimonides' intention with respect to this principle was that we ought to believe that God, because of His exalted state and power, is [alone] He Whom we ought to worship, exalt, and praise. This is not the commandment of worship, nor the actual, practical commandment of prayer. It is, rather, the belief that God alone is worthy of our worship and no other. Therefore, the prohibition of idolatry was founded upon this principle. Thus,

Maimonides said in explaining this principle: "We learn this fifth foundation from the commandment which we have been given prohibiting idolatry."[41] That is to say, we learn a true and fundamental[42] belief from the Torah's prohibition of worshipping other gods. It is that we ought to worship, magnify, exalt, and extoll God, and not do that to anything other than He. It thus established that this principle is not that we should actually worship God or pray to Him; these are all consequences of the principle that worship and praise are appropriate to God {alone}. It is known that a cause is not the same thing as its effect. This principle is the cause; worship and prayer are particular commandments which are consequences of it.

13

A Solution to the Fourth Objection

With respect to the fourth objection, concerning Maimonides' enumeration of the eternity of the Torah as a principle,[1] I respond and say that R. Sa'adia Gaon in his *Sefer ha-Emunot* wrote at length concerning the eternity of the Torah.[2] He discussed the arguments brought against this [belief] by perverse people who argued on the basis of reason[3] or Scriptural texts. He responded to them with simple answers, as is well known. It is not my intention here to copy his words, but to seek a strong and sufficient proof for the eternity of the Torah.

I say, therefore, that R. Ḥasdai wanted to demonstrate the eternity of the Torah when he said that our divine Torah is absolutely perfect.[4] For, [in the first instance], it is not possible for it to change into a less perfect Torah since God, by virtue of the nature of His perfection, perfects everything other than He as much as possible. It is therefore impossible for us to say that God might change the Torah into one less perfect than it [now] is. [In the second instance], if it were changed into a more perfect Torah then the divine Torah which we have would not be perfect since there could be another Torah more perfect than it. [In the third instance], if it were changed into an equally perfect Torah then the substitution and change would be an empty action, without any advantage. This cannot be conceived with respect to the nature of God. This is his argument.

Recent thinkers have objected to his position, saying that even if his arguments prove that it is impossible for the Torah to become more perfect or less perfect, it is still possible for the Torah to change to one of equivalent perfection.[5] This would not involve the absurdity he ascribed to it for the perfection which can be acquired through this Torah can be acquired in many ways. It is certainly possible that the means leading to this perfection can be changed and that the new means can lead to the same perfection. The need for such a change would be caused by a change in those guided by this Torah, who seek to arrive at this perfection. Because of a change in them a change in the means [leading to this perfection] is made necessary. Thus, the substitution and change would not be an empty action without any advantage, since there would be necessity and advantage to it.

Some have tried to demonstrate the eternity of the Torah in another way, as follows. Once it has been posited that this divine Torah is perfect [it must be held] that the mode of conduct it prescribes is perfect. It cannot be said to apply at one time and not at another; [it must apply] at every time and in every place. It is self-evidently true[5] that this Torah cannot change in any way at any time. They brought a proof [in support of this claim] from the practice of medicine. It is not verified on the basis of the experience of one man at one place but is, rather, appropriate[7] to all men at every time and in every place. This is all the more true with respect to the divine Torah which comes from God, Who is perfect, and which arouses one to love God and to cleave to Him. This is the end intended by the Torah. It is clear from the Torah itself that it perfects both the perfect and the deficient, each according to his nature and according to what is necessary for him. Thus, it is impossible for the Torah to change in any way.

But this argument is also susceptible to refutations and objections. One [refutation] relates to the claim that something which is perfect cannot change in any time or place. This is the way we ought to think of something which is absolutely perfect, which can be nothing other than God. For no thing other than He can include all perfection, since He is the cause of everything else. It is impossible for God to change in any way. The term "perfect," [however], may be used in a relative sense as when we say that man is the most perfect of all the species or that the heavenly bodies are the most perfect of all physical things. Similarly, we say that

Moses was the most perfect man conceivable. So we also say that our divine Torah is perfect, that is, the most perfect conceivable rule for behavior and the most perfect conceivable teaching. From this perspective it is possible for it to change or be destroyed, just as Moses was destroyed and changed,[8] notwithstanding his being the most perfect of all the prophets. Further, the Torah comes under the category of relation, it being the activity which teaches those who receive the instruction. That which falls under [the category of] relation can change as the relation changes. Thus the Torah, even though it is perfect, can change because of a change in its recipients with whom it is in relation, without this being a deficiency in its nature. It is true that this Torah arouses us to strive to love God and to cleave unto Him. But who makes it impossible for this goal to be reached through other means and by other commandments?

The analogy drawn between the Torah and medical practice is a sophistical argument for the practice of medicine is dependent upon natural things, the source of which is nature. One cannot [simultaneously] derive two opposites from them. It is not the case that heat will expand and cold contract at one time and do the opposite at another. But the Torah and, in general, all rules of behavior depend upon things which are caused by will and choice from which there can certainly be derived two opposites. For a man can desire something today which will disgust him at some other time. It is thus necessarily the case that [the Torah and medicine] are distinguished by the different things upon which they depend, namely, will and nature. Because of all this scholars have found this argument to be weak as well.

We thus see that the best way of proving the truth of the eternity of the Torah is from the aspect of the Agent Who gives it. For, since in its totality and in its parts this entity is the work of God, set down according to His wisdom, which does all things for an end which He knows, even if we do not know it, God in His wisdom arranged the matters upon which were to stand and endure all things after their creation, in accord with His mercy for them, just as He arranged nutrition for all living things in accordance with their needs.[9]

Similarly, God gave to all creatures, below and above,[10] that which would preserve their existence and enable them to fill out their appointed time, as His divine wisdom decreed. Just as He arranged the necessary nutrition for man's body, which cannot survive without it, so He arranged the necessary nutrition for the soul in the Torah. Just as the [proper] nutrition for the human body will never change or pass away, since it is ordered by God, so the divine Torah, which is the [proper] nutrition for the human soul, will not change since the two of them are nutrients arranged by one wisdom and one Agent.[11]

One may not object[12] on the basis of the law[13] of Adam and of the Noachides[14] for these are certainly not teachings which perfect the human soul. They were set down solely to preserve human society according to the nature of the times in which they were set down. They are at the level of conventional law.[15] The divine law,[16] however, which directs the soul to its final perfection, is none other than the Torah of Moses, for it is the nutrient necessary for the soul to acquire life and be saved from death.

One may not [further] object if it becomes necessary to change some element of the acts ordained by the Torah at some time. The nature of bread, as an appropriate nutrient for the human body, and so also meat and wine, will never change, even if at times the body is ill and they become inappropriate for it. For something which changes accidentally[17] will necessarily return to its essential nature[18] for nothing accidental is permanent. Even if it should be necessary to change some of the commandments, as if you would say that we will not recall the Exodus from Egypt in the days of the Messiah,[19] this should not be called a change in the Torah, just as there is no change in it for one who does not own a field or vineyard and who [therefore] does not give the tithe. The existence and eternity of commandments which are connected to other things lies in the fact that when these other things are found then these commandments apply; if those other things are not found to exist in actuality [at any given time] the commandments, in any event, remain in force. This is similar to the case of medicine, which depends upon the existence of disease. With the absence of sick people the art of medicine does not disappear, for it exists always. Its existence lies in the fact that when there are sick people, the remedies of medicine will be appropriate to them. Similarly, if it should come about that we recall the future redemption[20] but not the previous one[21] the commandment to recall the Exodus from Egypt will itself always remain in force, so long as the appropriate preconditions exist, namely that there will not have occurred a redemption greater than it.

The principle which arises from this is that any conceivable change in these matters does not reflect change in the [commandments] for they do not change in themselves. The change occurs in other things; this does not nullify the eternity of the Torah. In general, it is necessary to understand that a demonstration of the Torah's eternity can be had [only] with that which is ordered in relation to itself. This will not change at all, since it is the [proper] nutrient of the human soul set down by divine wisdom, just as the [proper] nutrients of the human body will not change, except accidentally.

It may still be urged against our position, however, that we have no right to assert that that which is found in the Torah is the specific nutrient of the soul. Perhaps that [nutrient] is something else, or more, or less than what is found in the Torah. It is necessary for this reason to establish the eternity of the Torah on the basis of the fact that the prophecy of Moses was superior to that of all the prophets. His prophecy occurred without the use of the faculty of imagination so that we can have no doubt that what he said is what God wanted him to say. No prophet can add to his words since it was he *whom the Lord knew face to face* [Deuteronomy 34:10] while [He knew] all the others through intermediaries.[22] How could one who speaks with God through an intermediary hear what he who spoke with God without an intermediary did not hear? This was made clear by Scripture, which said, *And there hath not arisen a prophet* [*since in Israel like unto Moses*] *whom the Lord knew face to face* [Deuteronomy 34:10]. Thus, no doubt can remain about [the possibility of] a prophet adding to the Torah. Therefore, it said above,[23] *And*

Joshua the son of Nun was full [of the spirit of wisdom; for Moses had laid his hands upon him; and the children of Israel hearkened unto him, and did as the Lord commanded Moses] [Deuteronomy 34:9]. This says that Joshua was full of the overflow[24] of wisdom in that he received it from Moses and that everything came from Moses' strength; therefore, *the children of Israel hearkened[25] unto him and did as the Lord commanded Moses.*

After all this there remain none of the objections which had been raised. For, since the Torah was set down by God, it may not be asked why this particular nutrient is necessary for the soul of man, no more than one may ask why bread in particular is the [proper] nutrient of man. The answer to both questions is that [the nutrient] is appropriate for the character of those being nourished. This characteristic[26] was given them by God, Who arranged everything according to the nature of His wisdom. The ways of God's wisdom are hidden from us in this case just as they are in the case of why He created man with his particular dispositions and not others. So it is with all other things.

Withal, the answer which satisfies all these [objections] is, as we have said, that everything is derived from the nature of God's wisdom and we are ignorant of the ways of that wisdom. Even if we comprehend many of the advantages [in the way God has arranged the world] to some degree[27] and even if we comprehend something about these two forms of nourishment,[28] we will not comprehend all [of the advantages in the way God has arranged the world], not even one in a million.[29] Philosophers and physicians have attested to this, asserting that up to this time only very little of the wisdom involved in the creation of man has been comprehended; this is all the more true of all other things.[30]

It is established by all this that the divine Torah in our hands is eternal. It is impossible for it ever to change for God made it and brought it into existence through His infinite wisdom. He saw that this Torah is appropriate for all men at every time. God's knowledge is not dependent upon a particular, defined, time but He knows things as they are appropriate for every time, man, and place. Because of this His general actions will never undergo permanent[31] change. If they should change for the needs of the hour, as was the case with what Elijah did on Mt. Carmel,[32] they do so in a way similar to the way in which parts of the universe are changed by miracles, for the needs of the hour, and according to the time and place in which the miracle occurred. For the form of the universe follows the form of the divine Torah: both *were given from one shepherd* [Ecclesiastes 12:11]. All [of the Torah] was [given] for the purpose of assuring the permanence[33] of the universe. Just as the form of the universe will not change in general, so the divine Torah will not change. And just as the human form differentiates and distinguishes the human species from the other species, so the Torah of Israel differentiates and distinguishes the nation [of Israel] from the other nations, as it says, [*And ye shall be holy unto Me; for I the Lord am holy*] *and have set you apart from the peoples* [*that ye should be mine*] [Leviticus 20:26].[34] Just as the human form is, with respect to itself, one and the same in the whole species, but will be found in different [degrees] among [different] individuals—some of whom perfectly embody the human form and some of whom are deficient with respect to it—but is nonetheless still the same in them all, so the Torah is one form which is, with respect to itself, equal with respect to the generality of Israelites, but is found in different degrees among different individuals, some of whom are perfect in it, and some of whom are deficient in it. Despite all this it is for all of them eternally one and there is nothing like it with respect to its equality. If those who follow it suffer wounds and illness there will be found in it all the potions and remedies through which the soul will be cured, returned to its natural balance, and made to continue in its existence. About this they said, "The Holy One, blessed be He, desired to benefit Israel and therefore increased the Torah and commandments for them."[35] This is to say [that God gave each Israelite] many ways in which to perfect himself. This is seen from him who asked, "How do I stand with the world to come?" They answered him, "Have you performed any commandments?"[36] That is to say, that with one commandment properly done he acquired the life of the world to come.

Resh Lakish and R. Johanan disputed this issue in Tractate Sanhedrin, with reference to the verse, *Therefore the nether world hath enlarged her desire and opened her mouth without measure* [Isaiah 5:14]: "Resh Lakish expounded: 'It means[37] for him who leaves undone even a single statute of the Torah.' R. Johanan said to him: 'It is not pleasing to their Master[38] that you say this. But, say, who has not fulfilled even one statute of the Torah.' "[39] Resh Lakish thus thought that [fulfillment of] all the commandments was necessary for spiritual regeneration and for the acquisition of perfection. He therefore said that the nether world, which is Gehinnom, opens its mouth for one who leaves even a single statute of the Torah undone. Rabbi Johanan, however, held that by properly keeping one commandment and one statute on the basis of rational choice, the soul will achieve complete regeneration. According to him, the increasing of the commandments reflects God's righteousness and great mercy since He created many paths and ways for human beings, by each of which it is possible to acquire perfection.

This is similar to the case of a sick person who is nauseated by food. The wise physician will prepare many different foods for him to eat. He will try them to see which of them pleases [the patient's] palate and is best for him. He will in this way find a food which pleases [the patient] and thus overcome his disgust for food. So God laid down many commandments in His Torah that we may take them one after another and do them as is fitting. When it occurs that we fulfill one of those commandments perfectly, with this rational choice, we are saved. This is even more the case if we do more than one perfectly and as it is fitting. Therefore the Sages said "that if Israel would properly observe two Sabbaths they would be redeemed immediately."[40]

The upshot of all this is that it is impossible for the Torah to change, whether in whole or in part, because of the wisdom and power of its Giver. This was the intention of the prophet when he said, *For I the Lord change not and ye, O sons of Jacob, are not consumed* [Malachi 3:6]. This is to say that the

Torah is eternal and does not change and that the nation [of Israel] is eternal also. Thus, the words of Maimonides in the principle of the eternity of the Torah have been proven.

The author of the *Sefer ha-Ikkarim* wrote [the following] in Book I, chapter 14, about Maimonides' proof for this [principle] from the verse, *Thou shalt not add thereto, nor diminish from it* [Deuteronomy 13:1]: "The same reason would lead us to say that the doctrine of the immutability of the Torah should not be reckoned as a principle if it is a specific command, as Maimonides thinks."[41] It is apparent from his words that he understood Maimonides to hold that this principle is a particular commandment, that we neither add to nor diminish from the Torah. But this is a mistake, as is clearly seen in the words of Maimonides, for the particular commandment is that we neither add to nor diminish from [the Torah] while the principle is that we believe in the eternity of the Torah, and that God will neither add to it nor diminish from it. The commandment itself, that Israel not add to nor diminish from [the Torah] is not the substance of the principle.

That this is the case is shown by Maimonides' words at the end of the principle: "We have already explained what needs explanation in this foundation in the beginning of this treatise."[42] He was referring to what he had written at the beginning of his *Commentary on the Mishnah*:

> All of the Sages and prophets were unable[43] to accomplish miracles like those of this prophet Moses and God implanted faith in him in our hearts[44] as it says, *And they will also believe in thee forever* [Exodus 19:9]. Moses related to us in the name of the Holy One, blessed be He, that no other Torah shall ever come from the Creator save this one, and this is what is meant by *It is not in Heaven* [Deuteronomy 30:12]; it [also says] *But the word is very nigh unto thee* [Deuteronomy 30:14].[45]

He further said there:

> Moses also warned us against adding to them or deleting from them as it is written, *Thou shalt not add thereto nor diminish from it* [Deuteronomy 13:1]. For this reason the Sages of blessed

memory stated, "No prophet may introduce any new law hereafter."[46]

Maimonides' statement that "God implanted faith in him in our hearts, etc." was made with reference to the principle and foundation that this Torah will never change and that no Torah other than it will ever be given by God. So, too, with his citation of *It is not in Heaven* [Deuteronomy 30:12].[47] The admonition against adding to or diminishing from [the Torah], however, which Maimonides cited after this, is the substance of the commandment. Thus, he phrased it in the form of an admonition. It has thus been established that the substance of the principle is different from that of the commandment.

The verse which Maimonides cited in his explanation of the principle, *Thou shalt not add thereto nor diminish from it* [Deuteronomy 13:1] was not presented in order to explain the belief [taught by] this principle, that God will neither change the Torah, nor substitute another for it, nor add to or diminish from it, for [the verse] was addressed to Israel.[48] Maimonides' intention, rather, was that we should believe that there will never be any addition to or diminution of this Torah. It is because of this that we were commanded neither to add to nor to diminish from the Torah.

Maimonides derived a number of the principles and foundations from the commandments. However the principle, a general belief, is one thing and the commandment, a particular action, is another. See his words at the end of the fifth foundation: "We learn this fifth foundation from the commandment which we have been given prohibiting idolatry."[49] Similarly, from God's commandment in the Torah, *Thou shalt not add thereto nor diminish from it* [Deuteronomy 13:1], we learn the general principle that the divine Torah will suffer neither addition nor diminution. [We learned this] from this command which God gave to Israel. This is in addition to our belief that God will neither add to nor diminish from the Torah which we learn from the statement, *It is not in heaven* [Deuteronomy 30:12]. This verse, however, *Thou shalt not add thereto nor diminish from it*

[Deuteronomy 13:1] includes any addition to or subtraction from the commandments. This is as the Sages said, "From whence do we learn that it is forbidden to add to the *lulav* or *ẓiẓit*? The Torah teaches, *Thou shalt not add thereto*."[50]

It was further urged against Maimonides' position that the Sages said that a court can abrogate something from the Torah in the case of abstaining from the performance of an action and that "Solomon ordained the laws of *eruv* and of [the washing of] hands." Are we to think that they violated *Thou shalt not . . . diminish* and *Thou shalt not add*?[51] Maimonides himself presented an answer to this in the *Sefer ha-Madda*.[52] We find "two biblical passages which contradict each other";[53] the first is *Thou shalt not add thereto nor diminish from it* [Deuteronomy 13:1], on which the Sages said, "No prophet may introduce any new law hereafter."[54] The second is *Thou shalt not turn aside from the sentence which they shall declare unto thee, to the right hand nor to the left* [Deuteronomy 17:11] on which the Sages said, "Even if they tell you that your right hand is left and your left hand is right."[55] Maimonides explained this [contradiction] according to Torah and true tradition. He said that *Thou shalt not add thereto nor diminish from it* [Deuteronomy 13:1] and "No prophet may introduce any new law hereafter" apply to something which has an element of idolatry in it, as is the plain intention of this passage. Even with respect to other commandments, we ought not to obey a prophet if he says that God commanded us to add to [the commandments] or to diminish from them. This is made clear by the verse, *And they will also believe in thee forever* [Exodus 19:9]. But the verse, *Thou shalt not turn aside from the sentence which they shall declare unto thee* [Deuteronomy 17:11] and the Sages' dictum, "Even if they tell you that your right hand is left" refer only to something which has no element of idolatry in it, and which is enacted only for the needs of the hour, not for all generations. The decrees, enactments, and hedges [about the law][56] promulgated by the Great Court and the Sages of each generation are of this type. They do not involve any change in the Torah, nor any addition to it or diminution of it, for this type of enactment is sanctioned by Torah and tradition. [This is an example] of divine wisdom [taking care] lest the order laid down in the Torah not be sufficient with respect to the various characters of its recipients [in the light of] their deficiencies. It therefore gave the prophets and the Great Court permission to enact decrees and to erect fences and hedges around the Torah in order to strengthen it in accord with the capabilities of its recipients. This should not be called a nullification of or change in the Torah, and it does not fall under the prohibition against adding to or diminishing from the Torah. Such addition or diminution only refers to a case where a man says, "I am adding to what the Torah says because it is deficient," or "I am removing something from the Torah because it is unnecessary and redundant." But when we made hedges and enactments, they came from the Torah itself and were for its observance. As they said, "Make safeguards to My charge."[57] Thus, it does not fall under the prohibition of adding to or diminishing from the Torah.

With respect to what the scholar[58] cited from Leviticus Rabbah, that all the holidays are destined to be abrogated except for Purim and the Day of Atonement,[59] [it should be noted] that this abrogation is not, heaven forfend, an abrogation of the holidays themselves, but only an abrogation of that which they recall, since they were all ordained "as a memorial to the Exodus from Egypt."[60] The point of the dictum is that in the time of the redemption Israel will not recall the miracles and wonders which God wrought for them in their Exodus from Egypt. For, in seeing *the great trials* [Deuteronomy 7:19] to which God will put them in the days of the Messiah they will forget the earlier ones and not recall them to mind. As Scripture says, [*Therefore behold, the days come, saith the Lord,*] *that they should no more say: "As the Lord liveth, that brought* [*up the children of Israel out of the land of Egypt"; but: "As the Lord liveth, that bought up*] *and that led* [*the seed of the House of Israel out of the north country, and from all the countries whither I had driven them; and they shall dwell in their own land"*] [Jeremiah 23:7–8]. Thus, the Sages said, "except for Purim and the Day of Atonement," for in the Day of Atonement they included both Rosh ha-Shana and the tenth[61]—for they are alike [in that they are both devoted] to repentance, forgiveness, and atonement, and were meant to stand by themselves—and Purim [was included] because it was one of the miracles performed in the Exile.[62]

Similarly, their dictum, "Why is it called 'swine' [ḥazir]? Because in the future God will return it [ha-ḥaziro] to Israel."[63] It has been explained in Yelamdenu[64] that Edom[65] is called "swine," as in [the verse], *The boar out of the wood doth ravage it* [Psalms 80:14].[66] Another explanation is that God might permit it to Israel during wartime, as a special dispensation,[67] as it was permitted to them during the time of the conquest of the Land—as they said, "*And houses full of all good things* [Deuteronomy 6:11], even bacon,"[68]—and it was on this basis that the Sages said that it would be returned. It is as the Sages said in Yelamdenu, "*The Lord looseneth the prisoners* [Psalms 146:7]—He makes the forbidden permitted."[69]

They brought a further objection from the names of the months which were changed during the days of Ezra.[70] But this is neither an abrogation nor a change, for who would stop us should we wish to give [new] names to the months, so long as we do not take them out of their sequence? This is no more than a form of translation and explanation of names found in Scripture, which does not abolish them, for, in any event, the names given in the Torah remain there in their place.

The scholar brought a further proof to the effect that our holy Torah might be changed from Midrash Ḥazit[71] on the verse, *Let Him kiss me with the kisses of His mouth* [Song of Songs 1:2];

> R. Judah said: When Israel heard the words, *I am the Lord thy God* [Exodus 20:2], the knowledge of the Torah was fixed in their heart and they learnt and forgot not. They came to Moses and said, "Our master, Moses, do thou become an intermediary[72] between us, as it says, *Speak thou with us, and we will hear* [. . . *now therefore why should we die* (Exodus 20:16; Deuteronomy 6:22). What profit is there in our perishing?]" Then they became liable to forget what they learnt. They said: Just as Moses, being flesh and blood, is transitory, so his teaching is transitory.[73] Forthwith they came a second time to Moses and

said: "[Our master,] Moses, would that God might be revealed to us a second time! Would that He might kiss us *with the kisses of His mouth* [Song of Songs 1:2]! [Would that He would fix the knowledge of Torah in our hearts as it was!]" He replied to them: "This cannot be now, but it will be in the days to come," as it says, *I will put My Torah in their inward parts* [*and in their heart will I write it*] [Jeremiah 31:33].[74]

I am amazed at this scholar for citing this passage as proof that the Torah will change. Israel's request was that they not forget the Torah which they had received through Moses. Therefore they asked to hear it from God's mouth a second time. They were referring to the same Torah which they had heard the first time, not another Torah, God forbid. We also learn this from Moses' response. He replied with the verse, *I will put my Torah in their inward parts* [Jeremiah 31:33]; that is, "My Torah, the Torah which I gave, not another one which they are now forgetting, will in the days of the Messiah be once again in their inward parts."

This objection in its entirety can also be solved in another way. [We may say] that the eternity of the Torah ought to be understood with respect to the Torah as a whole. [This includes] the written Torah with its explanation, as Moses received it on Sinai. Everything the Prophets and Sages did in every generation, whether as a special dispensation,[75] or as a hedge, whether by adding to or taking away from what is clearly written in the Torah, as well as the changes which they predicted would occur in the days of the Messiah—the abolition of the festivals, the permission to eat swine's flesh, etc.—are all from the Torah itself and all were given and commanded to Moses at Sinai, either by a particular or general command, to perform them in their [proper] time. He transmitted these things by oral tradition. Since it was from the Torah itself, it was permissible for Elijah to bring a sacrifice on a high place outside of the Sanctuary; he had a tradition to the effect that it was permitted to do this when the hour demanded it, as it did then. So also Solomon, who enacted the laws of *eruv* and of washing the hands did it in accordance with what was intended by the Explanation of the

Torah.[76] It was because of this that the Sages said a court can abrogate something from the Torah in the case of abstaining from the performance of an action, since this also was in the Torah itself which had been transmitted to them.

In witness to this God commanded, *Thou shalt not turn aside from the sentence which they shall declare unto thee, to the right hand, nor to the left* [Deuteronomy 17:11], on which the Sages said, "Even if they tell you that your right hand is left and your left hand is right."[77] This dictum is not meant to teach that the Sages would uproot anything from the Torah or make any decrees contrary to it [saying] that what it posits as right is left because that which is customary among us is not like that.[78] But that which the Sages decree is from the Torah itself according to the truth. This is the right hand according to its true explanation. It is no uprooting [of the Torah] for it is not the left hand. It is only a change or substitution from the point of view of our accustomed [reading] of the Torah as we have understood its literal meaning. Aside from all this, all these other things were commanded in the Tradition either specifically or by virtue of general commands and all that has been or will be done is from the Torah itself and is eternal through its eternity.

It is thus established by all the foregoing that the divine Torah in our hands is eternal and that it is impossible for it to be changed or replaced. This is what I wanted to establish.

14
A Solution to the Fifth Objection

With respect to the fifth objection—how is it possible that Maimonides could count the coming of the Messiah as a principle since, although it is a true belief, it is not a foundation in the sense that the Torah would collapse with its refutation—I respond and say that Maimonides was led to count the coming of the Messiah as a principle because of three[1] arguments.

First, since the coming of the Messiah is a type of retribution, as was shown in the fourth[2] proposition,[3] and since reward and punishment is itself a principle it is not impossible for the coming of the Messiah to be a principle also.

The second argument states that most of the prophets and all of those who spoke with divine inspiration[4] magnified their complaints with respect to the suffering of the righteous and the prosperity of the wicked. This is so to the extent that many scholars were led in their speculation to deny divine providence. Therefore, after Maimonides instilled the principles of God's knowledge and providence and of just reward and punishment in us he laid down the last two principles, those of the coming of the Messiah and the resurrection of the dead, in order to drive away any possible doubt or hesitation concerning divine providence and justice. All this is as I discussed in the fifth proposition.[5] From this perspective [also] it is proper to count this belief as a principle.

The third argument is that the coming of the Messiah is clearly stated in the Pentateuch, Prophets, and Hagiographa. Moses in his predictions, all the prophets who succeeded him, and all those who spoke with divine inspiration, predicted, prophesied, and spoke of the coming of the King Messiah. I proved this absolutely and clearly in my treatise *Mashmia Yeshua* on the coming of the Messiah.[6] Therefore, if one denies the coming of the Messiah, it is as if one denies the Torah, Prophets, and Hagiographa, since they all predict it. From this aspect [as well] this belief ought to be counted as one of the principles of the Torah.

With respect to R. Hillel's statement in *Perek Ḥelek*, "There will be no Messiah for Israel, because they have already enjoyed him in the days of Hezekiah,"[7] I have already written in the aforementioned treatise that it was not his intention to deny the coming of the Messiah, God forbid.[8] Nor was it his opinion, as some others have explained, that [he thought] that there would be no Messiah for Israel because all the verses about the Messiah in Isaiah must be interpreted as referring to Hezekiah, King of Judah. [On this interpretation] R. Hillel believed in the coming of the Redeemer, but on the basis of tradition and not on the basis of Scripture. All this is farfetched if we follow the simple meaning of the passage. His true intention was that the coming of the Messiah has two limits. The first relates to the possible time of his coming. Were Israel privileged to repent before God, then the Messiah's deeds would be speeded up and hastened and his coming advanced.[9] The second limit relates to the necessity that he will come at some time, known only to God, even should Israel not be privileged to repent since there is a definite time known by God which cannot pass without the Messiah coming. This is the subject of Daniel's prophecies at the end of his book.

It was with reference to these two limits that the Sages expounded on *I the Lord will hasten it in its time* [Isaiah 60:22] "If they are worthy, I will hasten it; if not [the Messiah will come] at the due time."[10] That is, even if they fail to repent, and do not merit [the coming of the Messiah] there is an appointed time at which he will come; he will not tarry past it. If they are privileged to repent, however, God will advance the coming of the Messiah before its time. They also hinted at this when they said, "The son of David[11] will only come in a generation that is either altogether righteous or altogether wicked."[12]

It was R. Hillel's opinion that "there shall be no Messiah for Israel"; that is, that the Messiah would not come by virtue of Israel's meriting him through repentance at any possible time "because they have already enjoyed him in the days of Hezekiah."[13] He mentioned "the days of Hezekiah" because God performed a great miracle for Hezekiah and acted with much grace toward him by killing one hundred eight-five thousand men in the Assyrian camp in one night. There was no other *day of the Lord's vengeance* [Isaiah 34:8] upon His enemies like that, and if his generation was not worthy [to receive the Messiah]—as Scripture says, *For I will defend this city to save it, for Mine own sake, and for My servant David's sake* [Isaiah 37:34], but it did not say, "for the sake of the generation of Hezekiah"—[then no subsequent generation will be worthy]. It is for this reason that R. Hillel thought that that miracle was restraining Israel from receiving the Messiah, since their merits have been diminished by that miracle and act of great grace which was done for them, since it is the kind of miracle fitting for the days of the Messiah.

Our Sages said in *Perek Ḥelek*, "The Holy One, blessed be He, wished to appoint Hezekiah as the Messiah and Sennacherib as Gog and Magog."[14] That is, God would fight Hezekiah's battles [for him] while he was at rest. This is what will be done in the future for the King Messiah in the wars of Gog and Magog, about which it is said, *Their flesh shall consume away while they stand upon their feet and their eyes shall consume away in their sockets* [Zechariah 14:12]. [The Talmud continues:] "Whereupon the attribute of Justice said before the Holy One, blessed be He: 'Sovereign of the Universe! If Thou didst not make David the Messiah, who uttered so many hymns and psalms before Thee'"[15]—that is to say, to fight his battles with miracles and wonders as will be done in the future for the King Messiah, about whom it is said, *and his resting place shall be glorious* [Isaiah 11:10], i.e., that he will tranquilly rest in his glory[16]—and now You wish to do this for Hezekiah! It says there, "But a heavenly voice cried out, 'It is My secret, it is My secret.'"[17] That is, the [time of the] coming of the Messiah *is laid up in store with Him, sealed up in His treasuries* [after Deuteronomy 32:34].

It has thus been established that R. Hillel thought that the miracle which God performed for Hezekiah harmed his descendants by diminishing their merits and thus lengthened the Exile, for now the Messiah will not come at any possible time, but only at the necessary time. For this reason he said, "There shall be no Messiah for Israel," i.e., that the Messiah will not come by virtue of the actions of the Jewish people, but that he will come at the necessary time, which God appointed and determined.

The truth of my interpretation is shown by the fact that in *Perek Ḥelek* it says many times, "The son of David will not come"[18] and "In the generation when the son of David comes"[19] for they commonly use those expressions.[20] R. Hillel, however, did not say, "The son of David will not come for they have already enjoyed him in the days of Hezekiah," for it was not his intention to deny the coming of the Messiah, heaven forfend. He said, rather, "There shall be no Messiah for Israel," that is, that the Messiah will not come by virtue of their own merit, on the basis of their repentance, but at the time of the end, appointed and determined by God.

R. Joseph responded to him: "May God forgive him [for saying so]."[21] R. Joseph deplored Hillel's denial that the Messiah could come at the possible time for this might cause Israel to lose hope in the efficacy of repentance and they would continue to sin, saying, *Our hope is lost* [Ezekiel 37:11]; no matter how much we pray, He does not hear." Therefore, R. Joseph sought God's forgiveness for him. R. Joseph's claim, "Now when did Hezekiah flourish? During the first Temple. Yet Zechariah, prophesying in the days of the second, proclaimed, *Rejoice greatly, O daughter of Zion; [shout, O daughter of Jerusalem;] behold thy king cometh unto thee* [Zechariah 9:9],"[22] would seem to contain nothing other than an argument against him.[23] But the truth of the matter is that R. Joseph said that Zechariah lived during the time of the second Temple, and prophesied about the coming of the Messiah, as he said, *behold thy king cometh unto thee* [Zechariah 9:9]. Immediately after this he said, *Return to the stronghold, ye prisoners of hope* [Zechariah 9:12]. This shows that he was reproving them and urging them to repent so that the divine salvation could come to them quickly.[24] [It also shows that R. Joseph held] that the issue did not accord with the words of R. Hillel, who denied that the Messiah would come in the possible time. Further, by saying, *thy king cometh unto thee* [Zechariah 9:9] he shows that the Messiah will come to Israel because of their merit and by virtue of their repentance. Thus, he contradicts what R. Hillel said, "There shall be no Messiah for Israel."

It is thus established on the basis of the foregoing that belief in the coming of the Messiah ought to be considered a great principle and foundation of our Torah.

15
A Solution to the Sixth Objection

The sixth objection relates to the fact that Maimonides counted belief in the resurrection of the dead as a principle even though if one were to believe in divine retribution in this world and in the next without believing in resurrection after death, the Torah in its generality would not collapse because of this, nor would its commandments be refuted.[1] To this I respond and say that even though the Torah in its generality would not collapse with the denial of this belief, it still should be counted as a principle and foundation among the foundations of the Torah for three[2] reasons.

The first reason is because it is a form of reward and punishment, as I wrote in the fifth proposition.[3] Since belief in reward and punishment is one of the principles of the religion it is proper that resurrection of the dead be counted as one of the principles insofar as it is a part of divine reward and punishment. One ought not wonder [at Maimonides] for counting both a genus and one of its species [as principles]; he did this because they were praiseworthy beliefs which one ought to know, as I have mentioned a number of times.[4]

The second reason is that this belief has been instilled in us by the divine Torah, by all the prophets, and by those who speak with divine inspiration. In *Perek Ḥelek* many proofs were brought from Scripture for this principle. The strongest of them are the following.

From the Torah: Moses said, *See now that I, even I, am He, and there is no god with Me; I kill and I make alive, I have wounded and I heal* [Deuteronomy 32:39]. They expounded there:[5]

I kill and I make alive. I might interpret I kill one person and give life to another, as the world goes on: therefore the Writ states, *I wound, and I heal.* Just as the wounding and healing [obviously] refer to the same person, so putting to death and bringing to life refer to the same person. This refutes those who maintain that resurrection is not intimated in the Torah.

We ought not to say that the explanation of *I kill and I make alive* is [only] that God *can* do so, not that He actually *will* do so, for the whole passage testifies about what will actually occur in the future.[6] Thus it says, *Is this not laid up in store with Me* [Deuteronomy 32:34], *Vengeance is Mine and recompense* [Deuteronomy 32:35], *For the day of their calamity is at hand* [Deuteronomy 32:35], and, *For the Lord will judge His people* [Deuteronomy 32:36]. Because of this the Talmud did not try to refute this proof, as it did with the other proofs which were brought [there in *Ḥelek*].

It says in Genesis Rabbah:[7] "*For dust thou art and unto dust thou shalt return* [Genesis 3:19]. R. Simeon b. Yoḥai said: Here Scripture hints at resurrection, for it does not say, For dust thou art, and to dust thou shalt go but *thou shalt return*."[8]

From the Prophets: [Isaiah said:] *Thy dead shall live, my dead bodies shall arise—Awake and sing, ye that dwell in the dust, for thy dew is as the dew of light, and the earth shall bring to life the shades* [26:19]. They questioned this proof in *Perek Ḥelek* and said, "But perhaps this refers to the dead whom Ezekiel resurrected?"[9] It is also possible to explain this verse as referring to the men of exile who live in the low-lying dust and that God would *raise up the poor out of the dust* [I Samuel 2:8].[10] But the style of this passage and its [specific] words prove absolutely that it is speaking of the resurrection of the dead in the literal sense, as was proved in the sequel.[11]

Malachi the prophet, predicting the Day of Resurrection and Judgment, said *For behold the day cometh, it burneth as a furnace* [3:19] and *Behold I will send you Elijah the prophet before the coming of the great and terrible day of the Lord. And he shall turn the heart of the fathers to the children and the heart of the children to their fathers* [3:23–24]. He said this because the resurrection will be effected through Elijah, since he still lives, in body and soul. Since when they are resurrected fathers will tell their children, or children their fathers, what happened when their souls parted from their bodies, he said, *And he shall turn the heart of the fathers to the children.*

From the Hagiographa: We find in the book of Daniel, *And many of them that sleep in the dust of the earth shall awake, [some to everlasting life and some to reproaches and everlasting abhorrence]* [12:2]. This proof was neither refuted nor qualified at all in *Perek Ḥelek.* Maimonides wrote in his *Treatise on Resurrection* that,

> . . . this resurrection of the dead, which involves the return of the soul to the body after death, was mentioned by Daniel in a way which cannot be interpreted [in another fashion or taken out of its literal sense]: *And many of them that sleep in the dust shall awake, some to everlasting life and some to reproaches and everlasting abhorrence* [12:2]. And the angel said to him, *But go thou thy way till the end be; and thou shalt rest, and shalt stand up to thy lot, at the end of the days* [Daniel 12:13].[12]

It has thus been established that this belief is found in the Torah, Prophets, and Hagiographa. It has therefore become a general belief, a great principle and foundation, such that if one denies it, it is as if one denies the Torah, the Prophets, and the Hagiographa. For this reason it has been laid down as a principle and as one of the foundations of the Torah.

The third reason is that this belief is hard[13] to conceive and hard for the human mind to accept. Since man's heart almost turns from it because of its difficulty, they said in the Mishnah that one who denies it has no share in the world to come.[14] Maimonides followed in the steps of the accepted mishnah.[15] See the statement of the Mishnah that the following have no share in the world to come: he who maintains that resurrection is not a biblical doctrine, he who denies that the Torah is divinely revealed, and[16] the *apikoros.* Since the authors of the Mishnah compared belief in the resurrection of the dead with belief in the divinely revealed character of the Torah and to belief in God's existence, knowledge, and providence, all of which are denied by the *apikoros*, [17] belief in the resurrection of the dead ought to be counted as a principle, like the other principles in that mishnah.

With this the sixth objection is rebutted.

16
Solutions for Eleven Other Objections

To the seventh objection—which relates to the claim that the Torah, its principles, and its foundations will never change, [and which states] that at the time of the coming of the Messiah and of the resurrection these two principles must necessarily change[1]—I respond and say that if we put forth [belief in] the coming of the Redeemer without connecting it with a [particular] time, future or past, and similarly with resurrection, if we do not connect it with any time, then these principles will not change even after the coming of the Messiah and the resurrection of the dead. For we will always believe that all the prophets spoke truthfully about the coming of the King Messiah and the resurrection of the dead. It is just as when Moses wrote in the Torah about the event of [the covenant] between the pieces, that Israel would be exiled to Egypt, and that they would leave there and inherit the land.[2] When all this actually occurred the Torah did not change, but was verified. So we ought to say with respect to these two roots that belief in them is not connected to any particular time. Thus, when they[3] actually occur, the matter will be verified, not changed. This is so even though the twelfth principle—about the coming of the Messiah—includes the claim that there shall be no king in Israel but of the House of David and the seed of Solomon and that all who dispute this kingship and this family deny God and the words of His prophets. This principle stands, unchanging, even after the coming of the Messiah. With respect to the last principle, resurrection of the dead, Maimonides wrote that after their resurrection people would eat and drink and die and be

144

perfected by the Torah.[4] According to this the principle will stand without change after the time of the resurrection.

The eighth objection—why Maimonides did not count as a principle [belief in] the immanence of God's presence in Israel through the Torah—has been answered by R. Moses ha-Kohen[5] who said that the indwelling of the Divine Presence depended upon a particular commandment, the building of the Tabernacle, as it says, *And I will sanctify the tent of meeting . . . and I will dwell among the Children of Israel* [Exodus 29:44, 45]. It was therefore not included among the principles.[6] We can support his opinion with what Maimonides wrote in the book enumerating the commandments in the principles with which he prefaced it, where he wrote that that which is derived from a commandment ought not to be counted as one and also ought not to be counted among the principles of the religion.[7] Thus, the indwelling of the Divine Presence, since it is dependent upon the activity of the Tabernacle, ought not to be counted among the principles.

It appears to me that the indwelling of the Divine Presence was the work of Moses.[8] As the Torah said, *And in all the mighty hand, and in all the great terror, which Moses wrought in the sight of Israel* [Deuteronomy 34:12]. It is taught by tradition that *"The great terror; this is the revelation of God's Presence."*[9] How could it not be thus for God, after the sin of the [Golden] Calf, said that He was going to send an angel to lead Israel [in His place]. Moses pleaded with Him until God said to him, *Behold I make a covenant; before all thy people will I do marvels [such as have not been wrought in all the earth, nor in any nation;] and all the people among which thou art shall see the work of the Lord that I am about to do with thee, that it is tremendous* [Exodus 34:10]. Since this [revelation of God's presence] was a mark of the exalted degree of Moses' prophecy, it is included in the seventh foundation, on the exalted character of his prophecy, according to the distinctions mentioned there by Maimonides.[10] It is also included in the eighth foundation, about revelation, for there is no possibility of it[11] without the immanence[12] of the Divine Presence.

With respect to the ninth objection—why Maimonides did not count creation among the principles[13]—I respond and say that Maimonides presented this belief in the fourth foundation, where he wrote, "that this aforementioned One is truly eternal *a parte ante* [*kadmon*] and that everything other than He is not eternal *a parte ante* when we compare them to Him."[14] The substance of this principle includes two things, as was explained in the third proposition.[15] The first is that God is eternal *a parte ante*, that is, that He has no beginning and does not exist in time. The second is that no things are eternal *a parte ante* "when we compare them to Him." that is, they are all created. We cannot say of any one of them that it is eternal *a parte ante*. If they are not eternal *a parte ante*, they must certainly be created. Maimonides therefore wrote, "when we compare them to Him," that is, even though we sometimes say that one thing is earlier [*kadmon*] than another thing, which was created after it, as we say that Methuselah was earlier than Noah who was earlier than Abraham, nothing but the Creator is called earliest absolutely since God created everything and He alone is eternal *a parte ante* and there is nothing other than He which is eternal *a parte ante*.[16] This is not simply the precedence of a cause [to its effect] but temporal precedence also, the precedence of a creator to that which it creates.[17] We have put it this way for heuristic purposes but in truth time is among the created things. Because of this Maimonides did not say that God is eternal *a parte post*,[18] the term which denotes uninterrupted existence, without beginning or end, but that He is eternal *a parte ante* to indicate that He precedes His works with every kind of precedence. This proves that in this principle Maimonides was not talking about God's eternity *a parte post* but, rather, about His being alone eternal *a parte ante*, and that all other things are created by Him.

It has thus been made clear to you that the creation of the world according to Maimonides' belief is an absolute creation, out of absolute nothingness. This is unlike the opinion of Plato who believed that there existed uncreated matter.[19] For, if this were so God would not alone be eternal *a parte ante* for that matter would be eternal *a parte ante* like Him.

However, since Maimonides believed in the absolute creation of the world according to the true tradition he wrote in this principle that God alone is eternal *a parte ante* and that there is nothing else which is eternal *a parte ante* "when we compare them to Him." He said that God was therefore called *Eternal God* [Deuteronomy 33:27] because He alone is the God Who is eternal *a parte ante*.[20]

A passage in the *Guide* about creation, at the end of chapter thirteen[21] in Part II, proves that Maimonides' intention in this principle was to establish the creation of the world. He wrote there: "And it is undoubtedly a foundation of Moses our Master, peace be on him. And it is second to the foundation that is the belief in the unity [of God]."[22] It seems that Maimonides did not count the principle of God's unity in this context, but said that the principle of creation was second to it. You see in the list of the principles that the first of the principles to come after the principle of [God's] unity was that of [God's] incorporeality. After it, the second one after the principle of [God's] unity, there comes the principle that God is eternal *a parte ante* and that nothing else is eternal *a parte ante* "when we compare them to Him." Since he wrote there in the *Guide* that this principle is the principle of creation it is clearly revealed that it was the intention of Maimonides that this principle [teach] that God is eternal *a parte ante* and that all other things are created by Him. I am amazed that these scholars[23] did not notice this.[24]

To the tenth objection—why Maimonides did not count that we ought to believe in all the miracles of the Torah according to their literal interpretation as a principle[25]— I respond and say that this is included in the eighth principle, which concerns revelation, since in its narratives the Torah testifies to all the miracles and wonders recounted in it. Since we believe that all the narratives in the Torah [were given] "from the mouth of the Almighty,"[26] we are obliged to believe them, as we [are obliged to] believe the commandments. It is also possible to say that this belief is included in the fifth foundation, that God alone ought to be worshipped. This is so for the intention of this principle is that we believe that God acts with intention and will and that He is omnipotent. It is therefore proper to worship Him, because of His power and because of His works in nature, which He does as He wills. This is the point of the miracles and wonders.

To the eleventh objection—why Maimonides did not count among the principles that one ought to follow the tradition of one's fathers[27]—I respond and say that this belief is explicitly included in the eighth principle, where Maimonides wrote, "that one is obliged to believe that the whole of the Torah which we possess today is the Torah which was given to Moses and is all of it from the mouth of the Almighty."[28] That is, that the Torah which we possess is itself the Torah which was given to Moses and that no change has been made in it up until today and that the Torah which Moses wrote for us he received "from the mouth of the Almighty" and wrote nothing of his own in it. In that principle he wrote that we ought to believe the accepted explanation of the Torah, which is the Talmud, since it, too, is "from the mouth of the Almighty." This is the tradition which we possess and which our fathers received one from the other back to Moses. This is the commentary on the Torah and its secrets which was passed on orally.

To the twelfth objection—why Maimonides did not count [human] choice[29] as a principle, since no religion can be imagined without it[30]— I respond and say that I have already pointed out in the ninth proposition[31] that these principles of Maimonides, which he established to serve as foundations for the house of the Lord and His Torah, are all beliefs about God and do not involve knowledge of human matters. Thus, Maimonides did not count among the principles [beliefs about] the essence of the human soul or that it is eternal by its nature for these beliefs relate to human beings and ought not to be counted as principles of the divine Torah since its principles and foundations are only things which we ought to believe about God and about His volitional works which relate to the [Jewish] people. Choice precedes the Torah and it precedes all human actions insofar as they are human. It is not a matter which is related to the Torah alone. It is like saying that man is rational. This is true of man *qua* man, not *qua* believer in the divine Torah.

Maimonides' words in the *Sefer ha-Madda,* in the fifth chapter of *"Hilkhot Teshuvah"* show this. He said, "This doctrine is an important principle, the pillar of the Torah and the Commandment."[32] Maimonides did not say that this was a "principle" of the Torah but that it was an "important principle." This is true, since it is a general principle, important to political order. He said that it was a "pillar" of the Torah. He did not say that it was a "principle" of the Torah, but a "pillar," upon which it rests. For it is a presupposition and general root for it,[33] for other faiths, and for human action [generally]. For idolatrous faiths, and all other faiths generally, also need this pillar. See his statement, "it is the pillar of the Torah." He did not say that this was a "principle" of the Torah for a principle is the essence of a thing and part of it, like the roots[34] of a tree which are parts of the tree according to its nature. A pillar [on the other hand] is not part of a building according to its nature but is outside of it, placed there for the building to lean upon. So it is with choice. It is not part of the essence of religion, nor one of its principles; it is outside of it and a pillar necessary to it. Maimonides therefore wrote in the same chapter:

> [Know that everything takes place according to His pleasure, notwithstanding that our acts are in our power. How so?] Just as it was the pleasure of the Creator that fire and air shall ascend, earth and water descend, and that the sphere shall revolve in a circle, and all the other things [in the Universe shall exist in their special ways which He desired, so it was His pleasure that man should have liberty of will, and all his acts should be left to his discretion; that nothing should coerce him or draw him to aught,] but that, of himself and by the exercise of his own mind which God had given him, he should do whatever it is in a man's power to do.[35]

This makes it clear that Maimonides did not consider choice as a principle of the Torah, but as a great principle of human action.

His statement at the end of the chapter, "And this is the principle on which all the words of Prophecy depend,"[36] should not be understood to imply that it was Maimonides' intention to call choice a principle. Rather, this refers back to what he said above it: "Hence it is said in the Prophetic writings that a man will be judged [for all his deeds] according to his deeds, whether they be good or evil."[37] It was about this that he said, "this is the principle." Choice, however, is the general presupposition of all religion without being in particular one of the principles of the divine Torah, for the reasons I have given.

To the thirteenth objection—why Maimonides did not record among the principles [the belief] that God acts by will[38]— I respond and say that, as I wrote in the third proposition,[39] this belief is included in the fifth foundation, [which teaches] that one ought to worship God and lift up one's voice in exalting Him since He has infinite power and acts by choice and will. Worship and praise are therefore appropriate to Him. Since this belief is included in the fifth principle it was not necessary for Maimonides to put it forth as a principle by itself.

To the fourteenth objection—why Maimonides does not count as a principle that God lives, is eternal, is powerful, has will, and [is endowed with] other divine attributes[40]— I respond and say that God's life, eternity, wisdom, and other attributes are included in the first principle, which teaches that God's existence is perfect. For were it not so His existence would not be absolutely perfect and necessary. God's power and will are included in the fifth principle, that He alone ought to be worshipped. This was stated in the third proposition. God's knowledge and the fact that in knowing Himself He knows all things are included in the tenth principle. All this shows that all these things are included in the words of Maimonides. Why the principles number thirteen has already been explained in the fifth proposition.[41]

To the fifteenth objection—why Maimonides did not list among the principles the issue of man's end and belief in the survival of the soul, as did R. Ḥasdai—I respond and say that all this is found in the eleventh foundation on reward and punishment, in which Maimonides wrote, "[the] greatest reward is the world to come and [the] greatest punishment is cutting off [the sinner]."[42] This being so, man's end is included in his reward, which is the world to come and the survival of the soul, this [latter] being the reward of the soul which he mentioned. Since they were included there Maimonides did not record them separately.

To the sixteenth objection—why Maimonides did not include the oracle of the *Urim* and *Tummim* among the principles as did R. Ḥasdai[43]— I respond and say that this also is included in the sixth principle, which is about the existence of prophecy. This is so because the *Urim* and *Tummim* are a species of [inspiration by] the holy spirit which is the second of the degrees of prophecy as Maimonides wrote in the *Guide,* Part II, chapter 45, where he discusses the degrees of prophecy. He mentioned the matter of the oracle of the *Urim* and *Tummim* in the second degree, that of [inspiration by] the holy spirit. This being so, the matter of the *Urim* and *Tummim* is a type of prophecy and is included in the sixth[44] principle.

To the seventeenth objection—why Maimonides did not count the efficacy of prayer, repentance, New Year, Day of Atonement, and the divisions of the year as principles as R. Ḥasdai did[45]—I respond and say that, as was established in this proposition,[46] one ought not to count as a principle any specific commandment of the Torah. One ought not to count prayer, repentance, and the meaning of the New Year, the Day of Atonement, and the divisions of the year [as principles], therefore, since they are all specific commandments. Only general matters ought to be counted among the principles. Moreover, all these things are already included in the fifth principle, that one ought to serve only God. The Sages said that the service of the heart is prayer.[47] These things are also included in the tenth principle, about God's knowledge and providence, and in the eleventh foundation, about reward and punishment. Thus, they were not counted among the principles.

17
Solutions for Two Other Objections

To the eighteenth objection, the first of those which R. Ḥasdai raised against Maimonides—why Maimonides counted *I am the Lord thy God* [Exodus 20:2] as a commandment when commandments are relational and cannot be conceived without a known God Who commands[1]—I respond and say that that objection occurred to R. Ḥasdai only because he failed perfectly to understand Maimonides' intention in his explanation of the first principle and the first commandment. He understood it to mean that we ought to believe that God exists. If this were Maimonides' opinion, then R. Ḥasdai's objection would be very hard to solve. But Maimonides' intention was, as I explained in the second proposition,[2] that God's existence is absolutely perfect and necessary, not contingent. This I proved from Maimonides' words. According to this truth, the one who commands would be the God Whose existence we posited, and His first command to us would be that we must believe that His existence is absolutely perfect, without any imperfection, and that He exists necessarily, not contingently. Thus, the commandment is related to the one who commands it and to others.[3] It is not the substance of this principle simply that God exists, as this scholar[4] thought, but that His existence is absolutely perfect and that He necessarily exists of Himself[5] and is not dependent upon anything else. Maimonides proved this from the first utterance,[6] which says, *I am the Lord thy God* [Exodus 20:2]. This statement, *I am the Lord,* teaches that He exists necessarily.

Maimonides wrote in the *Guide,* chapter 61[7] of Part I:

All the names of God, may He be exalted, that are to be found in any of the books derive from actions. There is nothing secret in this matter. The only exception is one name: namely, *Yod, He, Vav, He.* [8] This is the name of God, may He be exalted, that has been originated without any derivation and for this reason it is called the articulated name. This means that this name gives a clear, unequivocal indication of His essence, may He be exalted. [9]

He said further:

There can be do doubt about the fact that this great name, which as you know is not pronounced except in the Sanctuary by the sanctified Priests of the Lord and only in the benediction of the Priests and by the High Priest upon the day of fasting, is indicative of a notion with reference to which there is no association between God, may He be exalted, and what is other than He. Perhaps it indicates the notion of a necessary existence, according to the [Hebrew] language, of which today we know only a very scant portion and also with regard to its pronunciation. Generally speaking, the greatness of this name and the prohibition against pronouncing it are due to its being indicative of the essence of Him, may He be exalted, in such a way that none of the created things is associated with Him in this indication. As the Sages, may their memory be a blessing, have said of it: "My name that is peculiar to me." [10]

With this Maimonides made clear that when God said, *I am the Lord* [Exodus 20:2], he explained to the Israelites [11] that He existed necessarily, as is indicated by the name, *Yod, He, Vav, He.* However, that which He further said, *thy God, Who brought thee out of the land of Egypt,* was to make known to them that that Primary Existent, Who exists necessarily, is omnipotent. This is intended by *thy God* which is used here to show that God is the Ruler of Israel, the God Who brought them forth from the land of Egypt. It is as if He mentioned their exodus from Egypt so that they would recognize His divinity. The meaning of the verse, then, is as if it read, "Thy God Who brought thee forth from the land of Egypt out of the house of bondage, I am the Lord." That is to say, the powerful God Who watched over them and brought them out of Egypt, He is the Lord; that is, [He is] necessarily existent.

This, then, is Maimonides' belief concerning the first principle and the first commandment, as I have understood his words. *Unto thee it has been shown* [Deuteronomy 4:35] with what I have explained here that no room remains for R. Hasdai's objection.

The author of the *Sefer ha-Ikkarim*, however, resolves this objection in another way. He writes "that *the appearance of the glory of the Lord* [Exodus 24:17] which *was seen by Israel face to face* [after Numbers 14:14] on the day of the giving of the Torah taught the truth of God's existence and that that glory *which was encamped at the mount of God* [after Exodus 18:15] commanded them to believe in God's existence."[12] But these are empty words, for *I am the Lord thy God* [Exodus 20:2] is the statement of God, not of [His] glory.

Others said that the intention of the first utterance which God commanded the Israelites was to believe that He gave them the Torah and spoke with them and that He[13] is not something which receives emanations from the heavenly bodies nor the host on high. This is why He said, *I am the Lord thy God Who brought thee out* [Exodus 20:2]. What I have written, however, is more reasonable, true, and correct, according to the roots of Maimonides and his words.

To the nineteenth objection, which is the second which R. Hasdai raised with regard to the fact that Maimonides counted *I am the Lord thy God* [Exodus 20:2] as a commandment—he said, "the term 'commandment' according to its [proper] definition only applies to matters with respect to which will and choice obtain";[14] this is not the case with beliefs, which are not acquired by will and choice.[15] I respond [to this objection] and say that I have already explained in the ninth proposition that beliefs are actualized and fixed in man's heart and soul just as natural forms are fixed in their subjects, coming in an instant and by necessity, without choice and will.[16] But despite all this, it is impossible for these beliefs to be actualized if no preparation for them is made, with respect to knowing those things which bring one to those beliefs and which cause them to be accepted by the soul.

These facts, investigations, and examinations, and this study are the preparations which bring a person to belief.

There is no doubt that these preparations are an activity of will and choice and are acquired over time. For it is up to each person "to perceive, learn, teach,"[17] and know those things which necessitate and give birth to belief in his soul. If he does not wish to involve himself with this, {beliefs will not be born in his soul}.[18]

Now Maimonides did not count as a positive commandment the form of the belief and its truth,[19] but, rather, knowledge of those things which bring one to acquire beliefs. Therefore he wrote in the first chapter of the *Sefer ha-Madda*, in explaining the first foundation, which is about belief in the necessity of God's existence, that "to acknowledge this truth is an affirmative precept."[20] Maimonides did not say that *belief* in this truth is an affirmative precept, for he did not relate the commandment to belief but to knowing those things which bring one to belief.[21]

Thus he said in the second principle, about God's unity, that knowing it is a positive commandment[22] for he always connected commandment to knowledge and study of those things {which bring one to belief} but not to beliefs themselves, which are the forms which are fixed in the soul. Notwithstanding this, Maimonides wrote of these two commandments in his book enumerating the commandments "By this injunction we are commanded to believe in the unity of God."[23] But it was not his intention that there should be a commandment concerning the belief which is pictured by the soul. {But the commandment} only concerned those things which bring one to such belief. We may rely on what he wrote in the *Sefer ha-Madda*, as I said, for that is the only[24] proper place for a discussion of this matter while in the book enumerating the commandments Maimonides' only intention was to number the commandments, nothing else.

18

A Solution to the Twentieth Objection

The twentieth objection is the third of those raised by R. Ḥasdai.[1] It relates to the saying of R. Simlai in Tractate Makkot which Maimonides quoted to show that *I am the Lord thy God* is a commandment.[2] [R. Ḥasdai, however, sought] to prove [from R. Simlai's dictum] that it is not so. Know that this is the opinion of the author of the *Halakhot Gedolot* who did not count *I am the Lord thy God* among the 613 commandments.[3] Naḥmanides,[4] in his glosses to Maimonides' book enumerating the commandments cited this argument[5] to support the opinion of the [author of the] *Halakhot Gedolot*. R. Ḥasdai took the argument from there.

I respond as follows. Maimonides interpreted the dictum, "*I am* and *Thou shalt have no* we heard from the mouth of the Almighty," as referring only to the first two verses [of the Decalogue], *I am the Lord thy God, who brought thee out of the land of Egypt, out of the house of bondage. Thou shalt have no other gods before Me* [Exodus 20:2–3], and to no more than this. It was these two verses, according to [Maimonides' interpretation] of the opinion of the Sages, which the Israelites heard "from the mouth of Almighty" since they are great foundations and cornerstones of faith. But the Israelites heard the other verses, *Thou shalt not make unto thee a graven image,* etc. [Exodus 20:4 ff.]—according to the opinion of the Sages [as interpreted by Maimonides]—from the mouth of Moses, like the rest of the Decalogue.

Nahmanides[6] and R. Ḥasdai argued that it is not proper to separate the statement *Thou shalt have no* [Exodus 20:3] from the rest of the utterance continuing through . . . *of them that love Me and keep My commandments* [Exodus 20:6] since all

156

these verses are spoken in the first person while the rest were all spoken in the third person.

This contention has no substance, for why could not Moses have spoken these words in the name of God, Who sent him? We find this occurring in Scripture very often. Note, [for example,] the end of weekly reading Ki Tavo[7] in the passage beginning with *And Moses called unto all Israel* [Deuteronomy 29:1]. Even though Moses spoke in his own name, with his own mouth, as when he said, *Ye have seen all that the Lord did before your eyes* [Deuteronomy 29:1] and *But the Lord hath not given you a heart to know* [29:3] he continues immediately with *And I have led you in the wilderness forty years . . . that ye might know that I am the Lord thy God* [29:4–5, reversed]. He then resumes speaking in his own name with *And when you came unto this place . . . and Sihon came out against us into battle, and we smote them* [29:6].

There are many [other] places where Moses speaks in the name of Him who sent him. Thus it is when he says in our passage *for I the Lord am a jealous God* [Exodus 20:5] *and of them that love Me and keep My commandments* [20:6]. So it is with the other verses which [the Israelites] heard from Moses speaking in the name of Him Who sent him. [He spoke in this fashion] because he relayed the words in the exact style in which he heard them.

You will now see that one is forced to say this even according to the view of R. Ḥasdai and Naḥmanides.[8] For, were it their intention to say that *I am* and *Thou shalt have no* through . . . *of them that love Me and keep My commandments* [Exodus 20:2–6] constitute one utterance and even if we don't count *I am* and *Thou shalt have no* as commandments, since they are matters of faith,[9] there still remain three commandments in that utterance: *Thou shalt not make unto thee a graven image* [Exodus 20:4], *Thou shalt not bow down unto them* [20:5], and *nor serve them* [20:5]. How then could we have 613 commandments? [Counted this way] the number comes to 614 commandments.[10]

R. Ḥasdai sensed this objection and wrote in response that *Thou shalt not make unto thee a graven image* and *nor serve them* are [the only] two commandments [in Exodus 20:2–5] for *Thou shalt not bow down unto them* is included in *nor serve them* for bowing down is a form of worship.[11] But this is no answer[12] for all the scholars who enumerated the commandments counted *Thou shalt not make unto thee a graven image* as one commandment, *Thou shalt not bow down unto them* as another commandment by itself and *nor serve them* as a third commandment. It would have been better, on his own account, had he said that both *Thou shalt not bow down to them* and *nor serve them* were included in the utterance of *Thou shalt have no* and that they both fall under that general category.[13] There would then be two commandments: *Thou shalt have no* and *Thou shalt not make unto thee a graven image*.

But the simple sense of Scripture will not tolerate this [interpretation]. It cries out that *I am the Lord thy God* is one commandment and that the Israelites apprehended both—i.e., that God is absolutely perfect, existing necessarily and that He is one—"from the mouth of the Almighty." This is shown by Moses' statement in Deuteronomy, *Unto thee it was shown, that thou mightest know that the Lord, He is God; there is none beside Him* [4:35]. In saying *that the Lord, He is God,* Moses referred to the first root, that God exists necessarily, in absolute perfection.[14] In saying *there is none else beside Him* he referred to the root of unity.[15] It is said of both [of these doctrines] that [the Israelites] heard them *out of the midst of the fire* [Deuteronomy 4:36], for the purpose of the entire vision [at Sinai] was to perfect the people by means of these two valuable beliefs.[16] Thus, after *Unto thee it was shown, that thou mightest know that the Lord, He is God; there is none else beside Him* [Deuteronomy 4:35], Moses said, *Out of Heaven He made thee to hear His voice, that He might instruct thee; and upon earth He made thee to see His great fire; and thou didst hear His words out of the midst of the fire* [Deuteronomy 4:36]. There is no doubt but that it was from this source that the Sages derived [their dictum], "*I am* and *Thou shalt have no* we heard from the mouth of the Almighty," and that they meant by this only these two verses, as I have said.

You will find, therefore, that this view is generally accepted by the Sages, not only with respect to R. Simlai's dictum in Tractate Makkot—the proof presented by Maimonides—but in other places as well. Thus, they said in Midrash Ḥazit:[17]

[R. Joshua b. Levi and the Rabbis joined issue.] R. Joshua said: Israel heard two utterances from the mouth of the Holy One, blessed be He, viz., *I am* and *Thou shalt not have,* for so it is written, *Let Him kiss me with the kisses of His mouth* [Song of Songs 1:2]—with some and not all the kisses.[18] The Rabbis, however, say that Israel heard all the commandments from the mouth of the Holy One, blessed be He. R. Joshua of Siknin said in the name of R. Joshua b. Levi: the reason of the Rabbis is because it is written: *And they said to Moses: Speak thou with us and we will hear* [Exodus 20:16]. What does R. Joshua b. Levi do with this verse? He maintains in opposition to the Rabbis that strict chronological order is not followed in the Torah.[19] But perhaps the words *Speak with us, and we will hear* were spoken only after two or three commandments?—R. Azariah and R. Judah b. Simon speaking in the name of R. Joshua b. Levi followed his[20] view. They said: It is written, *Moses commanded us a law* [Torah] [Deuteronomy 33:4]. The whole Torah contains 613 commandments. The numerical value of the word "Torah" is 611, and so many commandments Moses spoke to us, but *I am* and *Thou shalt not have* Moses did not speak to us but we heard them from the mouth of the Holy One, blessed be He.[21]

We learn from this passage that many of the Sages of Israel erred in this matter and that some of them held that the Israelites heard all the utterances from the mouth of God. They did not find any difficulty in the fact that some of the utterances were said by God speaking for Himself in the first person and some by Moses in the third person. The consequence of this for our purposes is that the position of Maimonides is correct according to the roots [laid down by] the Sages and that the two commandments are *I am* and *Thou shalt have no.*

[This is true] whether we say that the statement *Thou shalt have no* includes *Thou shalt not make unto thee a graven image, thou shalt not bow down to them,* and *nor serve them* and was therefore called one commandment because of its general character or if we say that by *Thou shalt have no* they meant only that the prohibition itself [as expressed] in the verse was from the mouth of God and that they heard the other verses, *Thou shalt not make unto thee a graven image . . . thou shalt not bow down unto them, nor serve them* from the mouth of Moses, not the Almighty. Were this not so they would not constantly have spoken of *I am* and *Thou shalt have no,* never mentioning the other commandments by name.

A number of contemporary scholars from among our people[22] have emboldened themselves to prove from the sayings of the Sages that *I am the Lord thy God* is not a commandment.[23] This accords with the opinion of the author of the *Halakhot Gedolot,* who thinks that it is not proper to include in the list of specific commandments something which is a principle of the faith and from which all the commandments are derived.[24] For all the commandments are enactments decreed for us by God following from this belief. He who does not believe in divinity has no Torah at all. He thus thought that *I am the Lord thy God* is a principle of faith and its foundation since he maintained that the Torah had only one principle and that this was it. Therefore, he did not count it as a commandment while all the rest are commandments.

This is what they said in the Mekhilta:

> *Thou shalt not have other gods before Me.* Why is this said? Because it says, *I am the Lord thy God.* To give a parable: A king of flesh and blood entered a province. His attendants said to him: Issue some decrees upon the people. He, however, told them: No! When they will have accepted my sovereignty I shall issue decrees upon them. For it they do not accept my sovereignty how will they carry out my decrees? Likewise, God said to Israel: "I am the Lord thy God, thou shalt not have other gods—I am He whose sovereignty you have taken upon yourselves in Egypt." And when they said to Him: "Yes, yes," He continued: "Now, just as you accepted my sovereignty, you must also accept my decrees: *Thou shalt not have other gods before Me.*"[25]

It will be apparent from this statement of the Sages that the presupposition of the decrees and commandments is the utterance, *Thou shalt have no* and that the utterance *I am* refers to the belief in divinity, which is something they already believed in Egypt. Thus, the Sages said repeatedly that *I am the Lord thy God* signifies acceptance of the sovereignty of Heaven.

They[26] also brought proofs for this from what the Sages said in [Tractate] Horayot [8a-b]. [They asked] how we know that [the phrase] *And when you should err* [Numbers 15:22] refers to idolatry. [They said]:

> The school of R. Ishmael taught: *From the day that the Lord gave commandments, and onward throughout your generations. . . .* [Numbers 15:23]. Which is the commandment that was spoken at the very beginning? Surely it is that of idolatry. But did not a master state that Israel was given ten commandments at Marah![27]—But the best proof is that given at first.

Were the utterance *I am* a commandment [the argument runs], they would not have said that the utterance concerning idolatry was said first.

The answer which seems proper to me in all this is that our Sages did not deny that *I am the Lord thy God* is a commandment. They would say, rather, that it signifies the acceptance of the sovereignty of Heaven. This acceptance of the commandments was [itself] commanded by God. [He commanded the Israelites] to accept the yoke of His sovereignty[28] upon them. In their wisdom the Sages saw that the first commandment was all-inclusive and that it served as the pillar and principle for the other commandments. They therefore said, "When they will have accepted my sovereignty I will issue decrees upon them."[29] The acceptance of [God's] sovereignty is expressed in the utterance, *I am the Lord thy God.* It is, according to their opinion, a commandment with which God commanded the Jews to accept His sovereignty. After this general and fundamental commandment God said, "Now, just as you accepted My sovereignty, you must also accept my decrees."

Understand, that the decrees [of God] are called practical commandments while the acceptance of sovereignty of

Heaven is a commandment of faith.[30] It is as if they said that the commandment of faith, involving the acceptance of the sovereignty of Heaven, necessarily preceded all the decrees which are the practical commandments of the Torah. It is not that the Sages said that the acceptance of the sovereignty of Heaven was not a commandment but that the difference between it and the decrees is that it is a general and fundamental belief while the other commandments are decrees and particular practical commandments.

See the words of Naḥmanides in his commentary to the weekly reading *Yitro*[31] on the verse, *I am the Lord thy God.* He wrote:

> This divine utterance constitutes a positive commandment. He said *I am the Lord* thus teaching and commanding them that they should know and believe that the Lord exists and that He is God to them. That is to say, there exists an Eternal Being through Whom everything has come into existence by His will and power, and He is God to them who are obligated to worship Him.[32]

He continued:

> The commandment, in the words of our Rabbis, is called an obligation to "take upon oneself the yoke of the sovereignty of Heaven,"[33] for these words [i.e., *the Lord thy God*], which I have mentioned, indicate a king addressing his people. Thus the Rabbis have said in the *Mekhilta: "Thou shall have no other gods before Me.* Why is this said? Because it says, *I am the Lord thy God.* This can be illustrated by a parable: A king entered a country, etc."[34]

Thus Naḥmanides[35] cited the statement which I quoted from the Mekhilta and derived from it that *I am the Lord thy God* involves the acceptance of the sovereignty of Heaven and is a commandment.[36]

On the other hand, with respect to the claims made about this issue on the basis of the passage from Horayot which was cited above, namely,

> The school of R. Ishmael taught: *From the day that the Lord*

*gave commandments, and onward throughout your generations
. . .* [Numbers 15:23]. Which is the commandment that was
spoken at the very beginning? Surely it is that of idolatry.

which indicates that the first commandment was *Thou shalt
have no other gods before Me* which [in turn] proves that *I am
the Lord thy God* is not a commandment, I respond and say
that it was the opinion of R. Ishmael that *I am* and *Thou shalt
have no* were said in one utterance. It is as they expounded on
God hath spoken once, twice have I heard this [Psalms
62:12].[37] [On this basis it may be said] that the beginning
which he cited—*Thou shalt have no other gods before Me*—
was not precise. For the beginning is that utterance which
includes [both] *I am* and *Thou shalt have no.* Even though
they are two commandments, as Maimonides maintains, they
are united in that they both occur in one utterance. Thus one
of them, *I am the Lord thy God,* is a positive commandment
and the second, *Thou shalt have no,* is a negative commandment. We thus have a negative commandment corresponding
to a positive commandment.[38] Thus, Maimonides explained
Thou shalt have no as meaning that it is forbidden to think
that there is another god.[39]

Rashi's commentary on the passage proves the truth of this.
He wrote: "What is the commandment that was spoken at the
beginning? Surely it is that of idolatry since it is found in the
beginning of the Decalogue [with the words] *I am* and *Thou
shalt have no* which refer to idolatry."[40] He thus explained
that the phrase "Which is the command that was spoken at
the very beginning?" does not refer only to *Thou shalt have
no* but to both of the utterances at the beginning of the
Decalogue which relate to idolatry, namely *I am* and *Thou
shalt have no.*

One may not use [this passage from Horayot] to deny that
I am is a commandment especially in light of the fact that the
compiler of the Talmud[41] also had difficulty with this statement. This is shown by his question "But did not a master
state that Israel was given ten commandments at Marah!" He
decided the issue, stating that the dictum "Which is the
command that was spoken at the very beginning? . . ." ought

not to be accepted: "But the best proof is that given at first," that is to say, the clearest [proof]. That which was taught first seemed proper to him, not this dictum of "Which is the command that was spoken at the very beginning? . . ."[42]

There are other dicta of the Sages which show that they held *I am the Lord thy God* to be one of the commandments of the Decalogue. This is seen in Yelamdenu,[43] on the weekly reading *Naso*:[44] "The adulterer and adulteress transgress the Decalogue . . . How? They transgress *I am* for everyone that commits adultery with the wife of his fellow denies God as it is said, *They have belied the Lord and said, 'It is not He'* . . . [Jeremiah 5:12]." Further, in Leviticus Rabbah to the weekly reading *Kedoshim*[45] it is stated that the Decalogue is included in that weekly reading:

> R. Hiyya taught: This section was spoken in the presence of a gathering of the whole assembly, because most of the essential principles of the Torah are attached to it. R. Levi said: Because the Decalogue is included therein. Thus: (1) *I am the Lord thy God* and here it is written *I am the Lord your God* [Leviticus 19:3]; (2) *Thou shalt have no other gods* and here it is written, *Nor make to yourselves molten gods* [19:4]; (3) *Thou shalt not take the name of the Lord thy God in vain* and here it is written, *And ye shall not swear by My name falsely* [19:12]; (4) *Remember the Sabbath day* and here it is written, *And ye shall keep my Sabbaths* [19:3]; (5) *Honor thy father and thy mother* and here it is written, *Ye shall fear every man his mother and his father* [19:3]; (6) *Thou shalt not murder* and here it is written, *Neither shalt thou stand idly by the blood of thy neighbor* [19:16]; (7) *Thou shalt not commit adultery* and here it is written, *Both the adulterer and the adulteress shall surely be put to death* [20:10]; (8) *Thou shalt not steal* and here it is written, *Ye shall not steal* [19:11]; (9) *Thou shalt not bear false witness* and here it is written, *Thou shalt not go up and down as a talebearer* [19:16]; (10) *Thou shalt not covet . . . anything that is thy neighbor's* and here it is written, *Thou shalt love thy neighbor as thyself* [19:18].[46]

With this they establish that all the commandments in the Decalogue are found in the weekly reading *Kedoshim;* and they counted *I am* among them. All this shows that *I am the Lord thy God* is a commandment, as Maimonides maintains.

We ought not wonder that the author of the *Halakhot Gedolot* did not hit upon [the truth] for you will find that he did not count the commandment of unity[47] as did Naḥmanides[48] and all the other scholars. He counted it only as [an obligation] to recite the *Sh'ma*. He thought that the intent of the utterance *I am* and that of the commandment of unity were one, viz., acceptance of the sovereignty of Heaven, and that they are the principles of the Torah and (thus) not commandments. Perhaps he maintained this for R. Ḥasdai's reason[49] that the term "commandment" according to its [proper] definition does not apply to beliefs. Thus the Gaon[50] construed the commandment [as obliging one] to recite the *Sh'ma*, not [as obliging one] to believe in [God's] unity.

But the way of Maimonides is entirely reasonable. The Sages constantly refer to the commandment of unity and constantly prove it from the first verse of the *Sh'ma*.[51] All this proves that the words of Maimonides *are all plain to him that understandeth and right to them that find knowledge* [Proverbs 8:9].

19
Solutions to Three Other Objections

To the twenty-first and twenty-second objections, which are the first two which I raised,[1] and which are, [first], why did Maimonides in the *Sefer ha-Madda*, "*Hilkhot Yesodei ha-Torah*," include some of the foundations and principles from the *Commentary on the Mishnah* and exclude others, and [second,] why did he include other things in the "*Hilkhot Yesodei ha-Torah*" which are not among the foundations, such as to love God,[2] to fear Him,[3] to walk in His ways,[4] to sanctify His name,[5] not to profane His name,[6] not to destroy things with God's name upon them,[7] and other matters from physics and metaphysics mentioned there. I respond [to these objections] and say that in his *Commentary on the Mishnah* Maimonides mentioned those principles which should be believed by every religionist, to make known who should be called an Israelite with a share in the world to come, and to make known those who are heretics, who have no share in the world to come and who should not be called by the name "Israelite." He therefore wrote at the beginning of the principles that "what will suffice for what has to be mentioned here—and this is an appropriate place for it—is that the principles of our Torah and its foundations are thirteen."[8] He thus made clear that that place was fit and proper for explaining the principles of religion insofar as they are principles.

But in his *Mishneh Torah,* the great *Yad,*[9] it was his intention to clarify the commandments in the Book of God's Torah only, as he explained in the introduction to his commentary.[10] Therefore, he first listed all the commandments, one by one, *to find out the account* [Ecclesiastes 7:27] and after listing them he divided his composition into books and laws and listed the commandments discussed in each, for this was his intended aim there. Thus, he said in the table of contents of the book,

> Laws concerning the foundations of the Torah: These cover ten precepts, six of which are affirmative while four are negative. First, to know that there is a God. Second, not to permit the thought to enter the mind that there is any God but the Eternal. Third, to acknowledge His unity. Fourth, to love Him. Fifth, to revere Him. Sixth, to sanctify His name. Seventh, not to profane His name. Eighth, not to destroy things which bear His name. Ninth, to listen to [and accept] the prophet who speaks in His name. Tenth, not to tempt Him. The exposition of all these precepts forms the contents of the following chapters.[11]

It is thus clear from his words that his primary intention in these "Laws" was to clarify the commandments as opposed to clarifying the principles which were already explained in their proper place, the *Commentary on the Mishnah,* as I said. He presented these *"Hilkhot Yesodei ha-Torah,"* however, in order to explain those foundations which include commandments among them. He thus did not say, "all the foundations of the Torah," but only "Laws of the Foundations of the Torah," using indefinite language.[12] There is no difficulty posed, therefore, by the fact that he mentions only those foundations which include commandments or are related to them.

You will thus find that in the Introduction to the book, at the place where he divided it into fourteen parts, he said,

> First book: I include in it all the precepts which constitute the very essence and principle of the faith taught by Moses our teacher, and which it is necessary for one to know at the outset; as, for example, acceptance of the unity of God, and the prohibition of idolatry. I have called this book: the Book of Knowledge.[13]

He explains here that his primary goal was the explanation of the commandments. He thus presented only those foundations which related to the commandments, and no others.

Because of this he stated here that we should love God, fear Him, and sanctify Him, since these are fundamental commandments, connected with and related to those foundations. Since that place was set aside, first and foremost, for an explanation of the commandments, he presented them in these "Laws."

I say in further answer to this question that by careful study of those chapters in *"Hilkhot Yesodei ha-Torah,"* you will find references to all the principles and foundations. They are not presented here, however, in the same order in which they are presented in the *Commentary on the Mishnah,* according to the intention of each place, as I have indicated.[14]

Thus, in the first chapter, Maimonides explicitly discusses the first three principles, which are that God's existence is absolutely perfect and necessary, that God is one, and that God is neither a body nor the force of a body. In the second chapter he discusses all created things, especially the hierarchy of Separate Intellects. In the other chapters he discusses the heavenly bodies, the four elements, and the things composed of them. He presents all this to show that God is eternal *a parte ante* and that everything other than He is created, not eternal *a parte ante,* "when we compare them to Him."[15] For we learn this from Maimonides' description of all these created beings, from the upper, middle, and lower worlds, all of which are created. Since they are created, it is necessary that we posit some God, Who is eternal *a parte ante,* who created them.

The fifth principle, that we ought to worship God and raise our voices in exaltation of Him, also follows from this. We ought not to do this to any other being, for their actions are ordered and defined. They have neither the desire nor the choice to act in any way other than the way they do. This is true of both the spiritual and heavenly beings, even though they live and think, and of the nether beings which are not like that. Thus, in these three chapters—i.e., chapters two, three, and four—Maimonides described God's greatness, so that we should thereby know that we ought to worship Him and that all beings derive their existence from Him. He thus included among the commandments [that we ought] to love and fear God since we ought to worship God because of our love for and fear of Him. These are the two forms of worship mentioned by the Sages, "for its own sake from the aspect of love and not for its own sake from the aspect of awe."[16] Since one ought to love Him, one ought also to sanctify His name. And since one ought to fear Him, one ought not profane His name or destroy things on which His name is found. This being so, all these commandments are related to the fifth principle, that we ought to worship God.

In chapter seven Maimonides discusses two principles, the sixth[17] and the seventh,[18] which relate to the existence of prophecy and the superiority of Moses' prophecy. In chapters eight and nine Maimonides discusses the eighth principle, that of revelation,[19] and the ninth principle, that of the eternity of the Torah.[20]

You will further find that in chapter two Maimonides discusses the tenth principle, about divine knowledge and the way in which God knows things.[21] In the fifth chapter Maimonides commented on the eleventh principle, about reward and punishment.[22] It is for that reason that he discussed there the commandment of sanctifying God's name and other things for which the reward and punishment are great. But Maimonides did not discuss the last two principles, on the coming of the Messiah and the resurrection of the dead in the *"Hilkhot Yesodei ha-Torah,"* for they are types of the eleventh principle on reward and punishment, as I explained in the fifth proposition.[23] Maimonides discussed them in the *"Hilkhot Teshuvah,"* chapter nine, since they do not relate to commandments.[24]

It has been established by the foregoing that all thirteen of the principles mentioned by Maimonides in the *Commentary on the Mishnah* are found implicitly in the *Sefer ha-Madda*, in the *"Hilkhot Yesodei ha-Torah"* in the way in which I have discussed it and that the rest of the things found in those "Laws" relate to those principles and foundations and were therefore included there.

To the twenty-third objection, the third of those which I also raised[25]—why it is that of Maimonides' thirteen principles, the foundations of the Torah, only the first two, God's existence and unity, are included in the list of commandments while none of the other principles are counted among the commandments, whether positive or negative—I respond and say that the third principle, that the One is not a body nor the power of a body, was not counted as a commandment by Maimonides even though a verse was cited in proof of it, *Take ye therefore good heed unto yourselves* [*—for ye saw no manner of form on the day that the Lord spoke unto you in Horeb out of the midst of the fire*] [Deuteronomy 4:15], for only those things were counted among the commandments which God [specifically] commanded. For example, the commandment of unity, which God commanded us to believe by saying, *Hear, O Israel, the Lord our God, the Lord is one* [Deuteronomy 6:4], as if He said, "Hear and believe this thing." Thus Maimonides also counted *I am the Lord thy God* [Exodus 20:2] as a commandment, for he construed it as such. The negative element in the verse, *for ye saw no manner of form* [Deuteronomy 4:15] is a negation, not an admonition.[26] In the eighth of those principles with which he prefaced his *Sefer ha-Miẓvot* Maimonides wrote that we ought not to count the negative [counterpart] of a positive [commandment] as an admonition, as in *there is in the damsel no sin worthy of death* [Deuteronomy 22:26], *they shall not be put to death because she was not free* [Leviticus 19:20], and *the priest shall not seek* [Leviticus 13:36].[27] The author of the *Halakhot Gedolot* included *And the land shall not be sold in perpetuity* [Leviticus 25:23] in this class, understanding it as a negation, and not as an admonition.

Thus, the statement, *Take ye therefore good heed unto yourselves* [Deuteronomy 4:15] admonishes the Jewish people[28] in a general way not to be misled in their beliefs while *ye saw no manner of form* [Deuteronomy 4:15] is a negation, not an admonition. It is also the reason for the commandment, as it says, *FOR ye saw no manner of form.*[29] Maimonides also wrote in the fifth principle in the book enumerating the commandments that we ought not to count the reason of a commandment in the number of commandments. This is the case, for example, with *Her former husband who sent her away may not take her again to be his wife* [*after that she is defiled; for that is an abomination before the Lord;*] *and thou shalt not cause the land to sin,* [*which the Lord thy God giveth thee for an inheritance*] [Deuteronomy 24:3].[30] He therefore did not count them among the commandments.

Maimonides himself also explained in the first chapter of the *Sefer ha-Madda* that incorporeality is a branch of the principle of God's unity since, if God could be imagined to have a body, He would be divisible and thus many, not one.[31] Since incorporeality is included in [the principle] of God's unity, Maimonides found it sufficient to count [belief in] God's unity as a commandment and thus did not count incorporeality, which is included in it. In the eleventh of the thirteen principles from the aforementioned *Sefer ha-Miẓvot* Maimonides says that we ought not count the parts of a commandment separately but all together, as a unit.[32]

It is thus established by all these aspects that one ought not to count the third principle, that of God's incorporeality, as one of the commandments. The fourth foundation, however, that the One is eternal *a parte ante* "and that everything other than He is not eternal *a parte ante*"[33] we learn, as Maimonides wrote, from the verse, *The Eternal God is a dwelling place* [*and underneath are the everlasting arms*] [Deuteronomy 33:24]. Even though it is true, there is no mention of God commanding us with respect to this belief. Now, even though Maimonides derives "that everything other than He is not eternal *a parte ante*" from the verse, *For in six days the Lord made heaven and earth* [Exodus 20:11],[34] this is the reason for the Sabbath commandment, which teaches the creation of the world. I have already cited Maimonides' statement in his principles that it is not proper to count the reason of a commandment as a commandment itself.[35]

I have already written that Maimonides did not derive the fifth principle, that God alone ought to be worshipped, from the verses, *And ye shall serve the Lord your God* [Exodus 23:25] and *And Him shall ye serve* [Deuteronomy 13:5]. These verses admonish us with respect to service and prayer. The principle, [however,] is not that we are actually to worship God, but that we believe that He alone ought to be worshipped. Thus, Maimonides wrote in the explanation of this principle and foundation, "We learn this fifth foundation from the commandment which we have been given prohibiting idolatry, etc."[36] You thus see that while we learn this principle from a commandment it is not itself a commandment.

Now the sixth foundation, on the existence of prophecy among human beings generally, the seventh foundation, on the [exalted] degree of the prophecy of Moses, the eighth foundation, on revelation, the ninth foundation, on the eternity of the Torah, the tenth foundation, on divine knowledge, the eleventh foundation, on reward and punishment, the twelfth foundation, on the coming of the Messiah, and the thirteenth foundation, on resurrection, are all of them true beliefs since they were explained in the Pentateuch, Prophets, and Hagiographa. But they were not counted among the commandments since there are no verses in which God commands us to believe in them. But it does not follow from the fact that they are not commandments that they are not obligatory beliefs. For not all the narratives and teachings of the Torah are counted among the commandments and we are [still] obliged to believe them according to their literal sense. All these things are included in the dictum of the Sages, "that if one says that the whole Torah is from Heaven, excepting a particular verse, he is included in *because he hath despised the word of the Lord* [Numbers 15:31]."[37] For it is incumbent upon us to believe perfectly the entire Torah, with its narratives and commandments. This, despite the fact that some of its statements come in the form of admonitions and commandments, i.e., that God commanded and admonished us about them in particular, while the rest of them come in the form of predictions, narrative, and reproof. They are absolutely true, just like the commandments themselves.

20
Solutions for Three Other Objections

I have seen fit to respond to the twenty-fourth, -fifth, and -sixth objections, which are the fourth, fifth, and sixth [of the objections] which I raised—all of which deal with the beginning of the first chapter of the *Sefer ha-Madda*—with an explanation of the words of Maimonides there.[1]

He said:

> The foundation of all foundations and the pillar of all sciences is to realize that there is a First Being who brought every existing thing into being. All existing things, whether celestial, terrestrial, or belonging to an intermediate class, exist only through His true existence.
>
> If it could be supposed that He did not exist, it would follow that nothing else could possibly exist.
>
> If, however, it were supposed that all other beings were nonexistent, He alone would still exist. Their nonexistence would not involve His nonexistence. For all beings are in need of Him; but He, blessed be He, is not in need of them nor of any of them.[2]

Maimonides thus begins with the first principle, that God is the First Being. That is to say, He is the first in degree and perfection since He exists necessarily, as Maimonides made clear by his description. Since this principle is the first of all the principles and is the pillar upon which they all lean, Maimonides called it "the foundation of foundations." For, just as the foundations of the Torah are the principles and roots upon which the Torah is built, and the Torah is refuted with their refutation, so the first foundation is not only a foundation of the Torah, but is also a foundation for the rest of the foundations, all of which lean upon it and are founded upon it. If it should be thought that the first foundation is refuted, then all the other foundations would be refuted. It is because of this that this foundation is called the foundation of foundations. He therefore said afterwards that this doctrine is "the great principle on which everything depends."[3]

There is no contradiction in the fact that in the beginning of Part II of the *Guide*[4] Maimonides provided a demonstration for this principle and that in this chapter he established it on the basis of Scripture, for both reason and religion agree on this principle. Thus, according to the Torah it is the foundation of foundations and from this point of view he established it in this chapter on the basis of Scripture. According to demonstrative science it is the pillar of all sciences and from this point of view it was established in the *Guide* on the basis of philosophic propositions.

By saying "to realize that there is a First Being" Maimonides does not intend to specify a place but to indicate existence in general.[5] It is as if he said, "The foundation of foundations and of all the principles of the Torah, and the pillar of all investigative sciences, is to know that in the order of existents there exists a First Being which is prior to all [other] beings in the degree of its existence and in its priority, and that it creates all other existing things.[6] This Being is the first cause of them all. All the existing things in heaven—the celestial bodies moving in their uninterrupted circular motion and the separate intellects which move them—and earth, the center around which they revolve, and everything between them—the elements and things composed of them which exist between heaven and earth; all these could not exist without His true existence." This being so, he has established that God is the cause of causes.

By way of explaining the necessary character of God's existence Maimonides writes, "If it could be supposed that He did not exist [it would follow that nothing else could possibly exist]." That is, with the disappearance of the cause, all the effects will disappear; whereas if the effects disappear, the disappearance of their cause does not follow. But since this is imaginary and not really possible—I mean the disappearance of the First Cause—Maimonides wrote, "If it could be supposed that He did not exist" for this is something which one can imagine but which cannot be. The plain meaning of his words[7] is that while all existing things need God, He does not need any one of them. This is the meaning of necessary existence: God's existence is not dependent upon anything other than Him while the existence of all things depends upon Him.

> Hence His real essence is unlike any of them. This is what the prophet means when he says, *But the Lord is the true God* [Jeremiah 10:10]; that is, He alone is real,[8] and nothing else has reality like His reality. The same thought is expressed by the Torah in the text: *There is none else besides Him* [Deuteronomy 4:35]; that is: There is no being besides Him, that is really like Him.[9]

By this Maimonides wanted to establish a true point, that even though it is said of God that He exists and it is said of other things that they are existing things, the term "existence" may not be said of God and other things univocally[10] but only as an analogy[11] and by approximation. This is so because the way things are relative to actuality, so they are relative to existence; and the way things are relative to existence, so they are relative to the truth. For the truth depends upon existence and is overturned with it.[12] Since created things have potentiality mixed with actuality and possibility mixed with necessity, and are none of them absolutely actualized, it follows that their existence is not absolutely perfect. They are, therefore, not absolutely real.[13] The term "reality," however, is applicable to the First Cause absolutely since His existence is necessary of itself and not contingent. He is actual in every respect, there is no potentiality or contingency in Him at all. Thus, His existence is not like the existence of other things, and neither is His reality; that is, His actuality is not like the reality and actuality of other things, since His existence is necessary and His reality absolute, while the existence of other things is contingent per se. Their reality and actuality is mixed with potentiality and their existence with nonexistence. Thus it must be said that "existence" and "reality" apply to

God and to other things by homonymity or by amphiboly but not by shared definition.[14]

Maimonides proved this from the statement of the prophet Jeremiah, *But the Lord is the true God* [10:10]. The meaning of the verse can be made clear through an explanation of the [whole] passage there. At the beginning Jeremiah says, *Hear ye the word which the Lord speaketh unto you, O house of Israel. Thus saith the Lord: learn not the ways of the nations and be not dismayed at the signs of heaven; for the nations are dismayed at them* [Jeremiah 10:1–2]. With this he admonishes the Jews with respect to two things. First, that they learn not *the ways of the nations*, i.e., the worship of idols which have no reality. Second, that they be not dismayed at the signs of heaven as the nations are. For, as the nations are under the rule of the heavenly Princes—as it said, [*And lest thou lift up thine eyes unto the heaven, and when thou seest the sun and the moon and the stars, even all the host of heaven, thou be drawn away and worship them, and serve them*] *which the Lord thy God hath allotted unto all the peoples* [*under the whole heaven*] [Deuteronomy 4:19]—it is proper that they be dismayed by them. Israel, however, is set apart for divine rule, as it says, *But you the Lord hath taken* [*and brought forth out of the iron furnace, out of Egypt, to be unto Him a people of inheritance, as ye are this day*] [Deuteronomy 4:20], and should not, therefore, be dismayed by the signs of heaven, since they have no power or rule over the nation of Israel.

He then returned to explain that about which he had admonished them at first, that they keep away from the ways of the nations, and said, *For the customs of the peoples* [*are vanity; for it is but a tree which one cutteth out of the forest, the work of the hands of the workman with the axe.*] *They deck it with silver and gold* [*they fasten it with nails and hammers, that it move not.*] *They are like a pillar in a garden of cucumbers, and speak not;* [*they must needs be borne, because they cannot go.*] [Jeremiah 10:3–5]. That is, the idols do not have an animating spirit and are certainly not able to speak.[15] This being the case, *Be not afraid of them, for they cannot do evil, neither is it in them to do good* [Jeremiah

10:4]. That is, they have the power to do neither evil nor good for they are lifeless bodies. He continues, *There is none like unto Thee, O Lord; Thou art great, and Thy name is great in might* [Jeremiah 10:5]. This was said with respect to the signs of heaven, the subject of the second part of the prophet's admonition. That is, *There is none like unto Thee, O Lord,* neither among the celestial bodies nor the separate intellects. He said, *Thou art great, and Thy name is great in might* to affirm that God is great in and of Himself and does not receive any overflow from any other [thing] in the way in which all the existing things receive [an overflow] from Him. Thus, he said, *Thou art great.*

After this he said, *Who would not fear Thee, O King of the nations? For it befitteth Thee; forasmuch as among all the wise men of the nations, and in all their royalty, there is none like unto Thee* [Jeremiah 10:7]. This is a very strange verse. For God is not among the royalty of the nations nor among their wise men such that this statement could justifiably be said of Him. Its [proper] explanation, however, is that even the royalty of the nations and their wise men, upon whom the light of the divine Torah has not shone, will, on the basis of their investigations and speculation, recognize and understand His greatness and exalted rank. This is as it is said, *For from the rising of the sun even unto the going down of the same My name is great among the nations* [Malachi 1:11]. He therefore said here, *Who would not fear Thee, O King of the nations?* That is, who is this king of the nations who will not fear You? For fear befits You, for You are the Great Cause and not the heavens nor the moving bodies in them. *Forasmuch as among all the wise men of the nations, and in all their royalty, there is none like unto Thee.* That is, that their wise men and their royalty admit that there is none like You.

But they are altogether brutish and foolish; the vanities by which they are instructed [are but a stock] [Jeremiah 10:8]. That is, with respect to the First Cause, all the wise men of the nations admit to the exalted degree of its existence. Their foolishness, however, pertains to another matter, the heavenly intermediaries between them and the Creator. They make talismans to cause an overflow to descend from the celestial ones.[16] Thus, he said, *The vanities by which they are instructed [are but a stock. Silver] beaten into plates which is brought from Tarshish* [Jeremiah 10:8–9] and the end of his words, . . . *they are the work of wise men* [Jeremiah 10:9]. That is, it is not just the ignorant and the crude who confuse themselves with this, but the wise men of the nations also all err on this point by introducing intermediaries which are *the work of wise men*.

The prophet declared that this was an absolute mistake by saying *But the Lord is the true God* [Jeremiah 10:10]. I have already told you that the name *Yod He Vav He*[17] is said of the first cause only and not of any other existing thing.[18] But the name "Lord"[19] is said of the omnipotent Ruler. The wise men of the nations understood that God exists necessarily and thus it says, *there is none like unto Thee* but they did not think that He was the Ruler and Guardian of the sublunar world and thus did not mention the name "Lord." Therefore, the prophet granted them part of their claim[20] but added to their words, saying, *But the Lord is the true God.* That is, necessarily existent, powerful, ruling, and absolutely real.

As opposed to the idols he said, *He is the living God* [Jeremiah 10:10] for unlike God they have no life or sensation. As opposed to the celestial signs he said, *the everlasting King; at His wrath the earth trembleth* [Jeremiah 10:10] since He is the true Cause and Ruler of the world. *At His wrath the earth trembleth* and not [at the wrath of] the celestial signs.

He further said, *Thus shall ye say unto them: [The gods that have not made the heavens and the earth, these shall perish from the earth, and from under the heavens]* [Jeremiah 10:11]. [He said this] in Aramaic. The commentators[21] have said that this was because the Chaldeans were debating with the Jews [then] and Jeremiah was teaching them how to respond.[22] The correct [interpretation, however,] is that the prophet wished to give them an essential demonstration[23] and thus he spoke of God's divinity and that His existence is necessary, not contingent, like the heavens[24] and those which move them. Thus, he said, *Thus shall ye say unto them.* That is, you should say to those idolatrous nations and their wise men that a deity which did not create heaven and earth, and is not a cause which acts and creates should, even according to them, perish from beneath the heavens;[25] that is, they should not worship it. For it is the creation of heaven and earth which shows that they are all contingent, partially potential, not existing in absolute actuality, and that their reality is not absolutely real, like that of God Who created them. Thus, the verse which Maimonides cited, *But the Lord is the true God* [Jeremiah 10:10] is shown by an explanation of the [whole] passage [in which it occurs], to be consistent with his opinion.

With respect to the verse which he also cited from the Torah, *Unto thee it was shown that thou mightest know that the Lord, He is God; there is none else beside Him* [Deuteronomy 4:35] and which he explained as teaching that there is no real existent other than God, [it must be said] that there is no doubt that the word "real"[26] does not appear in the verse. But the context[27] indicates it. For the statement *there is none else beside Him* cannot possibly be interpreted as meaning that nothing other than God exists, because the multitude of existing things is evident to the senses. Nor may it be interpreted to mean that there is no deity other than He, because the separate intellects are called deities,[28] so how could one say that there is no deity but God? But Maimonides saw that the verse, *there is none else beside Him,* refers back to *the Lord He is God.* The name "God,"[29] the articulated name, indicates necessary existence while the name "Lord"[30] is said of a powerful, ruling entity.[31] It is as if [the verse] said that there is no other being which exists necessarily and is omnipotent. Necessary existence is the [only] absolutely true actuality, as I said.[32] Thus, he said, "there is no Being beside Him."[33] The name *Yod He Vav He* indicates reality.

Maimonides further wrote: "This being is the God of the Universe, *the Lord of all the earth.* [Joshua 3:11]. And He it is Who controls the Sphere [of the Universe] with a power that is without end or limit; with a power that is never intermitted. For the Sphere is always revolving; and it is impossible for it to revolve without someone making it revolve. God, blessed be He, it is, Who, without hand or body, causes it to revolve."[34] The explanation for this is that since Maimonides wrote at the beginning that this first principle was the foundation of the foundations of the Torah, and the pillar of investigative sciences, and since he further explained it in a conceptual way and from the implication of Scriptural verses, as is appropriate to the Torah, he therefore saw fit to make known that [the subject of] this principle is the One about which the philosophers said that He is the God of the Universe, Lord of all the Earth, and the Mover of the Sphere. It is as if he said: "This existent being which we have explained according to the Torah is the one whose existence has been established by investigation and speculation."

Maimonides' demonstrations of God's existence in the beginning of Part II of the *Guide* are based on the world as a whole and on the interrelationship of its parts, on generation and corruption, or on the movement of the Sphere. The demonstration is equally valid[35] for both believers in eternity and believers in creation, as he pointed out.[36] Therefore Maimonides here calls this Existent, "God of the Universe," with respect to the demonstrations drawn from the world as a whole. He calls Him "Lord of all the Earth" with respect to demonstrations drawn from generation and corruption. He says "He it is who Who controls the Sphere" with respect to the demonstrations drawn from the movements of the heavens, according to the opinion held in common by those who affirm eternity and those who affirm creation.

Infinity is either a matter of power or duration.[37] In writing "And He it is Who controls the Sphere [of the Universe] with a power that is without end or limit" Maimonides establishes [that God has] both kinds of infinity. "With a power that is without end or limit" refers to the first kind. "[With a power] that is never intermitted" refers to the second kind of infinity, which involves time and duration.

It is thus established that Maimonides referred to the movements of the heavens as having neither end nor limit [only] as following the opinion of Aristotle, but not that of the Torah. This is no refutation [of Maimonides' opinion] for he is only citing the demonstrations of the philosophers and their opinions here.[38]

We can also say that the infinity in time, to which

Maimonides refers here, can be understood in another way. That is, as referring to a being which has beginning in the past but will have no end or limit in the future and from that aspect is infinite. His statement "God, blessed be He, it is Who causes it to revolve" accords with the opinion of those who maintain that the First Mover is the First Cause. This is also the truth according to our holy Torah which says *And behold the Lord stood beside him* . . . [Genesis 28:13] . . . *Who rideth upon the heavens as thy help* . . . [Deuteronomy 33:26]. The Psalmist said, *Extol Him that rideth upon the skies* . . . [Psalms 68:5] [and] *To Him that rideth upon the heaven of heavens, which are of old* . . . [Psalms 68:34].[39]

Maimonides further wrote:

> To acknowledge this fact is an affirmative precept, as it is said, *I am the Lord thy God* [Exodus 20:2]. And whoever permits the thought to enter his mind that there is another deity besides this God, violates a prohibition; as it is said, *Thou shalt have no other gods before Me* [Exodus 20:3], and denies the essence of Religion[40]—this doctrine being the great principle on which everything depends.[41]

His words "to acknowledge this fact" do not refer back to "This being, etc."[42] but to what he said above about [God's] necessary existence which was proven from Scripture. I have already explained this terminology above.[43] The commandment is to seek to know all things, i.e., that God is the First Existent, that He brought all [other] things into existence and that He exists necessarily. All this depends upon knowledge and study. Knowledge and study are activities of will and choice. The term "commandment," therefore, according to its [proper] definition, applies to it even though the belief to which this knowledge and study gives birth and which it fixes in the soul, is acquired without choice or will. [All this is] as was established in the ninth proposition.[44] I also explained how Maimonides derived this commandment from the verse, *I am the Lord thy God* [Exodus 20:2] on the basis of the name *Yod He Vav He* which indicates necessary existence and [on the basis of] *Elohekha* which indicates omnipotence when linked to the name of being.[45]

After citing the positive commandment in this principle Maimonides cites its [corresponding] prohibition: "And whoever permits the thought to enter his mind that there is another deity besides this God, violates a prohibition." The explanation of this is that anyone who "permits the thought to enter his mind" that Israel has no God Who exists necessarily, as he described, but whose deity is another being, other than God, violates a prohibition and denies the first principle, which is the greatest of the principles since they all depend upon it. This being so, this prohibition does not correspond to the positive commandment of [God's] unity [as it would were it directed against those who] affirmed that there is another, second God. Rather, it corresponds to the positive commandment of the first principle and refers to one who thinks that the true God is not the aforementioned First Existent, but some deity other than it. This was all that Maimonides intended,[46] for such a person denies the first principle and does not admit to it. This is why Maimonides wrote "and denies the essence of Religion [ikkar]." That is, not that such a person affirms the existence of a second god but that he denies the first principle [ikkar] since he denies divinity to God and affirms it of something else, or is an atheist, like the *apikoros*.

Maimonides derived this from the verse, *Thou shalt have no other gods before Me* [Exodus 20:3]. In the *Guide*, I.37, Maimonides established that *panim*[47] refers to existence.[48] It is as if [the Torah] said, "Thou shalt have no other gods, and thou shalt not believe that any other existing thing is divine, as opposed to the absolutely real and necessarily existent Being." Alternatively, *have . . . before Me* may be taken in the sense of priority as in *Of old Thou didst lay the foundation of the earth* [Psalms 102:26] and like *In former time in Israel* [Ruth 4:7].[49] He said that one should not permit the thought to enter one's mind that there is a god prior to Him in any sense of "priority." For it is not so and they are without a doubt *other gods*,[50] subsequent to and derived from God. Their existence is after His existence, not *before Him*, that is, before His existence.

Maimonides wrote further:

> This God is One. He is not two nor more than two, but One; so that none of the things existing in the Universe to which the term one is applied is like unto His Unity; neither such a unit as a species which comprises many units, nor such a unit as a physical body which consists of parts and dimensions. His unity is such that there is no Unity like it in the world.[51]

After clarifying the first principle, about God's necessary existence, Maimonides then cites the second principle, about His unity. Since two things are included in [the idea of] God's unity—as I explained in the third proposition[52]—these being, first, that there is no second god or partner in divinity, and second, that there is no multiplicity or composition in Him at all, Maimonides pointed out these two teachings in the principle of unity. He intended the first of these, that there is no second god or partner in divinity, by his statement "This God is One. He is not two nor more than two." He intended the second of These in his statement "None of the things existing in the Universe to which the term one is applied is like unto His unity." Thus he said, "Neither such a unit as a species which comprises many units, nor such a unit as a physical body which consists of [many] parts and dimensions." For every body is divisible and cannot thus be one for it can be divided into many.

Maimonides further wrote:

> If there were plural deities, these would be physical bodies; because entities that can be enumerated and are equal in their essence, are only distinguishable from each other by the accidents that happen to physical bodies. If the Creator were a physical body, He would have bounds and limits, for it is impossible for a physical body to be without limits; and where a body is limited and finite, its energy is also limited and finite. And our God, blessed be His name, since His power is infinite and unceasing—for the Sphere [of the Universe] is continually revolving—His power is not the energy of a physical body. And since He is not a physical body, the accidents that happen to physical bodies do not apply to Him, so as to distinguish Him

from another being. Hence it is impossible that He can be anything but One. To realize this truth is an affirmative precept, as it is said, *The Lord our God, the Lord is One* [Deuteronomy 6:4].[53]

The explanation of this is that after Maimonides clarified the meaning of [God's] unity, he wanted to prove it on the basis of rational argument. He used it as the middle term in [the argument for God's] incorporeality since its meaning is the same as the meaning of [God's] unity. Both of them follow from necessary existence. He therefore said, "If there were plural deities, [it would follow of necessity that] these would be physical bodies." For, things which are equal in their existence are not different from one another except for their accidents. It is as if you would say that Reuben is distinguished from Simeon in that one is white and the other is black and that one is tall and the other short. Were we to admit that God is a body which bears accidents, He would then have an end and limit since no body can have infinite dimensions. If He had a finite body, He must necessarily have finite power. This accords with the eighth book of the *Physics* where it was established that it is impossible for there to be infinite power in a finite body.[54] We know that God's power is infinite. This is established by the uninterrupted circular motion of the Sphere which, from the beginning of creation, has revolved continuously and will not cease from revolving since the world and that motion are eternal, from which it follows necessarily that God is infinitely powerful. It follows from this that He is neither a body nor the force of a body for it He were so He would not be infinitely powerful. This is the proof which Maimonides brought for the matter of [God's unity].

You might say[55] that his argument does not include the two kinds of unity which he discussed since it only turns on the denial of the claim that God is two or more than two and does not involve the claim that God is not composite also. But see his words: "If the Creator were a physical body, he would have bounds and limits." The meaning of this is that he here included the second type of unity and from this derived the claim that it is impossible for God to be anything but one.

You may also question Maimonides' statement that if there were many gods, they would have bodies for entities that can be enumerated are distinguished from one another only by what happens to their bodies. But we find multiplicity and enumerability among the Intellects Separated from Matter and among the souls after death, according to the believers. Who is to stop this from being so with divinity?[56]

But the answer to this is clear for Maimonides holds the opinion of Avicenna that the Separate Intellects can be enumerated by virtue of the fact that they relate to each other as cause and effect. Even if the opinion of Averroës—who holds that they differ from one another with respect to the level of perfection unique to each one of them—is correct, it cannot obtain with respect to divinity.[57] The matter of equality of degree with respect to divinity differs from the matter of equality of degree with respect to souls in accordance with the concepts acquired by the soul through the body as if the difference in bodies were the cause of the difference [in souls]. But in the case of divinity it is not like this. Therefore, Maimonides wrote, "because entities that can be enumerated and are equal in their essence are [not] distinguishable." Whether Avicenna's opinion about the Separate Intellects is the true one, or whether the truth accords with the position of Averroës, who differs from him on this matter, is beyond the scope of this inquiry. This is also not the place for an inquiry into the proposition which says that every power found in a body is finite, since it involves much study. These matters were discussed in the *Sefer ha-Madda* simply, and without attention to specific detail, in accordance with the intention of that book.

Now Maimonides derived the commandment of unity from the verse, *Hear, O Israel, the Lord our God, the Lord is One* [Deuteronomy 6:4]. God commanded us to hear, that is, to understand and know that the Lord is our God. These latter are the names which indicate necessary existence and omnipotence. There is only one being with them. This accords with what has been established in metaphysics, that there can be only one necessary existent. Therefore, after it says, *the Lord our God*, the name is changed and it says, *the Lord is One*.[58] Thus Maimonides established the second principle, that of [God's] unity and the third, that of [God's] incorporeality, for both were established as one.

Since his proof from Scripture proved only God's unity, Maimonides brought a proof for the doctrine of incorporeality from the [Sacred] Writings as well. Thus, he said, "That the Holy One, blessed be He, is not a physical body is explicitly set forth in the Pentateuch and in the Prophets."[59]

After this he saw fit to anticipate those objections that are raised with respect to this principle on the basis of the literal sense of Scripture. He said, "[The reason for this is that] the Torah speaks in the language of men,"[60] and that the things found in the words of the prophets were said in a vision of prophecy.[61]

This [then] is the general meaning of the chapter. I did not see fit to comment on all of it, but, [rather, only those parts] which related to the solution of the twenty-fourth, twenty-fifth, and twenty-sixth objections which were solved through my explanation of Maimonides' words.

21
Solutions for the Remaining Objections to the Principles

With respect to the twenty-seventh objection, the seventh of those which I raised—why did Maimonides count [God's] unity and incorporeality as principles when they necessarily follow from and are included in the first principle, about God's necessary existence[1]—I respond and say that it has already been established in the fourth proposition[2] that some of these thirteen principles on which Maimonides established God's Torah in truth are included in some of the others. This is so with the second, third, and fourth [principles] which are included in the first. But Maimonides saw fit to make them all principles and discussed each one of them as a principle by itself. [He did this] because he was not laying down these principles of his for *the wise men who knew the times* [Esther 1:3] but *for all of the people from every quarter, both young and old* [Genesis 19:4, transposed]. Since these are praiseworthy beliefs of superior degree, he discussed each of them separately. In the *Guide* he called them "the great questions" and there he discussed God's existence and unity, [His] incorporeality, and the creation of the world.[3] It is from this point of view that Maimonides included these beliefs among the principles both in his *Commentary on the Mishnah* and in the *Sefer ha-Madda*.

With respect to the twenty-eighth objection, the eighth of those which I raised—why did Maimonides count as a principle [belief in] the resurrection of the dead simply when the principle should be to believe that resurrection of the dead is taught by the Torah, as it says in the mishnah, "He who maintains that resurrection is not a biblical doctrine."[4] In his commentary to that mishnah Rashi wrote that even if one believes in the resurrection on the basis of tradition, or because of his speculation, but says that it is not from the Torah he is a heretic and has no portion in the world to come for "what need have we of his faith" if he does not admit that it is from the Torah?—I respond to this and say that the explanation given by Rashi, whose dignity lies undisturbed in its place[5] accords with neither reason[6] nor the language of the mishnah. From the point of view of reason it is known that it is not a philosophical concept[7] for rational demonstration disavows it according to the natural roots.[8] Thus, it is not possible for a man to say that one can believe in resurrection on the basis of speculation. With respect to tradition, it is known that its roots are found in the Torah, either explicitly or implicitly.[9]

Because of this Maimonides understood that one who says that resurrection is not a biblical doctrine did not intend {only} to deny that {belief in resurrection} is from the Torah while admitting to its truth, whether on the basis of speculation or tradition. It is the opinion of such a person, rather, that we ought not to believe in the resurrection of the dead {at all} because of the rational arguments {against it} for it is something which speculation denies. Such a person further holds that the Torah, which is above reason, has not taught us this since {he holds} our Sages have—heaven forfend!—fabricated this opinion on their own authority.[10] Thus, when the heretic wished to deny this principle, he said, "Resurrection is not a biblical doctrine." That is, it has not been established on the basis of Scripture and is therefore not a traditional belief. Since it is also not a rational belief,[11] it follows that it is not a correct belief {at all}.

This interpretation of the mishnah, that it refers to the denial of resurrection simply, is shown to be correct by the Gemara on it: "And why such {severity}?—A Tanna taught: Since he denied the resurrection of the dead, therefore he shall not share in that resurrection."[12] They thus make clear that in saying that "resurrection is not a biblical doctrine" it is one's intention to deny resurrection absolutely and not {merely} to deny that it is taught by the Torah, as Rashi maintained. Therefore Maimonides made this true opinion a principle by itself.[13]

Thus have been solved the twenty-eight objections which I raised against the words of Maimonides about these principles and commandments which he posited in his books. My words have established that *All the words of his mouth are in righteousness, there is nothing perverse or crooked in them* [after Proverbs 8:8] and that the thirteen principles which he discussed are those which are appropriately posited on the level of principles, according to those intended lessons which I have discussed.[14]

22

A Study of the Opinions of Other Scholars on the Principles

I have already made clear that the principles and foundations presented by R. Ḥasdai are for the most part included in Maimonides' principles.[1] Some of them are also connected to particular commandments and thus ought not to be counted among the principles, as I made clear in the seventh proposition.[2] When you examine them [it becomes apparent] that some of them are foundations which are not unique to the divine Torah insofar as it is divine, since other laws, whether natural or conventional, share them. So it is with choice and others of the beliefs which he presented. It has already been shown in the eighth proposition that the principles of the divine Torah, insofar as it is divine, should be unique to it, and should not be shared by some other law. But careful examination and study of Maimonides' principles will show that they are unique to our divine Torah insofar as it is divine.

The three principles set up by the author of the *Sefer ha-Ikkarim*—which he thought were intended by the mishnah[3] when it said, "The following have no portion in the world to come: He who maintains that resurrection is not a biblical doctrine"; since such a person intended to deny divine reward and punishment; "He who maintains that the Torah was not divinely revealed," which is the second principle, and *"the apikoros"* who denies God's existence—will also be found, upon examination, not to be free of error and confusion. His first foundation was that God exists. This is subject to the first objection which Crescas raised against Maimonides.[4] He also made revelation a genus under which were subsumed prophecy and the [exalted] degree of Mosaic prophecy. But the existence of prophecy in general is the genus according to the truth and revelation is a species which comes under it. He sensed this objection himself in chapter 4 of the first treatise of his book, but did not answer it properly.

Even if we count revelation as a principle, as he posited it, it would still be a principle for itself. But the way of Maimonides, who [posited as a principle the belief] that the Torah in our possession today [is the same Torah given to Moses] is correct and *of sound body* [Psalms 73:4].

So, too, with the principle of reward and punishment, under which Albo included [God's] knowledge and providence. There is no doubt that providence is the genus and reward and punishment is one of its species. The mishnah[5] which he cited in support of his opinion did not at all intend what he thought it did for the resurrection of the dead is not the genus under which is included reward and punishment. How could it be construed as a genus under which are subsumed [God's] knowledge and providence and other things more general than it? [Moreover,] the *apikoros* does not only deny God's existence, but also His knowledge and providence, and reward and punishment, as Maimonides made clear in the *Guide* and other places.[6] All this shows that the number of principles posited by this scholar is not precise.

I have seen someone who thought that we ought to posit only one principle for the divine Torah, this being [belief in] God's existence. He called this "acceptance of the sovereignty of heaven." This is the opinion of the author of the *Halakhot Gedolot* as may be seen from his words which I quoted above in chapter 18.[7]

I think that this also was taken from the words of Maimonides, the source being what he wrote at the beginning of the *Sefer ha-Madda:* "The foundation of all foundations and the pillar of all sciences is to realize that there is a First Being, etc."[8] He thus showed that this cornerstone is the foundation of the other foundations and that it is therefore by itself the first foundation of the whole Torah. But this is not enough, for one can believe in God's existence while denying all the other cornerstones if the other foundations are not connected to this foundation.

There is also one [scholar] who thought that the divine Torah had only one principle, namely, that it is from heaven since in this are included and established all the principles.[9] But even if this were true it would then be a principle for itself; that is, that the principle of the divine Torah is that the Torah is from heaven. It is false that something can be its own principle.

Were I to choose principles to posit for the divine Torah I would only lay down one, the creation of the world. It is the root and foundation around which the divine Torah, its cornerstones, and its beliefs revolve and includes the creation at the beginning, the narratives about the Patriarchs, and the miracles and wonders which cannot be believed[10] without belief in creation. So, too, with belief in God's knowledge and providence, and reward and punishment according to [one's observance of] the commandments, none of which can one perfectly believe without believing in the volitional creation of the whole world. This is as Naḥmanides said at the beginning of his *Commentary to the Pentateuch,* that creation "is the root of faith, and he who does not believe in this and thinks the word was eternal denies the essential principle of the [Judaic] religion and has no Torah at all."[11] So, too, Maimonides, at *Guide,* II.13[12] wrote that belief in the creation of the world

> is undoubtedly a basis of the Torah of Moses our Master, peace be on him. And it is second to the basis that is the belief in the unity [of God]. Nothing other than this should come to your mind. It was Abraham, our Father, peace be on him, who began to proclaim in public this opinion to which speculation had led him. For this reason he made his proclamation *in the name of the Lord, God of the world* [Genesis 21:33]; he had also explicitly stated this opinion in saying: *Maker of heaven and earth* [Genesis 14:22].[13]

It is thus shown to you from the words of these rabbis that belief in the creation of the world is a great principle of our Torah *and it have I seen correct before me* [after Genesis 7:1] in the [matter of the] principles of the Torah; not God's existence, nor His unity, [nor His] incorporeality, nor all the other things which can be demonstrated and which are [thus] not unique to the divine Torah insofar as it is divine, for other laws and sciences also accept them.[14] It is certainly the case that through belief in creation the other foundations, or most of them, are verified, as they are through demonstration, as abu-Bakr showed in his book, *Hayy ben Yaktan*.[15] Perhaps Scripture hints at this by saying in the beginning of the Torah, *In the beginning God created the heaven and the earth* [Genesis 1:1], the word "beginning" signifying presupposition, principle, and root. It is as if it said that all the words of the divine Torah ought to be accepted by man on the basis of one primary presupposition and root, that God created the heaven and the earth. [Only] after this presupposition does [the Torah] present the narratives of the creation and the Patriarchs, the commandments, and other things. Since this belief is a root and presupposition of the Torah, it was set down as a matter of tradition and belief at the beginning of the Torah, before everything else, in the way of presuppositions.

23
An Explanation of the Correct Opinion in This Matter

That which I believe to be "true, certain, and established"[1] in this matter is that these men—Maimonides and those who follow after him[2]—*are peaceable with us* [Genesis 34:21]. They were brought to postulate principles in the divine Torah only because they were drawn after the custom of gentile scholars as described in their books. For they saw in every science, whether natural or mathematical, roots and principles which ought not to be denied or argued against. They further saw that it is incumbent upon the master of any science—to the extent that he is indeed a master of that science—to explain these roots and principles and to demonstrate them. Such principles are the accepted axioms of a science; they are already explained either in terms of another science, more general than and [logically] prior to this one, or through metaphysics, which precedes and is the first of all the sciences, the first principles of which are self-evident.

Thus, when one doubts one of the assumptions of a science and contradicts it, it can be clarified and proved with these general first principles since they are the roots on which that entire science is based. It is not fit for the student of a science to disagree with its principles, nor is it proper to dispute them since they are matters generally accepted in it which have already been explained in terms of a different science more general than it, or are self-evident. In this way physics takes its first principles from metaphysics and the science of music takes its first principles from mathematics.[3]

Our scholars, having been dispersed among the nations and

194

having studied their books and sciences, learned from their deeds and copied their ways and customs with respect to the divine Torah. They said: *"How do these gentiles pursue*[4] their sciences? By positing first principles and roots upon which a science is based. I will do so also and postulate principles and foundations for the divine Torah."

But to my eyes "the conclusion is not similar to the premise,"[5] for the sciences of the gentiles and their books are pursued by way of investigation and speculation. In order that their speculations would not become confused with the explanation of their premises they were forced to postulate accepted first principles which would be accepted by the student of science without the demand for demonstration and evidence. Those first principles in turn would be explained by a different, more general, science, or they would be self-evident, like the primary intelligibles.[6] God, however, understands the way of the divine Torah; He gave it to His people, to be accepted in faith, according to what He saw as necessary for their perfection. For this reason He did not have to set down in it some beliefs as more fundamental than others, or some as more acceptable than others; nor did He establish the relative importance of the commandments, since they were all given by one Shepherd. Nor is there any other Torah, or any science or divine understanding more general than or prior to our Torah, such that we could derive first principles for the Torah from it, or explain or validate them through it.

Therefore, I said, *this I recall to my mind* {Lamentations 3:21] that the divine Torah, with all its beliefs, is completely true. All of its commandments were divinely revealed. The validation and substantiation of all the beliefs and commandments, minor as well as major, is the same. The validation of one is like the validation of another. I, therefore, believe that it is not proper to postulate principles for the divine Torah, nor foundations in the matter of beliefs, for we are obliged to believe everything that is written in the Torah. We are not permitted to doubt even the smallest thing in it that it should be necessary to establish its truth with those principles and roots. For he who denies or doubts a belief or narrative of the Torah, be it small or great, is a sectarian and *apikoros*. For, since the Torah is true, no belief or narrative in it has any advantage over any other.

So it is said in *Perek Ḥelek:*

> Our Rabbis taught: *Because he hath despised the word of the Lord* [Numbers 15:31], this refers to him who maintains that the Torah is not from Heaven. . . . Another interpretation: *Because he hath despised the word of the Lord,*—even if he asserts that the whole Torah is from Heaven, excepting a particular verse, which he maintains was not uttered by God but by Moses himself, he is included in *because he hath despised the word of the Lord.* And even if he admits that the whole Torah is from Heaven, excepting a single point . . . or a comparison of similar expressions, he is still included in *because he hath despised the word of the Lord.*[7]

The Rabbis made it clear by saying that there is nothing in the divine Torah which a man may either deny or be obliged to believe, like the first principles of a science and its postulates. Rather, every Israelite is obliged to accept every single part of the Torah, the small as well as the great. There is no difference between denying the whole Torah, saying it is not from Heaven, and denying part of it, be it a verse, a derivation,[8] or a comparison of similar expressions.[9] Therefore the Rabbis said there that "Manasseh ben Hezekiah examined [biblical] narratives to prove them worthless. Thus, he jeered, 'Had Moses nothing [better] to write but *And Lotan's sister was Timna?*' [Genesis 36:22]."[10] Because of this they thought him to be a heretic and an *apikoros.*

Maimonides included his list of principles in his *Commentary on the Mishnah.* In the eighth principle, the one which asserts that the Torah is from Heaven, he writes that

> there is no difference between *And the sons of Ham: Cush and Mizraim* [Genesis 10:6], *I am the Lord your God* [Exodus 20:2], and *Hear, O Israel, the Lord our God,* [*the Lord is one*] [Deuteronomy 6:4]; it is all from the mouth of the Almighty and it is all the Torah of God, perfect, pure, holy, and true.[11]

He thus admitted with his mouth and lips that in the matter of beliefs the truth of the matter is that it is not proper that we postulate some beliefs as roots and first principles in the Torah of God which every religionist[12] must accept, and other beliefs which may be doubted, for all of them must be accepted and believed, since they are divine truth and one may not doubt or object to any one of them.

Just as we may not postulate principles and foundations among beliefs, so with commandments. We may not take some of them as fundamental, having greater importance than others. There are very general commandments of great significance relating both to man's relations with God and with his fellowman, among which are the commandment to remember the great day of the Assembly at Sinai,[13] the commandment to remember the Exodus from Egypt,[14] the commandment, *you shall do the right and the good* [Deuteronomy 6:8] and the commandment, *you shall love your neighbor as yourself* [Leviticus 19:18]. These authors did not mention even one of these among their principles. How can we presume to examine the commandments, choosing some from others? Did they not say in the Mishnah, "Be careful in the case of a light commandment as in that of a weighty one, since you do not know how the rewards of commandments are given"?[15] How then can we make distinctions among the commandments, postulating some of them as roots and some as branches?

We may say in defense of Maimonides that he did not intend to make principles and foundations of any of the commandments of the Torah, for he did not number among his principles any actional commandment, as I have noted.[16] With regard to beliefs also we may say that he did not choose principles among them in order to say that we are obliged to believe these principles but no others. His intention was, rather, correctly to guide those men who did not delve deeply in the Torah and who "neither studied nor served [their teachers] enough."[17] Since they could not comprehend or conceive of all the beliefs and sciences which are included in the divine Torah, Maimonides chose the thirteen most general beliefs, to teach them briefly those matters which I discussed in the fifth proposition,[18] in such a way that all men, even the ignorant, could become perfected through their acceptance.

From this point of view he called them principles and foundations, adapting [his language] to the thinking of the student, though it is not so according to the truth itself.

This will be confirmed by what Maimonides wrote after his principles, which principles I cited at the beginning of this treatise.[19] This explains why he did not list these principles in the *Guide*, in which he investigated deeply into the faith of Torah, but mentioned them rather in his *Commentary on the Mishnah*, which he wrote in his youth. He postulated the principles for the masses, and for beginners in the study of Mishnah, but not for those individuals who plumbed the knowledge of truth for whom he wrote the *Guide*. If this was his opinion, then his intentions were acceptable[20] and his actions were for the sake of heaven.

However, R. Ḥasdai, and the author of the *Ikkarim*, and *those after them who approve their sayings, selah* [Psalms 49:14], took these things literally and put those beliefs at the level of roots and principles, like the first principles of the sciences, as I have discussed.[21] This, in my eyes, is a great mistake and error. For even if we admit that there is a great difference among beliefs, some being of a higher degree than others according to the importance of their subject matter, since some of them deal with the separate intellects, some with the spheres, and some with the rest of things, we still ought not to think because of this that the belief about any one of them is a principle and a foundation while another belief is neither a principle nor a foundation, for all of them are true beliefs. The truth is that they are all principles upon which the divine Torah is based, for if a man denies or contradicts any one of them, even the smallest, it is as if he said that the Torah is not from Heaven. That being so, and since the divine Torah would collapse with the denial of any narrative, teaching, or belief in it, it follows necessarily that all the narratives, beliefs, teachings, and commandments in the Torah are, without exception, principles and foundations of it; we should not believe this of some of them but not of others.[22]

Among those things which teach the truth of this opinion are, [first,] that if there were roots and principles in the

Torah, it would have been appropriate that they be included in the Decalogue which God gave to His people at Sinai, so that everyone could have heard them and so that all Jews could ordain and accept them upon themselves and upon their descendants.[23] Of those thirteen principles which Maimonides listed, only one—or two, according to the opinion of Maimonides—is included in the Decalogue.[24]

[Second,] if there were principles and roots in the divine Torah, they would have been mentioned in the beginning of the Torah, just as the axioms and roots of a science are postulated at its beginning. I remarked in my commentary to Genesis that the creation account might be interpreted as a principle and foundation of the Torah, teaching the creation of the world at the beginning of the Torah. But inasmuch as we have seen that these first principles and roots [of Maimonides] were mentioned neither at the beginning of the Torah, nor in the account of Sinai, nor in the Decalogue, it is clear that there are no principles or foundations [in the Torah].

[Third,] if there were roots and principles in the Torah, it would be proper that the punishment for denying them be graver than the punishment for denying the other dicta of the Torah. Inasmuch as this is not the case, since the punishment of him who denies the lightest of the commandments, or the smallest of the verses, is equal to that of him who denies *I am the Lord your God* [Exodus 20:2], or the commandment of monotheism,[25] it is thus clearly explained that there is nothing in the Torah having the level of principles and roots.

Therefore, they said there in *Perek Ḥelek,* about him who denies that the Torah is from Heaven, that

R. Eliezer of Modi'im taught: He who defiles the sacred food, despises the festivals, abolishes the covenant of our Father Abraham, gives an interpretation of the Torah not according to the *halakaha* . . . even if he has Torah and good deeds to his credit, has no portion in the world to come.[26]

The Talmud mentioned other things there [which cost a person his share in the world to come] in addition to the foregoing, such as shaming one's fellow in public,[27] calling one's fellow by a [demeaning] nickname,[28] and glorying in one's fellow's shame.[29] The reason for this is not as was thought by Maimonides in his *Commentary on the Mishnah*, viz., that one who does one of these things has a deficient soul, lacking in perfection, and not worthy of the world to come.[30] For what is the deficiency in these things that is worse than that found in other things?

But the reason for this is as follows: all the commandments of the Torah, as well as the attributes and opinions taught therein, are divine. He who denies the smallest of them all, in that he uproots something from the Torah and denies it, is not worthy to be of the world to come.

[Fourth,] if there were principles and roots in the Torah, why were they never mentioned by the sages? It would have been more appropriate that they mention these and explain them in some special place than what they did with the commandments of the Torah and the ethical teachings of the Fathers.[31] Now, in that they directed us clearly beforehand, and did not feel the need to mention principles and foundations which a man ought to believe *that he might live by them* [Leviticus 18:5], it is clearly explained that in their wisdom the sages did not assent to the postulating of principles and roots in the divine Torah, for all of it is true and divine; there are no beliefs in it more fundamental than others.

24

On an Objection Which May Occur with Respect to This Position and Its Solution

Someone might object to this contention[1] and say that the Sages [themselves] laid down principles for the divine Torah in that first mishnah in *Perek Ḥelek* where they said:

> All Israel have a portion in the world to come, for it is written, *Thy people are all righteous; they shall inherit the land forever, the branch of My planting, the work of My hands, that I may be glorified* [Isaiah 60:22]. But the following have no portion therein: He who maintains that resurrection is not a biblical doctrine, the Torah was not divinely revealed, and an *apikoros*. R. Akiba added: one who reads uncanonical books. Also one who whispers [a charm] over a wound and says, *I will bring none of these diseases upon thee which I brought upon the Egyptians: for I am the Lord that healeth thee* [Exodus 15:26]. Abba Saul says: Also one who pronounces the divine name as it is spelled.[2]

In the Gemara it says, "And why such [severity]?—A Tanna taught: Since he denied the resurrection of the dead, therefore he shall not share in that resurrection, for in all measures [of punishment and reward] taken by the Holy One, blessed be He, the divine act befits the [human] deed."[3]

It would appear from their words that there are principles and foundations in the Torah about which they said that he who denies them has no portion in the world to come. Maimonides, in his commentary to that mishnah, presented his thirteen principles of faith, saying that he found that an appropriate place in which to discuss them.

In my study of that mishnah I have raised some difficulties

201

which were not noted by Rashi in his commentary there. Maimonides also did not raise them at all in his *Commentary on the Mishnah*. I see fit to mention them here and to respond to them *by the measure of the hand* [after Deuteronomy 16:10].[4] It is through the answers to them that this objection[5] will be clarified and solved.

The first difficulty relates to the statement in the mishnah, "All Israel have a portion in the world to come." The word "portion" is not appropriate in this context. It should better have said, "All Israel have the world to come" or that they are "sons of the world to come" or "inheritors of the world to come" or "destined for the life of the world to come."[6] Why did they use the expression "portion"?

The second difficulty is, why did the mishnah specify those who had no portion in the world to come, from the negative perspective, rather than [approaching it] from the positive perspective, saying, "These are those who have a portion in the world to come"? For, were it their intention to posit roots and foundations for the Torah which must be believed by every religionist, they should have posited and clarified those principles so that one could believe them, and [thereby] *live by them* [Leviticus 18:5], and have a portion in the world to come, just as they specified those foundations with respect to their denial by saying, "The following have no portion in the world to come." This is what Maimonides did with his principles. He specified those principles which a religionist has to believe in order to merit life in the world to come and thereby admonished the heretics not to sin by their heresy.

The third difficulty is, why did they include in that mishnah just those six things by which if one be caught up in their corruption, one has thereby no share in the world to come? Three of these are beliefs. They are, "He who maintains that resurrection is not a biblical doctrine, the Torah was not divinely revealed, and an *apikoros.*" Three of them are actions. They are, "One who reads uncanonical books and whispers [a charm] over a wound," according to R. Akiba, and "One who pronounces the divine name as it is spelled," according to Abba Saul. They mentioned no other beliefs, such as God's unity, the creation of the world, [God's] knowledge and providence, reward and punishment, and the coming of the Redeemer. In connection with the transgressions, also, they mentioned no others, such as idolatry, sexual immorality, and others.

The fourth difficulty relates to the order in which they[7] are presented. He who denies resurrection was listed first, after that, he who denies revelation, and after that, the *apikoros*. Despite the fact that the term *apikoros* is explained by the Gemara as one who mocks the Sages,[8] there is no doubt that it is an Aramaic word, naming those who follow after the opinion of Apikoros, one of those scholars who denied God's existence and other corner-stones including [God's] unity, knowledge, and providence, as Maimonides wrote in the *Guide*, Part II, chapter 13.[9] In the Talmud, however, it was interpreted to mean one who mocks the Sages. [This is so because] the intellect of every man does not suffice to know God's existence by itself. We know it, however, whether by tradition or by demonstration, from the teachings[10] of the Sages. Thus, he who mocks the Sages, who publicly announce and make God's existence known to all men generally, denies God's existence and is therefore called an *apikoros*. This being so, a difficulty arises with respect to the order in which these beliefs were set down in the mishnah. It ought first to have mentioned the *apikoros* and after him, "he who maintains that the Torah was not divinely revealed," and after him, "he who maintains that resurrection is not a Biblical doctrine." This is what Maimonides did, discussing the principle of resurrection last.

The fifth difficulty relates to what was asked in the Talmud about the one who denies resurrection, "And why such [severity]?" That is, why should his punishment be as great as was stated in the mishnah? You will not find that the Talmud asked this question about the other matters. It would, [however,] have been more appropriate to ask this with respect to "one who whispers [a charm] over a wound" or with respect to "one who pronounces the divine name as it is spelled." Why should they have no portion in the world to come because of this? This punishment for them is stranger and more out of proportion to the sin [than in other cases].

I say by way of solution to these problems that this mishnah informs us that every Israelite, whether poor or rich in the fulfillment of commandments, has a portion in the world to come. For, with the fulfillment of whatever commandment that comes to his hand, he will merit that exalted spiritual reward. It is as they said to the one who asked, "How do I stand with the world to come?" [They answered:] "Have you performed any commandments?"[11] to make known that one acquires life in the world to come with one commandment performed properly. This is so much the case that they stated in the Talmud,[12] "No one who is circumcised goes to Gehinnom."[13] Because of this they said, "All Israel have a share in the world to come." It is a general decree to the whole nation that everyone *called by the name Israel* [after Isaiah 44:5] will merit spiritual life.[14]

The reward in the world to come is not equal for all the righteous, but each receives it according to his deeds, as they said, "For each person they made a lodging as befits his honor."[15] Therefore they said here, "[All Israel] have a portion." That is, whether great or small, one *will receive a blessing from the Lord* [Psalms 24:5] according to his deeds and he will have some portion in the heavenly reward. They based this on the statement of the prophet, *For Thy people are all righteous; they shall inherit the land forever* [Isaiah 60:21]. That is, since they are the people of God, they are all on the level of the righteous and will inherit the land of life, which is the world to come.

It is also possible to explain the dictum "[All Israel] have a portion in the world to come" as referring to the rational soul. "The wicked are called dead in their lifetimes"[16] and their souls are destroyed with the destruction of their bodies and will have no immortality at all. But the children of Israel, since they are righteous in their faith[17] and in their Torah, have a portion prepared and set aside for them as their inheritance in the world to come. That portion is one's mind and soul which will exist, eternal and immortal, forever. They therefore said that "[All Israel] have a portion *of* the world to come" and did not say "*in* the world to come" with a *bet*.[18] Thus is the first difficulty solved.

There was no need for the Sages to specify those who have a portion in the world to come, and the beliefs which those who inherit it ought to hold since they already posited at the beginning of the mishnah that "All Israel have a portion in the world to come." This points toward what I have already recounted on the basis of my own opinion, that there is no need to lay down principles for the Torah of God which ought to be believed by every Israelite in order to merit life in the world to come as Maimonides and those who follow after him wrote, for the entire Torah, and every single verse, word, and letter in it is a principle and root which ought to be believed. Therefore they said that in order to acquire the world to come one only needs to be one of the Children of Israel who follow the Torah of God. With this, *his reward is with him* [Isaiah 40:10 and 62:4], *for the righteous shall live by his faith* [Habakkuk 2:4].

It was found necessary to clarify this in the mishnah, however, to the effect that even though "All Israel have a portion in the world to come" those *who have sinned at the cost of their lives* [Numbers 17:3][19] exclude themselves from it. These are "He who maintains that resurrection is not a biblical doctrine, the Torah was not divinely revealed, and an *apikoros.*" Since they are among the sinners of Israel they lose a great good and will not merit the life in the world to come.

They specified these three beliefs and these three transgressions and no others. One who denies Torah beliefs either denies the nature[20] of the Creator, Who gave him the Torah, and follows the opinion of the *apikoros* who denies God's existence, unity, power, knowledge, providence, and retribution and mocks and denigrates the Sages who make these truths known, or he denies the nature of the Torah itself in that he says it is not from heaven. For, even if such a person admits to God's existence and unity, and the other divine cornerstones, he denies that the Torah of Moses is divine, given by God from heaven. Conversely his denial might relate to the nature of the recipient, man.[21] This person denies his own immortality, saying that "resurrection is not a biblical doctrine." That is, the soul is a power of the body which passes away with the body and it has no immortality or resurrection after death. He thinks that because of this the Torah promises no spiritual rewards, but only physical goods. This teaches us [he holds] that there is no resurrection of the dead since speculation denies it, and since it is not established by the Torah, it follows necessarily that it is a belief which is neither true nor correct.

It is thus established that the mishnah specified these three heresies because they exhaust all rational possibilities, relating as they do to the giver of the Torah, to its recipient, or to the Torah itself. The mishnah mentions the heresy relating to the recipient first since "every man is close to himself";[22] it therefore mentioned how this heretic sinned against himself first, since *he doeth it that would destroy his own soul* [Proverbs 6:32]. After that it mentioned the second, intermediate heresy, about the divinity of the Torah. Last, it mentioned the heresy about God, as it says, "and an *apikoros.*"

R. Akiba, however, said that one is banished from life in the world to come not only for agreeing with the *apikoros,* but also if one "reads uncanonical books." These are the books of the sectarians, as explained in the Gemara.[23] This is his punishment for turning after the opinion of the sectarians and for *turning his heart from the Lord* [Jeremiah 17:5]. He said this by way of adding to the matter of the *apikoros.* He said further that one is called a heretic not only for denying the Torah and saying that "the Torah was not divinely revealed" and thus denying its divinity, but also if one mocks it and "whispers [a charm] over a wound and says, *I will bring none of these diseases upon thee which I brought upon the Egyptians: for I am the Lord that healeth thee* [Exodus 15:26]." Such a person has no portion in the world to come since, even though he doesn't deny the divinity of the Torah, he does mock it. The Gemara explains that this was because he expresses the Divine Name in conjunction with expectoration[24] and does other things which cause the divine Torah to be contemptible. Also, since he used the Torah as a shovel[25] this is included in the heresy. If he believed truthfully and simply that the Torah was divine he would treat it with reverence and respect.

We can also explain that "one who whispers [a charm] over a wound" refers to one who denies resurrection since "one who whispers [a charm] over a wound" thinks that he can resurrect the dead and heal the sick by the breath of his lips. That is heresy for, as the Sages said, the key of the resurrection of the dead was not entrusted to any messenger, as God said, *I kill and I make alive; I have wounded and I heal* [Deuteronomy 32:39].[26]

Abba Saul, seeing that R. Akiba added to the first two heresies, resurrection and the *apikoros*, wished to add to the third heresy which denies that the Torah is from heaven and said that one is banished from the Eden of the world to come not only for explicitly saying that "the Torah was not divinely revealed" and [not only for] treating it with contempt but also for revealing secrets of divine matters and the holy name. Such a person has no portion in the world to come. This is what is meant by his statement, "Also one who pronounces the divine name as it is spelled." This was explained in the Talmud[27] to mean that he says it in a foreign language, outside of the Sanctuary, since he was revealing the secrets of the divine name and he would only do this if he were a member of the sect of *apikoros* or a member of the sect which says that "the Torah is not from heaven"; he therefore made light of the honor due the sanctified name and said it in a foreign language and outside of its holy place.

It is thus shown that R. Akiba and Abba Saul spoke only of things which related to the first heresies which were mentioned by the first Tanna.[28] These are included in them so that he who denies resurrection, the divinity of the Torah and its honor, the divine beliefs, and the holy names, has no portion in the world to come. The punishments for other transgressions, however, are written in the Torah and he who violates them is not excluded from spiritual life, [unlike] those heretics and sinners who were specified [in the mishnah]. Thus are the second, third, and fourth questions solved.

The Gemara says "And why such [severity]?" about the one who denies resurrection since it is clearly revealed that one who denies God's existence and divinity will not inherit the world to come since this is the reward which God gives to those who love Him and *that think upon His name* [Malachi 3:16]. So, too, "he who maintains that the Torah was not divinely revealed" ought not to inherit the world to come since there is no way for a man to get there except by means of the Torah. He who denies it will not merit the reward which comes from it. But he who denies resurrection, that is, one who believes in God's existence, unity, and incorporeality, and [believes in] the creation of the world, in God's knowledge, providence, and retribution and [believes in] the eternity of the Torah, in the [exalted] degree of Moses, and in all the other principles, *not one faileth* [Isaiah 40:26] but concomitantly believes that the dead will not return to life, why should his punishment be so great that because of this he should not have a portion in the world to come? The merits and true beliefs will fall and he will not receive the final reward for them.

This objection which was raised in the Talmud is equivalent to one raised by the author of the *Sefer ha-Ikkarim* against Maimonides for counting resurrection as a principle, as was made clear in chapters 3 and 15 of this treatise.[29] He did not speak of "one who reads uncanonical books . . . and one who whispers [a charm] over a wound . . . and one who pronounces the divine name as it is spelled" since they have the same meaning as the first heresies mentioned there and are included in them as I explained. The answer of the Talmud was, "Since he denied the resurrection of the dead, therefore he shall not share in that resurrection."[30] Thus is the fifth difficulty solved.

As to what is meant by "the world to come" in this context—is it the world of souls, to which a man merits [admittance] immediately after death, or is it the time of the resurrection of the dead, or is it the final time that will come after the resurrection and the Day of Judgment? And how is it a matter of measure for measure?—this is a subject for much study and is a problem which great geniuses have striven to answer. I will discuss this matter at length in the treatise *Zedek Olamim* which I am composing.[31]

What follows from all of this is that our Sages did not posit roots for the Torah in this mishnah nor did they intend to do so. But by way of admonition they specified those heresies which will restrain a person from life in the world to come.

They said something similar to this in the first chapter of Rosh ha-Shana:

> But as for the sectarians, and the apostates, and the *apikorsim* and the informers who rejected the Torah and denied the resurrection of the dead, and those who abandoned the ways of the community, and those who *spread their terror in the land of the living* [after Ezekiel 32:23] and who sinned and made the masses sin, like Jereboam the son of Nebat and his fellows—these will go down to Gehinnom and be punished there for all generations.[32]

It is thus made clear that these things[33] were not mentioned because they are principles and foundations of religion, but because they are serious transgressions and reprehensible actions, *which cause the eyes of the mind to fail and the heart to languish* [after I Samuel 2:33] and which banish a man *from cleaving unto the inheritance of the Lord* [I Samuel 26:19], which is the life of the world to come.

With this the entire objection is solved and the opinion which I laid down with respect to the principles is strengthened. This is what I wished to establish in this treatise.

Praise and acclamation through every generation to the Lord, may He be exalted and blessed, Amen and Amen.

Completed in Naples at the end of the month of Marḥeshvan in the year *The voice of rejoicing and salvation* [Psalms 118:15].[34]

Table 1

The Twenty-eight Objections to Maimonides' Principles Listed in the Rosh Amanah

Objections one through seventeen are found in *Rosh Amanah* 3, objections eighteen through twenty in *Rosh Amanah* 4, and objections twenty-one through twenty-eight in *Rosh Amanah* 5.

1. If we define "principle" as "a term applied to a thing upon which the existence and duration of another thing depends and without which it cannot endure," then many of Maimonides' principles ought not to be called principles.
2. The fifth of Maimonides' principles, that God ought to be worshipped, is a particular commandment and as such ought not to be counted as a principle.
3. How would praying to an intermediary cause the Torah to collapse?
4. Contrary to the ninth principle [eternity of the Torah], why should not the Torah change if those who are guided by it change?
5. Given that R. Hillel denied the coming of the Messiah [Sanhedrin, 99a], how could belief in his coming be construed as a principle of faith?
6. Why would denying belief in resurrection cause the Torah to collapse?
7. How can we count belief in the Messiah and the resurrection of the dead as principles since, after they occur, there will be no need to *believe* in them?
8. Why did not Maimonides count as a principle the belief that the *Shekhina* dwells in Israel through the medium of the Torah?
9. Why did Maimonides fail to count as a principle belief in creation?

210

Table 1 211

10. Why did Maimonides fail to count as a principle that we ought to believe in the miracles of the Torah in their literal sense?

11. Why did Maimonides fail to count as a principle that we ought to accept ancestral tradition?

12. Why did Maimonides fail to count as a principle that we ought to believe in human choice?

13. Why did Maimonides fail to count as a principle that we ought to believe that God acts by will?

14. Why did Maimonides fail to count belief in more of God's attributes as principles? Why were his principles thirteen in number?

15. Why did Maimonides fail to count as principles belief in the end of man and survival of the soul after death?

16. Why did Maimonides fail to count as a principle belief in the oracular character of the *Urim* and *Tummim?*

17. Why did Maimonides fail to count as principles prayer and the other beliefs counted by Crescas?

18. Maimonides ought not to have counted belief in God as a commandment.

19. Beliefs cannot be commanded, yet two of Maimonides' principles are commandments.

20. Critique of Maimonides' proof from Makkot 23a–b that Exodus 20:2 is a commandment.

21. Why did Maimonides fail to include all of his principles in *Hilkhot Yesodei ha-Torah?*

22. Why did Maimonides include beliefs which are not principles of Judaism in *Hilkhot Yesodei ha-Torah?*

23. Why did Maimonides count only the first two principles, God's existence and unity, as commandments?

24. Why in the *Sefer ha-Madda* did Maimonides call the first principle "the foundation of all foundations and the pillar of the sciences" instead of calling it "*one* of the foundations"? Further, of what interest is it to us if this belief is the pillar of gentile sciences? Further still, why does Maimonides make the unnecessary claim "[God's] truth is not like the truth of any one of them" and why does he support this contention with an irrelevant verse?

25. Maimonides' statement in *Hilkhot Yesodei ha-Torah* that God moves the highest sphere is either unnecessary or heterodox.

26. Maimonides' discussion of God's unity in *Hilkhot Yesodei ha-Torah* raises many problems.

27. Ought not principles two, three, and four be included in principle one?

28. Why does Maimonides present the thirteenth principle as belief in the resurrection of the dead simply, as opposed to belief that the Torah teaches resurrection?

Table 2

Abravanel's Nine Propositions

1. The term *ikkar* denotes any important or essential belief, and not just the roots and axioms of faith. This proposition is discussed in *Rosh Amanah* 6. It is cited by Abravanel in his response to the first objection on p. 111.

2. Maimonides' first principle teaches that God exists necessarily, not just that He exists. This proposition is discussed in *Rosh Amanah* 7. It is cited by Abravanel in his response to the eighteenth objection on p. 152.

3. Each of Maimonides' principles teaches more than one belief. This proposition is discussed in *Rosh Amanah* 8. It is cited by Abravanel in his response to the second objection on p. 114, in his response to the ninth objection on p. 146, in his response to the thirteenth objection on p. 150, and in his response to the twentieth objection on p. 183.

4. Some of Maimonides' principles are included in others of his principles. This proposition is discussed in *Rosh Amanah* 9. It is cited by Abravanel in his response to the fifth objection on p. 135 and in his response to the twenty-seventh objection on p. 187.

5. One or more of three separate lessons may be learned from the order and number of Maimonides' principles. This proposition is discussed in *Rosh Amanah* 10. It is cited by Abravanel in his response to the first objection on p. 111, in his response to the fifth objection on p. 135, and in his response to the sixth objection on p. 140. It is also cited in chapter 23 on p. 197.

6. The principles of faith ought not to be taken from the practical commandments but ought to be taken from commandments of belief. This proposition is discussed in *Rosh Amanah* 11. It is cited by Abravanel in his response to the third objection on p. 118 and in his response to the seventeenth objection on p. 151. It is also cited in chapter 23 on p. 197.

7. The principles of the Torah ought to be unique to it and not

shared with other religions. This proposition is discussed in *Rosh Amanah* 11. It is cited by Abravanel in chapter 22 on p. 190.

8. All of Maimonides' principles are beliefs either in God or in His actions and in nothing else. This proposition is discussed in *Rosh Amanah* 11. It is cited by Abravanel in chapter 22 on p. 190.

9. Belief does not occur immediately but depends upon prior preparation. This proposition is discussed in *Rosh Amanah* 11. It is cited by Abravanel in his response to the twelfth objection on p. 148 and in his response to the nineteenth objection on p. 154.

Notes

Note on the Text and Translation

1. It was bound together with Abravanel's commentaries on the Passover Haggadah and Tractate Avot, *Zevaḥ Pesaḥ* and *Naḥlat Avot*. The book is fully described in Abraham Ya'ari, *Ha-Defus ha-Ivri bi-Kushta* (Jerusalem, 1967), pp. 60–61.

2. In their *Bet Eked Sefarim*, 2d ed. (Tel Aviv, 1954), 3: 927, C. B. and B. Friedberg list two further editions of the *Rosh Amanah:* Sabionetta, 1545 and Warsaw, 1785. I have not been able locate copies of these two alleged editions, nor have I been able to find any other references to them.

3. It is possible that this use of the verse suggested itself to Abravanel because of the comments on the verse of Midrash Rabbah and Rashi, both of which connect the verse with belief. I am grateful to Dr. Shalom Rosenberg for pointing this possibility out to me.

Introduction

1. On creed formulation in Judaism generally see David Neumark, *Toledot ha-Ikkarim bi-Yisrael* (Odessa, vol. 1, 1912, vol. 2, 1919), Solomon Schechter, "The Dogmas of Judaism," in his *Studies in Judaism*, 1st series (Philadelphia, 1905), pp. 147–81 and the extensive bibliographies in Louis Jacobs, *Principles of the Jewish Faith* (New York, 1964), pp. 7–8 and 30–32.

2. Sanhedrin, 90a. All quotations from the Talmud are taken from the Soncino edition (London, 1935). In the Babylonian Talmud the tenth and eleventh chapters of Sanhedrin are transposed.

3. The Arabic text of Maimonides' commentary to this mishnah (the first of what is called *Perek* [chapter] *Ḥelek*) may be found in J. Holzer, *Zur Geschichte der Dogmenlehre in der jüdischen Religionsphilosophie des Mittelalters: Mose Maimüni's Einleitung zu Chelek* (Berlin, 1901); Israel Friedlaender, *Selections from the Arabic writings of Maimonides* (Leiden, 1909 and 1951) and in Joseph Kafaḥ, *Mishnah im Perush Rabbenu Moshe ben Maimon*, vol. 4 (Jerusalem, 1964). The Holzer text includes the Hebrew translation of Solomon ben Joseph ibn Jacob while Kafaḥ presents a new Hebrew translation of his own. Mordecai Dov Rabinovitch edited the

translation of Solomon ben Joseph in *Rabbenu Moshe ben Maimon: Hakdamot li-Perush ha-Mishnah* (Jerusalem, 1961). There is also a modern Hebrew translation—which I have not seen—by M. Gottlieb in his *Perush ha-Mishnah la-Rambam, Masseket Sanhedrin* (Hanover, 1906). Maimonides's complete commentary to the first mishnah in *Perek Ḥelek* has been translated into English twice. Joshua Abelson's translation, "Maimonides on the Jewish Creed," appeared in the old series of the *JQR* 19 (1907): 24–58. Arnold Jacob Wolf retranslated the commentary in *Judaism* 15 (1966): 95–101, 211–16, and 337–42. This translation was reprinted in Isadore Twersky, ed., *A Maimonides Reader* (New York, 1972), 401–23, from which it will be cited below. On Maimonides' thirteen principles generally see Arthur Hyman, "Maimonides' 'Thirteen Principles,' " in Alexander Altmann, ed., *Jewish Medieval and Renaissance Studies* (Cambridge, Mass., 1967), 119–44.

4. Twersky, p. 422; Kafaḥ, p. 217. The reference to one "who cuts among the plantings" is to Elisha ben Abuyah. See Ḥagiga 14b.

5. See, for example, my "Gersonides and His Cultured Despisers: Arama and Abravanel," *Journal of Medieval and Renaissance Studies* 6 (1976): pp. 269–96.

6. Crescas is the author of *Or ha-Shem* (Light of the Lord) (Ferrara, 1555 [reprinted in London, 1969 and Jerusalem, 1972], Vienna, 1859 [reprinted in Tel Aviv, 1963], and Johannesburg, 1861). On his discussion of dogmas see, in addition to the sources cited in note 1 above, Eliezer Schweid, *Ha-Philosophia ha-Datit shel R. Ḥasdai Crescas* (Jerusalem, 1970), pp. 16–20, and S. B. Urbach, *Amudei ha-Maḥshava ha-Yisraelit*, vol. 3, *Mishnato ha-Philosophit shel Rabbi Ḥasdai Crescas* (Jerusalem, 1960), pp. 25–32. Albo is the author of the *Sefer ha-Ikkarim (Book of Principles)*, edited and translated by Isaac Husik in five volumes (Philadelphia, 1946). On his discussion of dogmas see, in addition to the sources cited in note 1 above, Eliezer Schweid, "Bein Mishnat ha-Ikkarim shel R. Joseph Albo li-Mishnat ha-Ikkarim shel ha-Rambam," *Tarbiz* 33 (1963–64): 74–84.

7. Arthur Hyman, "Maimonides' 'Thirteen Principles,' " p. 119n.

8. Abravanel introduces this translation with the claim that it is ibn Tibbon's. It most certainly is not. M. Gottlieb (see above, note 3) holds that it is a composite of two translations, one by ibn Tibbon and one by Judah al-Ḥarizi. Gottlieb is cited by Hyman on p. 120. See further Moshe Goshen-Gottstein, "Yod-Gimmel ha-Ikkarim shel ha-Rambam bi-Tirgum al-Ḥarizi," *Tarbiz* 26 (1946): 185–96.

9. Neumark, 2: 179.

10. Benzion Netanyahu, *Don Isaac Abravanel: Statesman and Philosopher*, 3d ed. (Philadelphia, 1972), p. 291.

11. "R. Isaac Abravanel on the Principles of Judaism," *Journal of the American Academy of Religion* 45, no. 4, Supplement (December 1977): 1183–1200, p. 1187.

12. Joseph Sarachek, *Don Isaac Abravanel* (New York, 1938), p. 151.

13. Eugene Mihaly, "Isaac Abravanel on the Principles of Faith," *Hebrew Union College Annual* 26 (1955): 484–85.

14. Maimonides, *Mishneh Torah, Sefer ha-Madda (Book of Knowledge), "Hilkhot Teshuvah"* ("Laws of Repentance"), III.6–8. All quotations from the *Sefer ha-Madda* will be taken from the translation of Moses Hyamson (Jerusalem–New York, 1974), sometimes with minor emendations. The present text appears on p. 84b.

15. *Guide of the Perplexed*, III.51. All quotations from the *Guide* are taken from the translation of Shlomo Pines (Chicago, 1963). The present text appears on p. 619.

16. On Abraham ben David (Rabad) see Isadore Twersky, *Rabad of Posquières* (Cambridge, Mass., 1962).

17. Gloss to *"Hilkhot Teshuvah,"* III.7. I cite the text as presented (and discussed) by Twersky, pp. 282–86.

18. On Duran see Heinrich Jaulus, "Simon ben Zemach Duran," *MGWJ* 23 (1874): 241–59, 308–17, 355–66, 398–412, 447–63, and 499–514; Jakob Guttmann, "Die Stellung des Simeon ben Zemach Duran in der jüdischen Religionsphilosophie," *MGWJ* 52 (1908): 641–72 and 53 (1909): 46–79 and 199–228; Isidore Epstein, *The Responsa of R. Simon ben Zemah Duran as a Source of the History of the Jews in North Africa* (London, 1930); and Naḥum Arieli, "Mishnato ha-Philosophit shel R. Shimon ben Ẓemaḥ Duran" (Ph.D. diss., Hebrew University, 1976).

19. *Ohev Mishpat* (Venice, 1590 and Tel Aviv, 1971), chapter 9 (p. 14b) I have corrected the text according to the copies of three mss. held at the Jewish National and University Library, Jerusalem.

20. *Or ha-Shem* (Vienna, 1859), Preface, p. 3b.

21. Ibid.

22. P. 27b.

23. P. 61a.

24. *Encyclopaedia Judaica* (Jerusalem, 1972), vol. 5, col. 1081.

25. *Ikkarim*, 1: 2 (Husik, p. 49).

26. Ibid., p. 52.

27. Ibid., p. 53.

28. Ibid., p. 2. Albo, unlike Crescas, is concerned, in the first instance, to determine the principles of divine law in general.

29. Ibid.

30. 1: 3 (pp. 55–56).

31. *Rosh Amanah* 24:205.

32. See below, pp. 33–36.

33. *Rosh Amanah* 23:195.

34. *Rosh Amanah* 12:112.

35. *Ikkarim*, 1:2 (p. 55). It is possible that Albo was reacting here to a suggestion of Duran's. See below, *Rosh Amanah* 12, note 11, and 23, note 22.

36. *Rosh Amanah* 23:195.

37. Ibid., 200.

38. See Netanyahu, p. 73, and Abravanel's introduction to the *Rosh Amanah*.

39. *Rosh Amanah* 6:80.

40. Ibid., p. 82. See also *Rosh Amanah* 6:82, 9:96–97, and 15:142.

41. Ibid., 9:97.

42. Ibid., 21:187.

43. Ibid., 23:197–98.

44. This seems to contradict his earlier statement (chapter 6, p. 82) to the effect that Maimonides rejects the axiomatic interpretation of the principles. Since Abravanel reiterates that claim immediately below (p. 198) I must assume that he did not mean to impute the axiomatic interpretation of the principles to Maimonides here.

45. *Rosh Amanah* 23:198.

46. Ibid.

47. Ibid. This is not to say that Abravanel thinks that Maimonides held only the heuristic interpretation of the principles (he again explicitly imputes the dogmatic interpretation of the principles to Maimonides in *Rosh Amanah* 24:201) but that he *also* holds that interpretation and he can defend him, therefore, on those grounds. For further on this, see immediately below.

48. For a survey of the various interpretations of Maimonides, see Marvin Fox, "Prolegomenon," in A. Cohen, *The Teachings of Maimonides* (New York, 1968), xv–xliii, and David Hartman, *Maimonides: Torah and Philosophic Quest* (Philadelphia, 1976), chapter 1.

49. See below, note 78.

50. See Arthur Hyman, "Maimonides' Thirteen Principles," and Fox, pp. xxxvi–xxxix.

51. *Shamayim Hadashim [New Heavens]* (Roedelheim, 1829), p. 2b.

52. *Madregah;* similarly in the rest of the passage.

53. *Mifalot Elohim [Deeds of God]* (Venice, 1592), p. 6a, col. 1.

54. On this, see Netanyahu, pp. 103–8 and p. 78.

55. *Rosh Amanah* 10:98.

56. This overflow or emanation (*shefa* in Hebrew) is discussed by Maimonides in the *Guide of the Perplexed*. It is, he says, sometimes call *ruah* (spirit) in Hebrew (I.40, p. 191); the world was created through this overflow and is kept in existence by it (I.58, p. 136 and I.69, p. 169). It is defined in II.12 as the term which denotes "the actions of one who is not a body" (p. 279). The term cannot be defined further "for we are not capable of finding the true reality of a term that would correspond to the true reality of the notion" (ibid.). The workings of the divine overflow may be beyond human ken, but its effects are evident, for it is the source of all knowledge. Commenting on the verse, "In Thy light do we see light" (Psalms 36:10), Maimonides writes "that through the overflow of the intellect that has overflowed from Thee, we intellectually cognize, and consequently we receive correct guidance, we draw inferences, and we apprehend the intellect" (p. 280). See Roger E. Herst, "Where God and Man Touch: An Inquiry into Maimonides' Doctrine of Divine

Overflow," *CCAR Journal* 23 (Autumn 1976): 16–21. This divine overflow is closely bound up with the subject of Maimonides's views of prophecy, on which issue see M. M. Kellner, "Maimonides and Gersonides on Mosaic Prophecy," *Speculum* 52 (1977): 62–79 and the sources cited in note 5 there (p. 63) as well as David R. Blumenthal, "Maimonides' Intellectualist Mysticism and the Superiority of the Prophecy of Moses," *Studies in Medieval Culture* 10 (1977): 51–67.

57. This phrase *(Torah min ha-Shamayim)* is missing in the printed edition but is found in the manuscripts. See above, note 19.

58. *Ohev Mishpat*, p. 14a.

59. Ibid.

60. *Magen Avot* (Livorno, 1785 and Jerusalem, n.d.), p. 2b, bottom.

61. See especially the articles by Jaulus and Guttmann cited above in note 18.

62. *Ikkarim*, I.4 (Husik, 1: 64).

63. Ibid. (p. 69).

64. On Bibago see Moritz Steinschneider, "Abraham Bibagos Schriften," *MGWJ* 32 (1883): 79–96 and 125–44; Allan Lazaroff, "The Theology of Abraham Bibago" (Ph.D. diss., Brandeis University, 1973); Abraham Nuriel, "Mishnato ha-Philosophit shel R. Abraham ben Shem Tov Bibago" (Ph.D. diss., Hebrew University, 1975); and Chava Fraenkel-Goldschmidt's introduction to her edition of selections from Bibago's *Derekh Emunah* (Jerusalem, 1978), pp. 7–40.

65. Abravanel's borrowings from Bibago were first noted by Eliakim Carmoly in "Annalecten 8: Plagiate," in Jost's *Israelitische Annalen* 1, no. 13 (March 29, 1839):101, and in "Toledot Don Yizḥak Abravanel," in Ignaz Blumenfeld, ed., *Oẓar Neḥmad* (Vienna, 1857) 2:55. Lazzaroff discusses Carmoly's claims and two defenses of Abravanel offered in the *Israelitische Annalen* (by "Tsarphati," 1:181, and by S. D. Luzzatto in 2:17 and 24–25) on pages 152–53 of his dissertation. Jacob Guttmann, *Die Religionsphilosophischen Lehren des Isaak Abravanel* (Breslau, 1916), pp. 39–40, provides further examples of Abravanel's dependence upon Bibago. The material here is taken from Bibago's *Derekh Emunah* (Constantinople, 1522; Jerusalem, 1970), pp. 99c–101d. These pages are missing from the Jerusalem reprint and I would like to thank Professor Allan Lazaroff of Boston University and Mr. James Neiger of the Klau Library at Hebrew Union College for their kindness in providing me with copies of them. The question of Abravanel's unattributed use of materials derived from other authors is a complicated one. He often criticizes others for doing it (see, for example, *Rosh Amanah* 7:87 for such a criticism of Albo) but seems to have been repeatedly guilty of the fault himself. Perhaps most notorious is the question of his dependence upon Isaac Arama (1420–94). Arama's son Meir (c. 1460–1545) wrote a letter in which he accused Abravanel of plagiarizing his father's work. The letter was published by Gabriel Polak in *Ha-Maggid* 2, no. 25 (June 30, 1858):99. Sarah Heller-Wilensky, in *R. Yizḥak Arama u-Mishnato ha-Philosophit* (Jerusalem, 1956), pp. 48–57, and in "Isaac Arama on the Creation and Structure of the World," *PAAJR* 22 (1953): 131–49, provides textual documentation for Abra-

vanel's dependence upon Arama. Benzion Netanyahu essays a defense of Abravanel in his *Don Isaac Abravanel: Statesman and Philosopher*, 3d ed. (Philadelphia, 1972), p. 296n. He argues that many of the ideas which Abravanel is claimed to have taken from Arama could more properly be attributed to both authors since they discussed many philosophical and theological topics together. One must question Netanyahu's suggestion, however, in the light of Abravanel's relationship to Bibago. In general, this is a subject which needs further study.

66. Neumark summarized his *Toledot ha-Ikkarim* in *The Principles of Judaism*, published as an appendix to 1, nos. 3 and 4 of the *Journal of Jewish Lore and Philosophy* (Cincinnati, 1919). It was republished independently a year later in the form of forty-six–page booklet (New York, 1920). Waxman based his critique of Neumark on this publication. See *Toledot ha-Ikkarim*, II, p. 151.

67. "Maimonides as Dogmatist," *CCAR Yearbook* 45 (1935):397–418. See especially p. 404. Waxman does not mention Duran.

68. "Yod-Gimmel ha-Ikkarim shel ha-Rambam," *Sinai* 58 (1965):58–61.

69. See above, note 3.

70. On the idea of the 613 commandments and its history see Abraham Hirsch Rabinowitz, *Taryag* (Jerusalem, 1967).

71. Each letter of the Hebrew alphabet has a numerical equivalent. The sum of the numerical equivalents of the letters in the word "Torah" is 611.

72. The Hebrew word which I translate as "Almighty" is *Gevurah*, literally "force," "power," or "might."

73. On the *Halakhot Gedolot* see the article by Yehoshua Horowitz in the *Encyclopaedia Judaica* (Jerusalem, 1972), vol. 7, cols. 1167–70.

74. On the *Azharot* see A. Z. Idelson, *Jewish Liturgy and Its Development* (New York, 1972), pp. 42, 197. It is interesting to note that the numerical value of the word *azharot*, written defectively, is 613.

75. *Sefer ha-Mitzvoth of Maimonides*, vol. 1, *The Positive Commandments*, translated by Charles B. Chavel (London, 1967), p. 1. All subsequent citations from the *Sefer ha-Miẓvot* will be taken from this source (as well as from vol. 2, *The Negative Commandments*), sometimes with minor emendations.

76. "*Hilkhot Yesodei ha-Torah*," I.1 and I.6, pp. 34a–b.

77. Wolf translation in Twersky, p. 417.

78. There is considerable debate over whether Maimonides understood the commandment to involve *belief* or *knowledge*. See Shlomo Goren, *Torat ha-Mo'adim* (Jerusalem, 1963/4), pp. 88–104; Simon Rawidowicz, "On Maimonides' *Sefer ha-Madda*," in his *Studies in Jewish Thought* (Philadelphia, 1974), pp. 317–23; and, very helpfully, Warren Harvey's Ph.D. dissertation, "Ḥasdai Crescas' Critique of the Theory of the Aquired Intellect" (Columbia University, 1973), pp. 218–19. Harvey analyzes the discussions of Goren and Rawidowicz. See also Arthur Hyman, "Maimonides' Thirteen Principles," pp. 133–34, 140, and the editions of the *Sefer ha-Miẓvot* by Chaim Heller (Jerusalem, 1946), p. 35, note 1, and Joseph Kafaḥ (Jerusalem, 1971), p. 53.

79. See David Hartman, *Maimonides: Torah and Philosophic Quest* (Philadelphia, 1976) for an exposition and defense of this theory. The whole book is relevant, but especially chapters 1 and 3 and, with respect to the present context, most especially p. 49.

80. See Eliezer Schweid, *Ha-Philosophia ha-Datit shel R. Ḥasdai Crescas* (Jerusalem, 1971), p. 23.

81. In his article on Crescas's philosophy in the *Encyclopaedia Judaica* (Jerusalem, 1972), vol. 5, col. 1081.

82. David Hartman, *Maimonides*, pp. 51–52, discusses the kind of position Crescas seems to be adopting.

83. The text of the *Or ha-Shem* is notoriously corrupt. See H. A. Wolfson, *Crescas' Critique of Aristotle* (Cambridge, Mass., 1929), pp. 703–5, and Warren Harvey's dissertation, pp. 230–32. In the translation that follows I have followed the text of the 1859 Vienna edition, checking it against the other two printed versions. Thus, since I have not established a critically edited text, my translation here must be regarded as provisional. But since Abravanel's paraphrase of Crescas's argument (see below) deviates from the Vienna text in no significant details, the issue is of little importance here.

84. The arguments are paraphrased by Abravanel in chapter 4 of the *Rosh Amanah* and analyzed by Warren Harvey on pp. 222–26. The first argument points out that a commandment presupposes a commander. The idea of a commandment to believe in the existence of the commander of that very commandment is logically incoherent. The second argument depends upon Crescas's analysis of the terms "will" and "choice" (*Or ha-Shem*, Treatise II, principle ii, chapter 5). Commandments, Crescas says, make sense only in contexts where will and choice obtain. But since one cannot will (or choose) to believe in something, there can be no commandments about beliefs. It should be pointed out here that Jewish commentators find many more than ten *commandments* in the Decalogue. They see it as a group of ten utterances or speeches, not a listing of ten discrete commandments. Abravanel, in his *Commentary on the Torah*, 3 vols. (Jerusalem, 1964), 2:178–86 (his commentary on the Decalogue) provides an exhaustive analysis of the opinions of his major predecessors on this subject.

85. Makkot, 23b–24a.

86. This is the view of Naḥmanides (1194–1270) as expressed in his commentary to Exodus 20:2. As will be seen below, Crescas was strongly influenced by Naḥmanides in his understanding of the verse.

87. *Sefer ha-Miẓvot*, 1:1.

88. See also Philip Birnbaum, *High Holiday Prayer Book* (New York, 1951), p. 537. In *Rosh Amanah* 7 Abravanel analyzes this passage of Crescas's and concludes that Crescas held that Maimonides contradicted himself. Abravanel writes: "This scholar thus thought that Maimonides' statements in these two places, i.e., the *Sefer ha-Madda* and the *Sefer ha-Miẓvot* were not in agreement. He thought that in the *Sefer ha-Madda* [Maimonides held] that the first commandment is simply that God

exists while he thought that in the *Sefer ha-Miẓvot* [Maimonides held] that the first commandment is to believe that God is the cause of the world and its Creator" (p. 88).

89. Exodus 31:17. I have no idea why this verse, which is not in the Decalogue, appears here. As will be seen below, Abravanel also cites it in his summary of Crescas's argument.

90. This is Crescas's crucial assumption; the rest of his arguments are based on it.

91. Namely, not to make a graven image (verse 4), not to bow down to such an image (verse 5), and to believe in God (verse 2).

92. On the assumption that Moses taught 611 commandments but none of those contained in the portion of the Decalogue (verses 2–6) in which God is presented as speaking in the first person.

93. Maimonides, *Sefer ha-Miẓvot,* negative commandment 1 (Chavel translation, 2:1).

94. Adding this admonition to the three listed in note 91 above.

95. Those who count the *Azharot* and, of course, Crescas himself. As will be seen below, Abravanel seizes on this question to argue that Crescas himself thought that his argument was weak.

96. Crescas's argument here may be explicated as follows: Commandments are not a matter of belief (because one cannot will or choose to believe something); if *Thou shalt have no other gods before Me* is a commandment, then it must be given an actional interpretation, such as forbidding the worship of other gods. In such a case, *Thou shalt have no other gods before Me* becomes equivalent to *Thou shalt not bow down unto them.*

97. Sanhedrin, 56b.

98. By way of summarizing the issue, it may be helpful to point out that both Crescas and Maimonides agree that Exodus 20:2–6 constitute the first two utterances of the Decalogue. According to Crescas these utterances contain two commandments: the commandment prohibiting the worship of idols and that prohibiting the bowing down to idols. According to Maimonides, the two utterances contain five commandments: *(a)* to believe (or know) that God exists (verse 2); *(b)* not to have other gods (verse 3); *(c)* not to make images for the purposes of worship (verse 4); *(d)* not to bow down before or serve idols (verse 5); and *(e)* not to worship idols (verse 5). These are, in Maimonides' *Sefer ha-Miẓvot,* positive commandment 1 and negative commandments 1, 2, 5, and 6.

99. Even to the extent of including the curious citation from Exodus 31:17 (see above, note 89).

100. In his gloss to positive commandment 1.

101. Ramban [Naḥmanides], *Commentary on the Torah,* vol. 2, *Exodus,* translated by Charles B. Chavel (New York, 1973), p. 285. All subsequent citations from Naḥmanides' commentary will be from the Chavel translation.

102. On the identity of the "contemporary scholars," see below, *Rosh Amanah* 18, note 22.

103. Abravanel's commentary on the Decalogue takes the form of an extended essay. It begins with thirteen questions, the seventh of which (p. 179, col. b), deals with our issue.

104. I.e., miracles, especially the deliverance from Egypt.

105. Abravanel, *Commentary on Exodus*, p. 185, col. a. It is entirely possible that Abravanel's usage of I Samuel 29:6 was prompted by Naḥmanides' use of the verse in his gloss to the first negative commandment in Maimonides' *Sefer ha-Miẓvot*, quoted above on page 48. Naḥmanides' position was "good in his eyes." Abravanel's position, however, was "best in his eyes."

106. *Commentary on Exodus*, p. 185, col. b. Abravanel's *Commentary on Exodus* was completed in 1505 (see Netanyahu, p. 289) while the *Rosh Amanah* was written in 1494 (see below, p. 209).

Table of Contents

1. *Editio princeps* reads "twenty-three."
2. Literally: "opinions."

Chapter 1

1. *Ha-Rav ha-Gadol.* Literally, "the great Rabbi," "the great Teacher," or "the great Master." I translate this and all similar expressions as "Maimonides."

2. *Yesodot.*

3. *Ikkareha* (from *ikkar*). Two motifs dominate the terminology of medieval Jewish discussions of the creed, the architectural and the botanical. Reflecting the former, we find words such as *pinah* ("cornerstone"), *ammud* ("column"), and *yesod* ("foundation"). The second motif is reflected in words such as *ikkar* ("root"), *shoresh* ("root"), *se'if* ("branch"), and *anaf* ("branch"). With the exception of *ikkar*, I have translated these words literally. I have translated *ikkar* as "principle" both because that now seems to be its accepted translation (as in Albo's *Book of Principles*) and in order to distinguish it from *shoresh*. Also, since I follow Netanyahu (p. 285) in calling this book *Principles of Faith* and since it is about the *ikkarim*, it makes further sense to translate *ikkar* as "principle."

4. Sanhedrin, X.1.

5. On the text of the commentary, see above, Introduction, note 3.

6. Thirteenth century. I have deleted the expression "of blessed memory" here and do so throughout the translation.

7. As noted above (Introduction, note 8), the translation is not ibn Tibbon's.

8. The Separate Intellects in medieval Jewish Aristotelianism are those bodiless entities which mediate between God and the world. See Maimonides' *Guide of the Perplexed*, II.2–12, and Harry Blumberg, "Ha-Sekhalim ha-Nivdalim bi-Mishnato

shel ha-Rambam, *Tarbiz* 40 (1971): 216–45. Abravanel's text of Maimonides here has *deot ha-nivdalot.* The Separate Intellects, however, are more commonly called *sekhalim nivdalim.*

9. *Dibbur,* one of the elements of the Decalogue. Ordinarily and incorrectly translated as "commandment."

10. Ḥagiga, 15a: "On High there is neither sitting nor standing, neither want nor weariness."

11. Berakhot, 31b.

12. *Kadmon* ("uncreated"). This word for "eternity" should be distinguished from *nizḥi,* "eternal *a parte post.*"

13. For a general description of Maimonides' view of the structure of the Universe, see his *"Hilkhot Yesodei ha-Torah"* ("Laws of the Foundations of the Torah") in *Sefer ha-Madda.*

14. That Maimonides took this literally seems to be the point of the last several chapters of the *Guide* (III.51–54) and of the famous parable of the palace (III.51).

15. Exodus 20:3–6.

16. See *Guide,* III.29 (p. 521).

17. The tenth Emanation. On the Agent Intelligence (or "Active Intellect") in Maimonides, see *Guide,* II.4 (p. 257), II.6 (p. 262), and II.36 (p. 369). See also his *"Hilkhot Yesodei ha-Torah"* II.7 and IV.6. See further Joseph Heller, "Mahuto vi-Tafkido shel ha-Sekhel ha-Poel lifi Torat ha-Rambam," in *Sefer ha-Yovel Likhvod S.K. Mirsky* (New York, 1958) pp. 26–42.

18. I have deleted the expression "our Teacher, peace upon him" and do so henceforth.

19. There are some words missing here. In M. D. Rabinovitch's text we find: ". . . attained the rank of an angel and was included among them. There remained no veil which he did not pierce and penetrate. No material hindrance troubled him and no deficiency, whether great or small, was mingled with him."

20. This is a Kabbalistic term referring to a highly anthropomorphic conception of God. See Gershom Sholem, *Major Trends in Jewish Mysticism* (New York, 1954), pp. 63–67.

21. Sifra to Leviticus 16:2.

22. Literally: "Torah from Heaven."

23. See Makkot, 24a.

24. Numbers Rabbah, 10.21.

25. See Psalms 19:8.

26. *Kofer.* Literally: "denier."

27. Sanhedrin, X.1.

28. Sanhedrin, 99a.

29. See Fred Rosner, trans., *Moses Maimonides' Commentary on the Mishnah, Introduction to Seder Zeraim and Commentary on Tractate Berachoth* (New York, 1975), pp. 45ff.

30. Sanhedrin, 97b. I follow the standard text, and not that of Abravanel, which deviates slightly from it.

31. Numbers 23–24.

32. *Attem Niẓavim;* Deuteronomy 29:9–30:20, especially 30:1–10.

33. Abravanel's text here has *ikkar.* The other Hebrew versions all have *yesod.*

34. Earlier in the commentary to the first mishnah in *Ḥelek.*

35. *Klal Yisrael.*

36. *Kafar bi-ikkar.*

37. *Min.* On Maimonides' use of the term, see *"Hilkhot Teshuvah"* ("Laws of Repentance"), III.7.

38. On Maimonides' use of this term, see *"Hilkhot Teshuvah,"* III.8.

39. Ḥagiga, 15a. This is a reference to Elisha ben Abuyah.

40. Abravanel's text here is difficult to follow and appears to be corrupt. I follow Rabinovitch's text here.

41. I.1 (Hyamson, p. 34a).

42. I.6 (p. 34b).

43. I.7 (p. 34b).

44. I.8 (p. 34b).

45. Abravanel discusses which principles are found in *"Hilkhot Yesodei ha-Torah"* below in *Rosh Amanah* 20.

46. Abravanel is referring to Maimonides' *Sefer ha-Miẓvot (Book of Commandments).*

47. Makkot, 23a–b.

Chapter 2

1. Literally: "He is neither a body nor the power in a body."

2. Although Abravanel does not introduce this as a quotation, it is taken from the Introduction to Treatise II of Crescas's *Or ha-Shem* (p. 27b).

3. Oracular device on the breastplate of the High Priest. See Exodus 28:15–30. Leviticus 8:8, *Yoma,* VII.5 and *Yoma,* 73b. See further Maimonides' *"Hilkhot Kele ha-Mikdash"* ("Laws of the Temple Implements"), X.11.

4. *Or ha-Shem,* III, Introduction (p. 61a). The difference between this group of beliefs and the previous one is that the existence of the Torah can be conceived without them.

5. Numbers 6:24–26.

6. *Or ha-Shem,* III.ii, Introduction (p. 82b) has *"Yom Kippur"* ("Day of Atonement") where Abravanel has *"Rosh ha-Shana."*

7. Ibid. On the "four divisions of the year" see Rosh ha-Shana, I.2. They are the four times a year when the world is judged by God.

8. *Sugim elyonim.* The term often means "category" in the Aristotelian sense, but that would make little sense in the present context.

9. *Ikkarim*, I.4 (pp. 64–65).

10. Or: ". . . peaceable as they are with us in their opinions diverged from the position of Maimonides."

11. *Sefekot.*

Chapter 3

1. In its literal sense of "root."

2. Albo, *Ikkarim*, I.2 (p. 55).

3. Albo, I.3 (p. 47). See also Crescas, *Or ha-Shem*, III, Introduction (p. 61a).

4. This is taken almost word for word from Albo, I.3 (pp. 57–58).

5. I.e., that *only* God is to be worshipped.

6. Sifri *ad locum* and Ta'anit, 2a.

7. At I.14 (pp. 124–25) Albo states: "The truth of the matter is that none of the specific commandments of the Torah should be regarded as principles, fundamental or derived. It follows from this that the duty to worship God alone, which is in Maimonides' list, should not be counted as a principle, primary or secondary, for it is a specific command." In a note to this text, Husik points out Albo's dependence upon Duran for this doctrine.

8. Literally: "that this not be done to anything else."

9. Albo, I.3 (p. 58).

10. II.39, p. 380.

11. I.e., because it is perfect.

12. Albo, III.13 (pp. 113–14).

13. *Datot.* On this term see Albo, I.7 (p. 78).

14. Albo, III.14 (p. 118); see also p. 127. See also Crescas, *Or ha-Shem*, III. v. 1 (p. 78b).

15. Ketubot II.2. I.e., the physician allows the patient to change his diet.

16. *Hok.*

17. Based on Albo, III.13 (p. 114).

18. Albo, III.14 (p. 121).

19. Yevamot, 91a–b.

20. Law pertaining to the movement of objects and to traveling on the Sabbath.

21. Eruvin, 21b. Albo, III.14 (p. 126), cites both these cases.

22. I have not been able to find this in Leviticus Rabbah. Husik (*Ikkarim*, III.16, p. 141) cites as its source Yalkut Shim'oni on Proverbs 9:2 (section 944), where it actually occurs as it does in Midrash Rabbah on Proverbs 9:2. Albo cites this passage as coming from Leviticus Rabbah.

23. The point of this statement is that in the messianic future the flesh of swine will be permitted to Jews. The statement, however, does not occur in Leviticus Rabbah as we have it (although a similar play on words occurs at XIII.5). Rabbi Moshe Sever in his *Mikhlol ha-Ma'amarim vi-ha-Pitgamim* (Jerusalem, 1961),

2:1095, cites a wide variety of medieval Jewish sources which quote this midrash.

24. Albo, III. 16 (pp. 142–43).

25. Emphasis added.

26. Sanhedrin, 99a.

27. Albo, I.1 (p. 44) and IV.42 (p. 413).

28. Albo, I.3 (p. 58).

29. I have not found this objection in either Albo or Crescas. I have found it, however, in Bibago's *Derekh Emunah*, III.5 (p. 102a). Abravanel borrows the passage from Bibago almost verbatim.

30. God's immanent presence.

31. Albo, I.3 (p. 59). The point of this and the rest of the objections in the chapter is that Maimonides, who did not accept the definition of *ikkar* offered by Crescas and Albo, did not seem to have any criterion whereby he chose his principles.

32. Maimonides says (*Guide*, II.25, p. 328): "The belief in eternity the way Aristotle sees it . . . destroys the Law in its principle."

33. Albo, I.3 (p. 59). This objection is cited by Duran in *Ohev Mishpat*, chapter 8, p. 13b.

34. Albo, I.3 (p. 59).

35. Ibid.

36. Ibid.

37. Ibid. At *"Hilkhot Teshuva,"* V.3 (p. 87a), Maimonides writes: "This is an important principle, the pillar of the Torah and the Commandment."

38. Emending the text from *zakhah* to *zakhar*.

39. I.e., miracles. The literal translation of the last phrase is "creation of signs and demonstrations."

40. I.e., Crescas and Albo.

41. Abravanel here refers to Bibago, who raises this objection at the end of *Derekh Emunah* (p. 102d).

42. See Albo, I.4 (p. 70).

43. See Exodus 34:6–7. Duran, *Ohev Mishpat*, p. 13b, quotes just such an explanation from an anonymous source.

44. These thirteen rules are attributed to R. Ishmael (Sifra, Introduction, section 5). They are translated, with illustrative examples, in Philip Birnbaum, *Daily Prayer Book* (New York, 1949), pp. 41–45. See also Louis Jacobs, *Studies in Talmudic Logic and Methodology* (London, 1961).

45. Literally: "numbers." These two suggestions are cited (without approval) by Albo, I.3 (p. 60) and Duran, *Ohev Mishpat*, Introduction, chapter 8, p. 13b. It is likely that Duran is Albo's source.

46. *Hasharat ha-nefesh.*

47. *Or ha-Shem*, II, Introduction (p. 27b).

48. *Or ha-Shem*, III, Introduction (p. 61a).

49. Ibid.

50. Ibid.

Chapter 4

1. Maimonides does this both in the *Sefer ha-Miẓvot* (positive commandments 1 and 2) and in *"Hilkhot Yesodei ha-Torah,"* I.6–7.
2. I.e., in the *haẓa'a* (preface) to the *Or ha-Shem* (pp. 2a–b).
3. Correcting *editio princeps*, which has "ii" here. The passage is on pp. 49a–50b.
4. Above, p. 63.
5. Exodus 31:17. I do now know why Crescas (and Abravanel, following him) cite this verse in this context since it is not in the Decalogue.
6. Crescas refers explicitly to the writers of the *Azharot*. See above, introduction, note 74.
7. *Sefer ha-Miẓvot,* negative commandment one: "By this prohibition we are forbidden to believe in or ascribe deity to, any but Him."
8. For the text of Crescas's argument here, see above, introduction, pp. 45–47.

Chapter 5

1. I.e., the preceding twenty objections listed in chapters 3 and 4.
2. Literally: "the first ones."
3. I.1–6. I.7, and I.8–12, respectively (pp. 34a–35b).
4. Prophecy is discussed in VII.1–5 and 7; Mosaic prophecy in VII.6 (pp. 42a–43b). There is no discussion of revelation per se in the chapter.
5. Pp. 44b–45a.
6. X.1 (p. 45b) and possibly VIII.3 (p. 44a).
7. It is surprising that Abravanel wholly fails to mention Maimonides' listing of the principles in the *Sefer ha-Madda, "Hilkhot Teshuvah"* ("Laws of Repentance"). III.6–8 (pp. 84a–85a). It is possible that he did not consider this summary listing as a formal statement of the principles of Judaism.
8. I.e., The "foundations" of the Torah ought to be identical with its "principles."
9. On both love and fear of God, see II.1–2 (p. 35b) and IV.12 (p. 39b).
10. Maimonides discusses this, not in *"Hilkhot Yesodei ha-Torah,"* but in the very next section of the *Mishneh Torah, "Hilkhot Deot"* ("Laws of Ethics"), I.5–7 (pp. 47b–48a).
11. VI.7 (p. 42a).
12. *Yediot.*
13. When he introduced the principles. See above, p. 56.
14. *"Hilkhot Yesodei ha-Torah,"* I.6 and 7 (p. 34b).
15. Positive commandments 1 and 2.
16. See above, *Rosh Amanah* 4:72.
17. Literally: "here is."

18. Eruvin 96b and Shavuot 7a. The point of all this is that Deuteronomy 4:15 is a commandment.

19. Maimonides' fourth principle; see above, *Rosh Amanah* 1: 57.

20. See below, *Rosh Amanah* 16:146.

21. Abravanel's text has the plural.

22. I.e., the connection between the verses and the commandments is weaker.

23. *"Hilkhot Yesodei ha-Torah,"* I.1 (p. 34a).

24. Ibid., I.3 (p. 34a). Hyamson translates this as "Hence His real essence is unlike any of them."

25. *"Hilkhot Yesodei ha-Torah,"* I.4 (p. 34a).

26. I.5 in our printed editions; I.2 in the ms. which formed the basis for Hyamson's edition (p. 34a).

27. *Ḥakhmei iyyun.*

28. Abravanel does not refer specifically to the *Guide* in this sentence; he says "his book." But since he calls Maimonides "the Rabbi and Guide" here *(ha-Rav ha-Moreh),* the inference is obvious. *Ateret Zekenim (Crown of the Elders)* was first published in Sabionetta in 1557 and in Warsaw in 1894. This latter edition was reprinted in Jerusalem in 1968. *Ateret Zekenim* deals largely with God and prophecy; on it, see Netanyahu, p. 17. The reference here is to chapter 8 (pp. 22–28 in the Warsaw edition).

29. *Guide,* II, Introduction (p. 240).

30. In the *Guide of the Perplexed* Maimonides presents a disjunctive proof of God's existence, unity, and incorporeality. He argues (I.71–76) that if the world is created, then God exists, is one, and is incorporeal. He then argues (II, Introduction and chapter 1) that if the world is uncreated, then God exists, is one, and is incorporeal. Abravanel's point here is that, while Maimonides may have assumed the eternity of the world only for the sake of argument, he ought not to have cited a corollary of that opinion in the *Sefer ha-Madda* both because it was unnecessary and because it was heterodox.

31. *"Hilkhot Yesodei ha-Torah,"* I.6 (p. 34b).

32. Ibid., I.7 (p. 34b).

33. See *Guide,* II.1 in general, and p. 248 in particular.

34. Sanhedrin, X.1.

35. The numerical equivalent of the Hebrew word for "power" *(koaḥ)* being twenty-eight.

Chapter 6

1. In *Physics* IV.4 (212a 20–24) Aristotle says: "So the center of the universe and the inner surface of the revolving heavens constitute the supreme 'below' and the supreme 'above'; the former being absolutely stable, and the latter constant in its

position as a whole." Aristotle, *The Physics,* trans. P. H. Wickstead and F. Cornford (Cambridge, Mass., 1929), 1:315.

2. I.e., the revolving object.

3. Albo, *Sefer ha-Ikkarim,* I.3 (p. 55).

4. Genesis Rabbah 53:15, Soncino translation (London, 1939), 1:474. See also Midrash Tanḥuma, *Balak,* 17.

5. Albo, I.3 (p. 56). See also Sanhedrin, 88b.

6. *Aẓmi.*

7. *Vi-zeh ikkar.*

8. Berakhot, VI.1 (44a in the Talmud).

9. Berakhot, VI.

10. Berakhot, 44a.

11. The salted food which it is necessary to eat in order to dilute the excessive sweetness of the fruits of Ginnosar. See *Tosafot* there, *s.v., "Bi–okhlei."*

12. Berakhot, 12b–13a.

13. Avot, I.7.

14. P. 55.

15. Albo, III.12 (vol. 3, p. 109).

16. Emending the text from "he did not consider."

17. Albo argues as follows: "The truth is this. If the purpose of the prophetic institution among men were that people may know the particular events of the world or that by means of it signs and wonders may be produced for a particular purpose, as might seem at first sight, then the objection would be well taken. But since we have made clear that the necessity of prophecy is that men may be guided toward eternal happiness, that they may know through it what is agreeable to God and what is not, and that they may attain to the destiny intended for mankind by those things which are agreeable to God, the above objection does not hold. For since the purpose of prophecy is that the human race be guided by God, which means revelation of the Torah, the latter must be a fundamental principle, because it is that which makes prophecy necessary. For this reason we consider prophecy a derivative principle dependent upon revelation." See Albo, III.12 (pp. 109–10). He goes on to make a similar argument with respect to providence.

18. As in the case of revelation, which is the purpose of prophecy, and the case of reward and punishment, which is the purpose of providence.

19. These are the words with which Maimonides introduces the principles. See above, *Rosh Amanah* 1:56.

20. *Shorashim azmi'im.*

21. I have added the negation. Neumark, *Toledot ha-Ikkarim,* 1:5, discusses this passage and emends it in the same way.

22. Abravanel reiterates this claim below in *Rosh Amanah* 23:197–98. He defends Maimonides to the extent that the latter's principles were put forward for heuristic purposes.

23. I.e., the principles which he lists.

24. Albo proposes his dogmas as principles of faith in general, not just of Judaism. See *Sefer ha-Ikkarim,* table of contents, p. 2.

25. See *Rosh Amanah* 1:62.

26. In *Ohev Mishpat,* 10, and in *Magen Avot* (p. 2b, bottom) Duran explicitly links Maimonides' thirteen principles to the mishnah in Sanhedrin such that they can be construed as a commentary upon it.

27. Shabbat, 31a; Bava Mezia, 84a.

Chapter 7

1. *Sefer ha-Mizvot,* 1:1.

2. Moses ben Jacob of Coucy (thirteenth century) was the author of the *Sefer Mizvot Gadol (Great Book of Commandments),* an enumeration of the 613 commandments. There are some minor variations between the standard text and Abravanel's version.

3. *Sefer Mizvot Gadol* (Kopys, 1807), p. 11.

4. *Amudei Golah (Pillars of Exile)* is another name for the *Sefer Mizvot Katan* (or *Kazar*), the *Small* (or *Short) Book of Commandments* by Isaac ben Joseph of Corbeil (d. 1280). It is, basically, an abridgement of the *Sefer Mizvot Gadol* arranged in seven parts for daily study.

5. Literally: "winds of the world."

6. *Mazalot.*

7. Hullin, 7b. The whole passage comes from *Amudei Golah* (Jerusalem, 1960), pp. 1–2. Abravanel's text differs slightly from the text presented there.

8. See below, *Rosh Amanah* 8:94.

9. 1089–1164. On ibn Ezra in general and his exegetical works in particular, see Michael Friedlaender, *Essays in the Writings of Abraham ibn Ezra* (London 1877; reprinted in Jerusalem, 1964).

10. Literally: "Never allow awe of Him to turn from one's face." On the whole issue here, see Friedlaender, pp. 110–14.

11. *Editio princeps* has "Maimonides."

12. On Exodus 20:2.

13. *Hasagot al Sefer ha-Mizvot (Glosses on the Book of Commandments),* negative commandment 1.

14. Chavel translation, p. 285. Chavel follows his own critically edited text of Nahmanides' commentary as given in *Perush ha-Ramban al ha-Torah* (revised edition, Jerusalem, 1977), 1:385. That text differs in some minor details from Abravanel's.

15. *Dibbur;* ordinarily mistranslated as "commandment."

16. 1288–1344; on Gersonides see M. M. Kellner, "R. Levi ben Gerson: A Bibliographical Essay," *Studies in Bibliography and Booklore* 12 (1979):13–23.

17. *Perush ha-Ralbag al ha-Torah* (Venice, 1547; reproduced photographically in Israel in two volumes, n.d.), 1:85d.

18. I.e., Crescas.

19. In his *haza'a* (p. 3a).

20. Nissim ben Reuben Gerondi (c. 1310–1375) was the teacher of Hasdai Crescas. His commentary on Genesis was edited by Leon Feldman (Jerusalem, 1968). On Gerondi, see Feldman's introduction, pp. 7–92.

21. I.e., Albo.

22. I.e., those who took issue with Maimonides.

23. See Avot, VI.6, and Megilla, 15a.

24. Albo, I.14 (p. 128) writes: "The meaning of it [Exodus 20:2] is that we should believe that the same God Who took us out of Egypt from the house of bondage, gave us the Torah on Mt. Sinai." See also III.8 (p. 163).

25. *Haza'a*, p. 3a.

26. *"Hilkhot Yesodei ha-Torah,"* I.1 (p. 34a).

27. *Ma'amad har Sinai.*

28. Makkot, 24a.

29. P. 364.

30. Positive commandment 1 (p. 1).

31. *Or ha-Shem, haza'a,* p. 3a.

32. Or: "His essence." Similarly at the end of the sentence.

33. See above, *Rosh Amanah* 1:56.

34. *"Hilkhot Yesodei ha-Torah,"* I.1 (p. 34a).

35. This is a paraphrase of Maimonides' statement in the first principle. See above, *Rosh Amanah* 1:56.

36. Positive commandment 1 (p. 1).

37. At *Guide,* I.69 (p. 168), Maimonides writes: "My purpose in this chapter is to make it clear to you in what respect it is said of Him, may He be exalted, that He is the efficient cause, that He is the form of the world, and that He is its end."

38. Rather than "metaphysics" because Abravanel says *Hakhmat ha-Elokut, yit'aleh.*

39. This is very likely a reference to al-Ghazzali's *Makasid al-falasifa (Intentions of the Philosophers),* Part I, tractate two. In the Latin translation of the *Makasid* published by J. T. Muckle under the title *Al-Gazel's Metaphysics* (Toronto, 1933), this passage is found on pp. 52–61. Abravanel would have had access to this text in the Hebrew translation of Isaac Albalag, called *Kavanot ha-Philosophim.* That Abravanel knew this text is evidenced by the fact that he cites it in his *Zurot ha-Yesodot* (Sabionetta, 1557), folio 1b. See Jacob Guttmann, *Die Religionsphilosophischen Lehren des Isaak Abravanel* (Breslau, 1916), p. 43.

40. Positive commandment 1 (p. 1). Abravanel adds the bracketed words.

41. In the *Sefer ha-Miẓvot*.

42. Literally, "the philosopher."

43. I.e., creation *ex nihilo*.

44. P. 364. See above in this chapter, p. 87.

45. *"Hilkhot Yesodei ha-Torah,"* I.1 (p. 34a).

46. See below, *Rosh Amanah* 17:152–55.

Chapter 8

1. *Hoda'a* here and throughout the chapter.

2. Abravanel does not present the second teaching included in the first principle. This may have been an oversight on his part or a printer's error. In general, the third proposition maintains that there are at least two beliefs taught by each of Maimonides' thirteen principles. Abravanel states this clearly at the end of the present chapter.

3. *Kadmon* here and throughout the paragraph.

4. Maimonides describes Aristotle's theory of creation in the *Guide* (II.13, 284) as follows:

> He asserts—though he does not do so textually, but this is what his opinion comes to—that in his opinion it would be an impossibility that will should change in God or a new volition arise in Him; and that all that exists has been brought into existence, in the state in which it is at present, by God through His volition; but that it was not produced after having been in a state of nonexistence. He thinks that just as it is impossible that the deity should become nonexistent or that His essence should undergo a change, it is impossible that a volition should undergo a change in Him or a new will arise in Him. Accordingly it follows necessarily that his being as a whole has never ceased to be as it is at present and will be as it is in the future eternity.

5. As expressed in the *Timaeus*. Plato held that the world was created out of a preexisting, eternal matter.

6. See below, *Rosh Amanah* 16:146–47.

7. *Ḥefeẓ*.

8. On these two teachings concerning prophecy, see *Guide*, II.36 (p. 371) and II.32 (p. 361).

9. See above, *Rosh Amanah* 1:58.

10. See *Guide*, II.32 (p. 361).

11. *Shittuf ha-shem*. At *Guide*, II.35 (p. 367), Maimonides says: "For to my mind the term prophet used with reference to Moses and the others is amphibolous."

12. Seventh principle of faith (see above, *Rosh Amanah* 1:58–60), and *"Hilkhot Yesodei ha-Torah,"* VII.6 (p. 43a).

13. This book *(Vision of God)* is lost. See Netanyahu, p. 85.

14. Makkot, 24a.

15. See above, *Rosh Amanah* 1:61.

16. This book *(Eternal Justice)* is lost. See Netanyahu, p. 289, n. 12 and p. 297, n. 14.

17. I.e., in that part of the *Commentary* where he lists the principles.

18. Edited by Joshua Finkel in the *PAAJR* 9 (1938–39). Abravanel did not realize, apparently, that the *Treatise on Resurrection* was written after the *Commentary on the Mishnah*.

19. See above, *Rosh Amanah* 1:62.

20. See below, *Rosh Amanah* 10:100–101 and 16:140–43.

Chapter 9

1. *Ha-sekhel ha-yashar.*

2. *"Hilkhot Yesodei ha-Torah,"* I.7 (p. 34b).

3. *Ḥakhamot.*

4. See below, *Rosh Amanah* 10. Here, too, we see that Abravanel imputes the pedagogic or heuristic interpretation of the principles to Maimonides.

Chapter 10

1. Maimonides himself makes this claim just after presenting the principles. See above, p. 62. The point of this chapter seems to be that Maimonides did not lack criteria by which to choose his principles. See above, chapter 3, note 31.

2. See Exodus 34:6–7. Duran, *Ohev Mishpat*, p. 13b, quotes just such an explanation from an anonymous source. See also Albo, I.3 (p. 60).

3. These thirteen rules are attributed to Rabbi Ishmael (Sifra, Introduction, section 5). They are translated, with illustrative examples, in Philip Birnbaum, *Daily Prayer Book* (New York, 1949), pp. 41–45. See also Louis Jacobs, *Studies in Talmudic Logic and Methodology* (London, 1961).

4. *Ḥakhamot.*

5. Taken from the synagogue hymn *Adon Olam,* attributed to Solomon ben Judah ibn Gabirol (1021–58).

6. I.e., the Talmud. See above, *Rosh Amanah* 8:94.

7. See Avot, I.3.

8. See above, *Rosh Amanah* 9:96.

9. See below, *Rosh Amanah* 14:135.

10. Literally: "the philosopher." Similarly in the rest of the passage.

11. See above, *Rosh Amanah* 6:82–83.

12. Literally: "there is nothing in existence other than God and His works."

13. *Guide,* I.51–60.

14. Literally: "absolutely invisible to us."

15. A play on the word for "few" in the verse just quoted.

16. The preceding paragraph is taken, almost word for word, from Bibago's *Derekh Emunah*, p. 99c. See above, Introduction, pp. 39, 40–41.

17. Maimonides calls the first principle "the foundation of all foundations" in "*Hilkhot Yesodei ha-Torah*," I.1 (p. 34a).

18. The preceding paragraph, starting with "Limitation may occur in one of three ways," is taken, almost word for word, from Bibago's *Derekh Emunah*, p. 101d.

19. Literally: "after absolute nothingness."

20. That is to say, the beginning of his commentary to the first mishnah in *Ḥelek*. In Wolf's translation (Twersky, p. 414): "However, resurrection is only for the righteous."

21. Genesis Rabbah 13.6 reads: "It [the might of rain] is as important as resurrection. . . . R. Ḥiyya b. Aba said: It is greater than resurrection, for whereas resurrection is for man alone, this is for man and beast; again, resurrection is for Israel, whereas this is for Israel and the nations." At Ta'anit 7a we read: "R. Abbahu said: The day when rain falls is greater than the day of the revival of the dead for the revival of the dead is for the righteous only whereas rain is both for the righteous and the wicked." See also Sifri Deuteronomy 32 and 306 and Midrash Tehilim 117.

22. Ta'anit 25a. There are some minor variations between the text cited by Abravanel, that found in the standard editions of the Talmud, and that given by Henry Malter in his scientifically edited edition of *The Tractate Ta'anit of the Babylonian Talmud* (Philadelphia, 1928). I present here the translation of the Soncino edition, bracketing words not found in Abravanel's text. The "thirteen rivers of balsam oil" are mentioned in the Palestinian Talmud (Avodah Zarah III.1) and several places in the *Zohar*. See R. J. Z. Werblowsky, *Joseph Karo: Lawyer and Mystic* (Philadelphia, 1977), p. 130n.

23. The preceding paragraph is taken, almost word for word, from Bibago's *Derekh Emunah*, p. 101b.

24. *Editio princeps* has the obviously incorrect reading, "Rabbi Joshua b. Yoḥai."

25. I deviate from the Soncino text here (which has "thirteen stools of gold") to follow Abravanel's reading.

26. Rashi, *ad. loc.*: "It is not proper to proclaim you in this fashion because I have heard that the rainbow is nothing but a sign of the covenant that the world will not be destroyed and if there is a perfect saint in a generation, there is no need for this sign."

27. I.e., the appearance of a rainbow.

28. P. 77b.

Chapter 11

1. *Miẓvot ma'asiyot*.

2. *Takhlit* here and throughout the chapter.

3. Albo has "those who profess the Torah." See note 6 below.

4. Sanhedrin, 99a.

5. Deuteronomy 22:6–7.

6. This passage is taken almost word for word from *Sefer ha-Ikkarim* I.14 (pp. 123–24), although it is not introduced as a quotation. The bracketed material is found in Albo's text, not Abravanel's.

7. *Hitba'er bi-ḥakhmah.*

8. Abravanel might mean Maimonides' *"Hilkhot Avodah Zarah"* ("Laws of Idolatry"), but this is unlikely because principle 5 forms the substance of *"Hilkhot Avodah Zarah,"* II.1 (p. 67a).

9. Pp. 123–24. See above, note 6.

10. Exodus 22:35 and Deuteronomy 11:13 (on which latter see Ta'anit 2a).

11. I.14 (p. 127).

12. I.14 (p. 128).

13. *Dat.* This proposition is directed against Albo, who held that the principles ought to be common to all divine laws *(datot).*

14. On the distinction between natural and conventional law in Albo, see *Sefer ha-Ikkarim,* I.7 (pp. 78–80), and Ralph Lerner, "Natural Law in Albo's *Book of Roots,*" in Joseph Cropsey, ed., *Ancients and Moderns* (New York, 1964), pp. 132–47.

15. *Ikkarim,* I.3 (p. 62). The rest of the paragraph paraphrases Albo's text.

16. *Ko'aḥ ha-middaber.*

17. *Middaber.*

18. *Hakdamot tiviyot.* In this proposition Abravanel appears to be arguing against the axiomatic interpretation of the principles.

19. *Ha-ẓurot ha-tiviyot.* On this expression see H. A. Wolfson, *Crescas' Critique of Aristotle* (Cambridge, Mass., 1929), p. 578.

20. *Ẓiyur.*

21. I.e., the substratum.

22. Literally, "to the beliefs."

23. *Tekhunatah;* i.e., that toward which one is disposed by one's disposition.

24. This work, *Vision of God* in English, is lost; see Netanyahu, p. 85. This ninth proposition is directed against Crescas's second objection to Maimonides. See above, *Rosh Amanah* 4:72.

25. Here, *ma'amarot;* everywhere else in the *Rosh Amanah, hakdamot.*

Chapter 12

1. See above, *Rosh Amanah* 3:66 and 6:80–84.

2. Possibly a reference to Aristotle's discussion of *sophia* and *phronesis* toward the end of book 6 of the *Nichomachean Ethics.*

3. See above, *Rosh Amanah* 10:102–104.

4. French Talmudist. See above, Introduction, pp. 22–23.

5. I.e., that God is incorporeal.

6. Albo: "This seems to be correct view as held by the Rabbis of the Talmud. For in speaking of Elisha ben Abuyah they quote the biblical expression." See below, note 11.

7. Elisha, an apostate Tanna, was called *Aḥer,* "the other one."

8. Albo: "his Creator." See below, note 11.

9. Ḥagiga 15a.

10. Albo: "but whose sole intention is to interpret the texts according to his opinion." See following note.

11. Abravanel follows the text of Rabad's statement, his gloss to *"Hilkhot Teshuvah,"* III.7, as it is cited by Albo (I.2, p. 53), not as it is found in the printed editions of the *Mishneh Torah.* See Twersky, *Rabad,* pp. 282–86 and Joseph Karo's *Kesef Mishnah* to *"Hilkhot Teshuvah,"* III.7. Karo quotes Albo's version, saying that it might be the correct text. The rest of the passage, which Abravanel presents as a continuation of Rabad's gloss (beginning with "This view . . ."), is actually Albo's (pp. 53–54).

12. The words "of the Christians" *(ha-Noẓerim)* were censored from the Cremona edition and a blank spot was left where the word should have been. See Meir Benihu, *Ha-Defus ha-Ivri bi-Cremona* (Jerusalem, 1971), p. 73. Subsequent editions, most of which appear to have been based on the Cremona text, supply the want in various ways. Koenigsberg, 1860, reads "their faith" while Tel Aviv, 1958, has "the belief of Ẓadok and Boethus."

13. Literally: "dispute the true felicity [*haẓlaḥa*]."

14. The two preceding paragraphs are largely based on Bibago's *Derekh Emunah* III.5 (p. 102c).

15. Emending *meẓuyar* to *meẓuyah.*

16. *Ḥok.*

17. The preceding paragraph is taken almost verbatim from Bibago's *Derekh Emunah,* III.5 (p. 102c).

18. This sentence presents several syntactical difficulties and may very well be corrupt. I have rearranged its parts and translated it according to the best interpretation I could give it.

19. Literally: "Perfection of his mind." That is, Elisha was neither ignorant nor insane.

20. *Ha-sevara ha-goveret.*

21. See above, *Rosh Amanah* 3: 66–67.

22. Emending the text from "fifth proposition." See above, *Rosh Amanah* 8:92–95.

23. That is not to say that they desire to act differently, but that they have no desires at all.

24. Maimonides' fifth principle; see above, *Rosh Amanah* 1:57.

25. "Ordered" in the sense of "prearranged."

26. The bracketed words are not found in the verse.

27. *Sar.*

28. Commentary to Deuteronomy 4:19.

29. See Gerald Friedlander, trans., *Pirke de [Chapters of] Rabbi Eliezer* (London, 1916), pp. 176–77.

30. See *Ateret Zekenim,* chapter 16 (Warsaw edition, pp. 60–61).

31. See above, *Rosh Amanah* 1:57.

32. See T. J. Berakhot, IX.1.

33. See *Ateret Zekenim,* chapter 16 (p. 60).

34. Sanhedrin, 38b.

35. Joshua 5:13–15.

36. Rachel was pleading the cause of her children and so, it was thought, the dead could be asked to intercede on behalf of the living.

37. Menaḥot 110a. The terms "westwards" and "eastwards" seem to be transposed here. See the note to the Soncino edition.

38. The word "Christian" was censored from the Cremona text. See above, note 12. In the copy of that edition held in the library of the Hebrew Union College—Jewish Institute of Religion (Cincinnati), the entire sentence was inked over.

39. Ta'anit 2a.

40. See above, *Rosh Amanah* 11:106–7.

41. See above, *Rosh Amanah* 1:57.

42. *Ikkarit.*

Chapter 13

1. In this context Abravanel uses the word *niẓḥi* for "eternal." In *Rosh Amanah* 16 (p. 146) Abravanel defines it as "uninterrupted existence." It means "eternity *a parte post*" as distinguished from *kadmon,* which I usually translate as "eternity *a parte ante*" and which Abravanel (*Rosh Amanah* 16:146) defines as pertaining to something which "has no beginning and does not exist in time." The objection may be found above, *Rosh Amanah* 3:67–69.

2. S. Rosenblatt, trans., *Book of Beliefs and Opinions* (New Haven, 1948), III.7 (pp. 157–67).

3. *Ha-sekhel vi-ha-sevara.*

4. *Or ha-Shem,* III.5.1 (p. 78a).

5. *Ikkarim,* III.13 (pp. 114–17).

6. *Mevuar bi-aẓmo.*

7. Following Aryeh Albert (editor of the Tel Aviv, 1958, edition), I emend the text from *tivaser* to *tikhasher.*

8. I.e., he died.

9. *Al mah shehu alav.*

10. *Kol beruei matah uma'alah.* For a similar expression, and possibly Abravanel's source, see Philip Birnbaum, *High Holiday Prayer Book* (New York, 1951), p. 657.

11. I follow the Cremona edition in emending the text from *aḥer* to *eḥad.*

12. To this argument for the eternity of the Torah.

13. *Torah.*

14. Which were changed and superseded.

15. For a definition of the term "conventional law" see Albo, *Ikkarim,* I.7 (pp. 78–80) and above, chapter 11, note 14.

16. *Torah.*

17. *Mikri* ("accidental" in the philosophic sense).

18. *Li-azmuto.*

19. The commandment to recall the Exodus is found at Exodus 13:3.

20. I.e., of the Messiah.

21. I.e., from Egypt.

22. For a general discussion of Abravanel's views on prophecy see Alvin Reines, *Maimonides and Abarbanel on Prophecy* (Cincinnati, 1970).

23. I.e., just before the previously cited verse.

24. *Shefa.*

25. Abravanel uses the perfect tense. The biblical text, however, has the imperfect with *vav*-consecutive.

26. *Ha-otot,* following Cremona.

27. *Bi-matkonet zot ha-beḥina.*

28. I.e., Torah and bread.

29. This phrase is taken from the *Nishmat* prayer. See Philip Birnbaum, *Daily Prayer Book* (New York, 1949), p. 331.

30. I.e., even less of the wisdom involved in the creation of all the rest of the universe is understood.

31. *Heḥliti.*

32. See I Kings 18.

33. Following Cremona in emending the text from *l'ha'amid* to *l'hatmid.*

34. Abravanel alters the verse slightly.

35. Makkot III.16.

36. Avodah Zarah 18a. Abravanel's text, which I follow, varies slightly from the standard version. See Albo, III.29, p. 273.

37. The verse means that hell waits.

38. I.e., God.

39. Sanhedrin, 111a. Abravanel's text, which I follow, differs from the standard version in some important particulars. See Albo, III.29, p. 269.

40. Shabbat, 118b. Abravanel's text, which I follow, varies slightly from the standard version.

41. P. 127. "The same reason" refers to Albo's claim that none of the specific commandments of the Torah should be construed as principles.

42. See above, *Rosh Amanah* 1:61.

43. Literally: "were shorthanded." See Isaiah 59:1.

44. Abravanel's text to this point differs from the standard version. I follow Abravanel.

45. Fred Rosner, trans., *Moses Maimonides' Commentary on the Mishnah: Introduction to Seder Zeraim and Commentary on Tractate Berachoth* (New York, 1975), p. 48.

46. Rosner, pp. 48–49. The rabbinic reference is to Megillah, 2b.

47. The citing of the verse here makes sense in the context of a passage at Bava Meẓia 59b in which the verse is quoted and which Maimonides (*"Hilkhot Yesodei ha-Torah,"* IX.1) construes as teaching that no prophet may innovate in the Torah.

48. While the principle asserts that *God* will never change the Torah.

49. See above, *Rosh Amanah* 1:61.

50. Sifri to Deuteronomy 13:1.

51. See above, *Rosh Amanah* 3:68.

52. *"Hilkhot Yesodei ha-Torah,"* IX.1–5.

53. This phrase is part of one of the hermeneutical principles attributed to R. Ishmael. See Philip Birnbaum, *Daily Prayer Book* (New York, 1949), p. 45.

54. Megillah, 2b.

55. See Sifri on Deuteronomy 17:11 and T. J. Horayot, I.1. Abravanel quotes the version of this statement given by Rashi in his comment on the verse.

56. See Avot, I.1.

57. Moed Katan, 5a. I.e., build fences around the Torah.

58. I.e., Albo.

59. See above, *Rosh Amanah* 3:68.

60. This phrase is taken from the Sabbath Eve Kiddush. See Philip Birnbaum, *Daily Prayer Book* (New York, 1949), p. 289.

61. I.e., the tenth day of Tishrei, the Day of Atonement.

62. In other words, Purim and the Day of Atonement will not be abrogated because they do not recall events which will be superceded by the Messianic redemption.

63. See above, *Rosh Amanah* 3:68.

64. Midrash Tanḥuma.

65. I.e., Rome.

66. Tanḥuma on Leviticus 11:17. Ed. Solomon Buber (Vilna, 1885), p. 32. The point is that the law prohibiting swine's flesh will not change.

67. *Hora'at sha'ah.* See Horayot 6a and *Enzyklopedia Talmudit* (Jerusalem, 1957), vol. 8, col. 512.

68. Ḥullin, 17a.

69. Although this dictum does not seem to appear in Tanḥuma, very similar

expressions are found in Leviticus Rabbah 22.10 and Deuteronomy Rabbah 4.9. Albo cites it at III.16 (p. 148).

70. See above, *Rosh Amanah* 3:68.

71. Song of Songs Rabbah.

72. Abravanel adds a phrase here, explaining the midrash's term for "intermediary."

73. Abravanel adds here: "i.e., is likely to be forgotten."

74. *Song of Songs Rabbah,* I.2,4 (Soncino ed., pp. 25–26). Albo cites this passage at III.19 (pp. 180–81).

75. See note 67 above.

76. I.e., the Oral Torah.

77. See above, note 55.

78. Abravanel's meaning here is not clear to me.

Chapter 14

1. Following Albert's addition. The word is lacking in the *editio princeps.* The objection itself is found above, *Rosh Amanah* 3:69.

2. The text reads "fifth," which is obviously incorrect.

3. See above, *Rosh Amanah* 9:96–97.

4. *Meddabberim b'ruah ha-kodesh.* I.e., the authors of the Hagiographa. On this phrase see Husik's comment in his edition of the *Sefer ha-Ikkarim,* vol. 4, part ii, p. 556.

5. See above, *Rosh Amanah* 10:99–100.

6. *Announcer of Redemption* is the third of Abravanel's three messianic works. It was first published in Salonika in 1526 (republished in Amsterdam in 1643 and in Offenbach, 1767).

7. Sanhedrin, 99a.

8. *Mashmia Yeshuah,* Introduction. Page 2c of the Offenbach, 1767, edition.

9. By the "possible time" of the Messiah's coming, Abravanel means that in one sense the coming of the Messiah is dependent upon the behavior of the Jews. Should they repent of their sins and merit the coming of the Messiah, he will come immediately, even if it is before the time ordained for his coming by God.

10. Sanhedrin, 98a. The passage in question is a discussion of Isaiah 60:22: . . . *I the Lord will hasten it in its time.* It reads as follows: "R. Alexandri said: "R. Joshua b. Levi pointed out a contradiction. It is written, *in its time* [will the Messiah come], whilst it is also written, *I the Lord will hasten it!*—If they are worthy, I will hasten it; if not he will come at the due time.'" Abravanel's text reverses the dictum, putting the negative possibility before the positive one. See also Exodus Rabbah XXV.12, Saadia Gaon's *Emunot vi-Deot,* VIII.2 (pp. 294–95 in the Rosenblatt translation), *Mashmia Yeshua,* p. 34a, and *Yeshuot Meshiho* (Koenigsberg, 1860), pp. 11b–12a and 25b–26a.

11. I.e., the Messiah.

12. Sanhedrin, 98a.

13. I.e., before the final time appointed by God. The point is that Israel has "used up" the possibility of bringing about the coming of the Messiah by virtue of its own behavior and must now wait for the time ordained by God.

14. Sanhedrin, 94a.

15. Ibid. Abravanel's text varies slightly from the standard version.

16. I.e., that he will not have to fight because God will be fighting his battles for him.

17. Sanhedrin, 94a.

18. Sanhedrin, 98a.

19. Sanhedrin, 97a.

20. I.e., in referring to the Messiah they commonly used those expressions. So, R. Hillel was not referring to the actual coming of the Messiah.

21. Sanhedrin, 99a.

22. Ibid.

23. R. Hillel. The argument, as Abravanel explains at *Yeshuot Meshiḥo* 26a, is that the phrase *unto thee* can be interpreted to mean, "by your merit."

24. The point being that according to the prophet, who lived after Hezekiah, repentance will bring the Messiah. This proves that even after Hezekiah Israel can still cause the coming of the Messiah through its own deeds.

Chapter 15

1. The sixth objection may be found above, *Rosh Amanah* 3:69.

2. Following Albert's addition. The word is lacking in the *editio princeps*.

3. See above, *Rosh Amanah* 10:100.

4. See above, *Rosh Amanah* 6:82–83, 9:96–97. See also below, *Rosh Amanah* 21:187, and 23:198.

5. Sanhedrin, 91b.

6. Emphasis added.

7. XX.10 (Soncino edition, p. 169).

8. I.e., after the resurrection.

9. See Ezekiel 27 and Sanhedrin, 90b.

10. I do not know to what Abravanel is referring here. It is possible that this statement is related to Albo, IV, 35, pp. 349–51.

11. I.e., in the subsequent discussion in the Talmud.

12. Joshua Finkel, ed., *Maimonides' Treatise on Resurrection (PAAJR, 1939)*, section 22 (p. 15). The bracketed words do not appear in Finkel's text.

13. Emending the text from *keshet* to *kasheh*.

14. I.e., so that people would believe in it, notwithstanding the difficulties such belief presents.

15. *Ha-mishnah ha-mekubelet.* This idea that the doctrine of the resurrection is hard to accept is found in Saadia's *Emunot vi-Deot,* VII.3 (p. 238 of the Rosenblatt translation).

16. Emending the text from *hu* to *ve-ha.*

17. See *"Hilkhot Teshuvah,"* III, 8.

Chapter 16

1. Because one will no longer have to accept the Messiah and the resurrection as matters of faith. For the objection, see above, *Rosh Amanah* 3:69.

2. See Genesis 15.

3. I.e., the coming of the Messiah and the resurrection.

4. Joshua Finkel, ed., *Maimonides' Treatise on Resurrection* (New York, 1939), section 23 (p. 16).

5. On Moses ha-Kohen, see I. Twersky, *Rabad of Posquières* (Cambridge, 1962), p. 179.

6. In proposition six (*Rosh Amanah* 11:106–107), Abravanel says that the principles are not taken from particular commandments. The eighth objection may be found above, *Rosh Amanah* 3:69–70.

7. *Sefer ha-Miẓvot,* Principle VII (Chavel edition, vol. 2, pp. 384–90).

8. This is the beginning of Abravanel's own answer to the problem as distinguished from that of R. Moses ha-Kohen.

9. This is taken from the Passover Haggadah. See E. D. Goldschmidt, *The Passover Haggadah* (Jerusalem, 1960), pp. 46, 122.

10. See above, *Rosh Amanah* 1:58–60.

11. I.e., revelation.

12. *Devekut.*

13. See above, *Rosh Amanah* 3:70.

14. See above, *Rosh Amanah* 1:57.

15. See above, *Rosh Amanah* 8:92–95.

16. The discussion here turns on the fact that the Hebrew *kadmon* can mean either "eternal *a parte ante*" or "earlier."

17. Abravanel is here arguing against the claim of those Neoplatonic and Aristotelian philosophers who argued that God was the Creator of the world in the sense of being its cause, but that the world was at the same time actually uncreated, coexisting eternally with God.

18. *Niẓḥi.*

19. Plato's doctrine of creation is set forth in his *Timaeus.*

20. Maimonides made this statement in the fourth principle. See above, *Rosh Amanah* 1:57.

21. *Editio princeps* has "fourteen."

22. P. 282.

23. Albo and Crescas.

24. The point of all this is that Abravanel is trying to show that Maimonides holds that the principle of creation is the second principle after the principle of unity.

25. See above, *Rosh Amanah* 3:70.

26. Makkot, 24a.

27. See above, *Rosh Amanah* 3:70.

28. See above, *Rosh Amanah* 1:60.

29. *Beḥira.*

30. See above, *Rosh Amanah* 3:70.

31. See above, *Rosh Amanah* 11:108–10.

32. "*Hilkhot Teshuvah,*" V.3 (p. 87a).

33. I.e., the Torah.

34. *Ikkarim.*

35. "*Hilkhot Teshuvah,*" V.4 (p. 87b).

36. "*Hilkhot Teshuvah,*" V.5 (p. 88a).

37. Ibid. (87b–88a). Abravanel's text lacks the bracketed words.

38. See above, *Rosh Amanah* 3:70.

39. See above, *Rosh Amanah* 8:92–95.

40. See above, *Rosh Amanah* 3:70–71.

41. See above, *Rosh Amanah* 10:98–105.

42. See above, *Rosh Amanah* 1:61.

43. See above, *Rosh Amanah* 3:71.

44. See above, *Rosh Amanah* 1:58. *Editio princeps* has "tenth principle."

45. See above, *Rosh Amanah* 3:71.

46. The sixth proposition. See above, *Rosh Amanah* 11:106–7.

47. Ta'anit, 2a.

Chapter 17

1. See above, *Rosh Amanah* 4:72.

2. See above, *Rosh Amanah* 7:85–91.

3. I.e., the commandment related to God, the Commander, and to the Jewish people, the commanded.

4. I.e., Crescas.

5. *Miẓad aẓmo.*

6. Of the Decalogue.

7. *Editio princeps* reads "60."

8. The Hebrew letters of the tetragrammaton.

9. P. 147.

10. *Guide,* I.61, p. 148. The rabbinic reference is to Sotah 38a. Abravanel's text varies slightly from the ibn Tibbon version of the *Guide.*

11. Literally: "to them."

12. I.e., that it wasn't God but His glory which commanded belief in His existence. I have not been able to find this passage in the *Sefer ha-Ikkarim*. Albo discusses Maimonides's interpretation of Exodus 20:2 at I.14 (pp. 128–29). He cites Exodus 20:17 at II.17 (p. 102) and II.28 (p. 178). He cites Numbers 14:14 at IV.47 (p. 460).

13. The antecedent is unclear. That God, not the Torah, is the correct antecedent is evidenced by a parallel passage in Rosh Amanah 20:177.

14. *Or ha-Shem, "Haza'a"* (p. 2a).

15. See above, *Rosh Amanah* 4:72.

16. See above, *Rosh Amanah* 11:108–10.

17. This phrase is taken from the *"Ahavah Rabbah"* prayer. See Philip Birnbaum, *Daily Prayer Book* (New York, 1949), p. 76.

18. The phrase in brackets is added by Albert in his edition.

19. I.e., its content.

20. *"Hilkhot Yesodei ha-Torah,"* I.6 (p. 34b).

21. Emphasis added.

22. See above, *Rosh Amanah* 1:56. This is not exactly what Maimonides says. He wrote, "This is a positive commandment," but does not specify if the commandment relates to *belief* or to *knowledge*. On this, see Introduction, note 78.

23. *Sefer ha-Mizvot*, vol. 1, p. 2. Maimonides uses this phrase there with regard to the first commandment (belief in God's existence) as well. See p. 1.

24. *Azmi.*

Chapter 18

1. See above, *Rosh Amanah* 4:73.

2. *Sefer ha-Mizvot*, positive commandment 1.

3. On the *Halakhot Gedolot* see above, Introduction, p. 42.

4. *Editio princeps* has "Maimonides."

5. The argument of the twentieth objection.

6. *Editio princeps* has "Maimonides."

7. Deuteronomy 26:1–29:8.

8. *Editio princeps* has "Maimonides."

9. According to Crescas (see above, *Rosh Amanah* 4:72), matters of faith cannot be commanded.

10. Because there are three commandments in the utterance which the Israelites heard from God. Adding those to the 611 taught by Moses, one gets 614.

11. Crescas does not make this last claim explicitly. That Abravanel did not mean this to be a quotation is shown by the fact that he did not introduce it with the term

"*zeh leshono,*" with which he almost invariably introduces direct quotations. Abravanel seems to be making explicit an argument he finds implicit in Crescas's position.

12. *Aval zeh ein inyan lo.*

13. It would have been better for Crescas, because then the total would still come to 613. This turns Crescas's argument around, for he also cited the authors of the *Azharot* to support *his* position.

14. The "first root" is Maimonides' first principle of faith which Abravanel (see above, *Rosh Amanah* 7:85–89) construes as affirming, not simply that God exists, but that He exists necessarily and perfectly.

15. The "root of unity" is Maimonides' second principle of faith, that God is one.

16. This claim makes excellent sense in the context of a position which maintains that all Israel were taught these two beliefs directly by God. See *Guide,* II.33 (p. 364).

17. Shir ha-Shirim [Song of Songs] Rabbah 1:2, 2. I quote from the Soncino edition (London, 1939), pp. 22–23.

18. I.e., commandments heard directly from God are like "the kisses of His mouth."

19. Following the Talmudic principle that the Torah follows no chronological order. See, for example, Pesaḥim 6b.

20. I.e., that of R. Joshua of Siknin.

21. Abravanel's text continues with the words, "Thus it said, *Let him kiss me with the kisses of His mouth.*"

22. It is not known to whom Abravanel is referring. I would like to suggest, however, that he is actually referring to himself! In his parallel discussion in his *Commentary on Exodus* (see above, Introduction, note 84) he introduces both these passages in support of the position which he adopts there; but he introduces them there, however, in his own name. Reading Abravanel's response to the "contemporary scholars" carefully, we see that he understands the passage as affirming that *I am the Lord thy God* "signifies the acceptance of the sovereignty of Heaven," and that it serves as "the pillar and principle of all the commandments." This is his true opinion as expressed in the *Commentary.* To it he only adds here that God "commanded the Israelites to accept the yoke of His sovereignty." I would suggest that Abravanel does not introduce the arguments as his own here because he feels obliged to continue in the role he adopted, that of defender of Maimonides. See above, Introduction, p. 49–50, and below, *Rosh Amanah* 23, note 24.

23. This introduces a new argument against Maimonides, one not directly grounded in the exegesis of the Decalogue.

24. This, at least, is the way Naḥmanides (in his gloss to the first positive commandment in Maimonides' *Sefer ha-Miẓvot*) represents the thinking of the author of the *Halakhot Gedolot.*

25. Mekhilta, Tractate Baḥodesh, VI. Translated by Jacob Z. Lauterbach in

Mekilta de Rabbi Ishmael, 3 vols. (Philadelphia, 1933), 2:237–38. Abravanel's text presents the colloquy as taking place between the king and his subjects (e.g., "Issue decrees upon *us*"). I have translated the Hebrew word *malkhut* as "sovereignty" where Lauterbach has "reign."

26. I.e., the "contemporary scholars" (see note 22 above) who attacked Maimonides on the basis of rabbinic material which they present and which they claim does not interpret Exodus 20:2 as he does.

27. See Sanhedrin, 56b.

28. *Ol Malkhuto.* See Berakhot, 13a, b.

29. Following Lauterbach's text (see note 25 above).

30. Abravanel distinguishes commandments which involve some actual practice or action from those which involve matters of faith alone above in *Rosh Amanah* 11:106–7. All of Maimonides' principles of faith, he says there, relate to the second kind of commandment.

31. Exodus 14–20.

32. Chavel translation, p. 285.

33. Berakhot, 13a, b.

34. Chavel translation, pp. 286–87.

35. Literally, "the Rabbi."

36. Which is just the opposite of what the "contemporary scholars" sought to prove from this passage. David Hartman, *Maimonides: Torah and Philosophic Quest* (Philadelphia, 1976), p. 221, note 51, points out that Naḥmanides understands the first commandment as establishing God's *juridical* authority while Maimonides understands the commandment in an *ontological* sense, relating directly to belief in God's existence, not only His right to command. Hartman says: "The fundamental, logical difference between a juridical and ontological understanding of the first commandment of the Decalogue is that the former implies a necessary connection between the first and the rest of the commandments, whereas to Maimonides, one could understand the meaning of *I am the Lord* independent of further legislation." Hartman's interpretation is strengthened by the fact that Naḥmanides adduces the passage from the Mekhilta concerning a king entering a country as support for his position. This passage clearly relates to God's *right* to promulgate commandments.

37. This verse is cited at Sanhedrin, 34a. It is used to prove that one biblical verse may "convey several teachings."

38. On the relationship between commandments containing both positive and negative injunctions, see Maimonides's *Sefer ha-Miẓvot,* principle 6 (Chavel translation, vol. 2, pp. 383–84).

39. *Sefer ha-Miẓvot,* vol. 2, p. 1.

40. Horayot 8b, *s.v. "li-min ha-yom."*

41. *Ba'al ha-Talmud.*

42. The question raised in the Talmud here is how can we know that Numbers

15:29–30 refers to idolatry. Two other answers [offered by R. Judah the Prince and R. Joshua ben Levi] precede that of the School of R. Ishmael. The phrase, "the best proof was given at first" refers to their answers. The point of all this is that Abravanel first offers an interpretation of the School of R. Ishmael's suggestion which makes it compatible with Maimonides' position and then points out [in case that interpretation should be rejected] that the School of R. Ishmael's suggestion is in any event not accepted by the Talmud.

43. Midrash Tanḥuma on Numbers, ed. Buber (Vilna, 1885), pp. 26–27.

44. Numbers 4:17–6:59.

45. Leviticus 19–21.

46. Leviticus Rabbah XXIV.5 (Soncino edition [London, 1939], pp. 307–8).

47. The *Sh'ma* (Deuteronomy 6:4).

48. Nahmanides raises no objection to Maimonides' claim (*Sefer ha-Miẓvot*, positive commandment two) that Deuteronomy 6:4 commands belief in God's unity. Also, in his commentary to the verse he writes, "This, too is a commandment . . ." See Chavel translation, p. 76.

49. Adopting Albert's textual emendation (from "*man'an*" to "*mi-ta'-am*").

50. I.e., the author of the *Halakhot Gedolot*.

51. E.g., Berakhot, 6a; Sukkah, 53b; Ḥagigah, 3a; and Gittin, 57b.

Chapter 19

1. See above, *Rosh Amanah* 5:74–75.

2. II.1 (p. 35b).

3. Ibid.

4. "*Hilkhot Deot*" ("Laws of Ethics"), I.6 (p. 48a). I do not know why Abravanel cites this as being in "*Hilkhot Yesodei ha-Torah*," unless he was using the name in a very general sense to refer to all the earlier parts of the *Sefer ha-Madda*.

5. V.1 (p. 40a).

6. Ibid.

7. VI.1 (p. 41b).

8. See above, *Rosh Amanah* 1:56.

9. The *Mishneh Torah* is also called the *Yad ha-Ḥazakah* ("Strong Hand") because it is divided into fourteen books and the numerical equivalent of the Hebrew word *yad* (hand) is fourteen.

10. Introduction to the *Mishneh Torah* (p. 4b). I do not know why Abravanel calls this work a "commentary" *(perush)*. His use of this term is particularly curious in the light of Maimonides' insistence that the *Mishneh Torah* was a *ḥibbur* (composition) as opposed to a *perush*. See I. Twersky, "Some Non-Halakhic Aspects of the *Mishneh Torah*," A. Altmann, ed., *Jewish Medieval and Renaissance Studies* (Cambridge, Mass., 1967), p. 109.

11. P. 18a.

12. *Lashon stami.*

13. P. 18a.

14. I.e., the intentions of the *Sefer ha-Miẓvot* and the *Mishneh Torah* are different. Therefore they are structured differently.

15. See above, *Rosh Amanah* 1:57.

16. I have not been able to locate the source of this citation, if indeed it is a reference to any particular text. For similar expressions, see Sotah 31a. It is possible that Abravanel's source here was Maimonides' discussion of the love of God near the beginning of his commentary to *Ḥelek*. See the Wolf translation in Twersky, p. 406.

17. VII.1–5 (pp. 42a–42b).

18. VII.6 (p. 43a).

19. VIII.1 (p. 43b).

20. IX.1 (p. 44b).

21. II.8 (p. 36a).

22. V.4 (p. 40a–40b).

23. See above, *Rosh Amanah* 10:100.

24. Pp. 91a–92a.

25. See above, *Rosh Amanah* 5:75–76.

26. On the distinction between negation *(shelilah)* and admonition *(azharah)* see *Sefer ha-Miẓvot,* principle eight (Chavel, vol. 2, pp. 390–96). Negations are simple negative statements while admonitions are negative commands.

27. P. 392.

28. Literally: "them."

29. Emphasis added.

30. Pp. 383–84.

31. I.7 (p. 34b).

32. Pp. 409–11.

33. See above, *Rosh Amanah* 1:57.

34. See *Guide* II.31 (p. 359).

35. See above, note 30.

36. See above, *Rosh Amanah* 1:57.

37. Sanhedrin, 99a. Abravanel's text, which I follow, differs somewhat from the standard version.

Chapter 20

1. For statements of the twenty-fourth, -fifth, and -sixth objections, see above, *Rosh Amanah* 5:76–78.

2. *"Hilkhot Yesodei ha-Torah,"* I.1–3 (p. 34a).

3. Ibid., I.6 (p. 34b).

4. Pp. 235–41.

5. The Hebrew expression here translated includes the word *sham*, usually a spatial designation.

6. The *editio princeps* has the singular.

7. *Vi–stam devarav.*

8. *Emet.* In the present context I follow Hyamson in translating this word as "real" instead of the more customary "true."

9. *"Hilkhot Yesodei ha-Torah,"* I.4 (p. 34a).

10. *Bi-haskama u-vi-shivui.*

11. *Sippuk.* On the technical terms in this paragraph see Shalom Rosenberg, "Torat ha-Shemot bi-Philosophia ha-Yehudit bimei ha-Benayim," *Iyyun* 27 (1976–77):105–44.

12. Abravanel is adumbrating a correspondence theory of truth; that appears to be the point of his discussion here.

13. *Emet.* See above, note 8.

14. *Bi-shem u-vi-gader.*

15. Possibly: "are not rational."

16. Certain forms of idolatry were thought to involve attempts to manipulate the celestial beings *(elyonim).*

17. The tetragrammaton.

18. In *Rosh Amanah* 17:153, Abravanel says that the tetragrammaton indicates necessary existence.

19. *Elohim.*

20. This is a play on a common Talmudic expression. See, for example, Bava Kamma, 107a.

21. See Rashi and Radak *ad. loc.*

22. See Avot II.19.

23. *Mofet azmi.*

24. Emending the text from "in the heavens . . ."

25. Abravanel here uses the Hebrew of the Aramaic expression in Jeremiah 10:11.

26. *Emet.* See above, note 8.

27. Literally: "style of the words."

28. See Guide, II.6 (pp. 261–65).

29. Tetragrammaton.

30. *Elohim.*

31. See above, *Rosh Amanah* 17:153.

32. See the beginning of the present chapter.

33. *"Hilkhot Yesodei ha-Torah,"* I.4 (p. 34a).

34. *"Hilkhot Yesodei ha-Torah,"* I.5 (pp. 34a–b).

35. *Meshutaf.*

36. In his introduction to Part II of the *Guide* (pp. 235–41) Maimonides assumes

the eternity of the world for the sake of showing that God's existence, unity, and incorporeality can be demonstrated even on that assumption. His own position, however, as far as Abravanel is concerned, is that the world is created and that God's existence, unity, and incorporeality can also be demonstrated on that assumption.

37. See Crescas, *Or ha-Shem*, II.iii.1 (p. 40b).

38. I.e., without adopting these opinions himself.

39. Abravanel's discussion here, and his citation of these verses, may be better understood if it is pointed out that Maimonides cites two of these verses [Deuteronomy 33:26 and Psalms 68:5] at *Guide*, I.70 (p. 171), to prove that God dominates and rules the earth. At the end of that chapter Maimonides says that the phrase *The Rider of the Heavens* (Pslams 68:5) signifies: "He Who makes the encompassing heaven revolve and Who moves it in virtue of His power and will" (p. 175).

40. So Hyamson. Hebrew: *Kafar bi-ikkar.*

41. *"Hilkhot Yesodei ha-Torah,"* I.6 (p. 34b).

42. Ibid., I.5 (pp. 34a–b).

43. See above, *Rosh Amanah* 17:153–54.

44. See above, *Rosh Amanah* 11:108–10. The *editio princeps* reads "tenth proposition."

45. I.e., the tetragrammaton.

46. Literally: "Maimonides said nothing but this."

47. The Hebrew root of the word translated as "before" in Exodus 20:3.

48. Pp. 85–87.

49. "Of old" and "In former time" are translations of words related to *panim.*

50. This is a play on the Hebrew words for "other" and "later."

51. *"Hilkhot Yesodei ha-Torah,"* I.7 (p. 34b).

52. See above, *Rosh Amanah* 8:92–95.

53. *"Hilkhot Yesodei ha-Torah,"* I.7 (p. 34b).

54. *Physics* 8.10. See the translation of P. Wickstead and F. Cornford (London, 1929), 2:411.

55. *Vi-im Tomar.* This is a common rabbinic expression used to introduce questions. Based on Leviticus 25:20, it was widely used by the Tosafists.

56. Possibly: "gods."

57. Abravanel here refers to a dispute discussed by Albo at *Ikkarim*, II.12–13 (pp. 66–81), especially p. 80). See also Harry A. Wolfson, "The Plurality of Immovable Movers in Aristotle and Averroës," *Harvard Studies in Classical Philology* 63 (1958): 233–53, especially pp. 243–45.

58. I.e., the omnipotent God is the necessarily existent Lord.

59. *"Hilkhot Yesodei ha-Torah,"* I.8 (p. 34b).

60. Ibid., I.9 (p. 34b). Maimonides is quoting a rabbinic expression here. See, for example, Berakhot, 31b.

61. Ibid.

Chapter 21

1. See above, *Rosh Amanah* 5:78.

2. See above, *Rosh Amanah* 9:96–97.

3. This seems to be a reference to *Guide,* I.35, although Maimonides does not use the expression *"ha-she'elot ha-yekarot"* ("the great questions") there.

4. Sanhedrin, X.1. The twenty-eighth objection may be found above, *Rosh Amanah* 5:78–79.

5. Bekhorot, 30b. Abravanel is saying that in disagreeing with Rashi he means no disrespect and that Rashi's reputation will not be harmed by his criticism of him.

6. *Sevara.*

7. *Musag bi-iyyun.*

8. *Ha-shorashim ha-tiv'iyim.*

9. Thus, if one claims to believe in resurrection on the basis of tradition, one's claim is ultimately based on the Torah.

10. Literally: "from their hearts."

11. *Muskelet.*

12. Sanhedrin, 90a.

13. The "true opinion" refers to resurrection. This claim does not seem to follow directly from the preceding unless one understands "by itself" to mean "without reference to whether or not it is taught by the Torah."

14. Abravanel discusses the lessons contained in the order and interrelationship of the principles in proposition five (see above, *Rosh Amanah* 10:98–105). That discussion seems to be object of the reference here.

Chapter 22

1. See above, *Rosh Amanah* 16:144–51.

2. See above, *Rosh Amanah* 11:107–8.

3. Sanhedrin, X.1.

4. See above, *Rosh Amanah* 4:72.

5. Sanhedrin, X.1.

6. *Guide,* III.17 (p. 464) and *"Hilkhot Teshuvah"* ("Laws of Repentance"), III.8 (p. 84b).

7. See above, p. 156.

8. *"Hilkhot Yesodei ha-Torah,"* I.1 (p. 34a).

9. This is possibly a reference to Duran who says (*Ohev Mishpat,* Introduction, chapter 9, p. 14b): "It would also be correct to say that the Torah only has one principle and that is to believe that everything included in the Torah is true." On this, see below, *Rosh Amanah* 23, note 22.

10. Literally: "for which there is no room."

11. Chavel translation, 1:17.

12. *Editio princeps* reads "II.14."

13. P. 282.

14. I do not understand how Abravanel can say this when just above (p. 190) he said, "But careful examination and study of Maimonides' principles will show that they are unique to our divine Torah insofar as it is divine."

15. Abu Bakr (Abubacer) is the Arabic philosophical allegorist ibn Tufayl (d. 1185). See Lenn Evan Goodman, trans., *Ibn Tufayl's Hayy ibn Yaqzan* (New York, 1972).

Chapter 23

1. This phrase is taken from the first blessing after the *Sh'ma* in the morning prayer. See Philip Birnbaum, *Daily Prayer Book* (New York, 1949), p. 78.

2. Crescas and Albo.

3. This passage appears to be based on *Sefer ha-Ikkarim*, I.17 (pp. 145–46), which, in turn, as Husik notes there, is based on Aristotle's *Posterior Analytics* I.10 and 13. Eliezer Schweid, "Bein Mishnat ha-Ikkarim shel R. Joseph Albo li-Mishnat ha-Ikkarim shel ha-Rambam," *Tarbiz* 33 (1963–64): 81, traces the attempt to establish a "science" of Torah to Duran.

4. The partial verse is Deuteronomy 12:30. The context of this verse, dealing as it does with idol worship, is instructive.

5. See Pesaḥim, 15a. The phrase means that the cases are dissimilar.

6. *Muskal Rishon.* Abravanel is here taking explicit issue with the axiomatic interpretation of the principles.

7. Sanhedrin, 99a.

8. *Dikduk.*

9. *Gezera shava.*

10. Sanhedrin, 99a.

11. See above, *Rosh Amanah* 1:60.

12. *Ba'al dat.*

13. Deuteronomy 4:9.

14. Deuteronomy 16:3.

15. Avot, II.1.

16. See above, *Rosh Amanah* 11:106.

17. See Sotah, 47b. Abravanel here imputes the pedagogical interpretation of the principles to Maimonides.

18. See above, *Rosh Amanah* 10:98–105.

19. Maimonides wrote: "For I have expatiated on these points precisely in order to teach those with no training in theology, a subject which not every man can understand" (Wolf translation in Twersky, p. 417).

20. See Judah Halevy, *Kuzari*, I.1.

21. At the beginning of the present chapter. Abravanel here distinguishes Maimonides from Crescas and Albo, exculpating the former and condemning the latter. Abravanel thus continues his defense of Maimonides.

22. This is Abravanel's statement of his own position on the question of the principles of Judaism. Although this position is usually associated with Abravanel it should be noted that the idea is anticipated by Duran and mentioned (scornfully) by Albo. Duran (*Ohev Mishpat,* Introduction, chapter 9, p. 14b) wrote:

> Know this, O reader, that the great principle in all this is to believe what is in included in the Torah about these matters. One who knowingly denies something included in the Torah is a heretic and not one of Israel. It is therefore correct to say that the [number of the] principles of the Torah is equivalent to the number of letters, words, verses, or commandments in the Torah. For he who does not admit their truth is a heretic and not one of Israel. It would also be correct to say that the Torah has only one principle and that is to believe that everything included in the Torah is true.

For Albo's rejection of this position see *Sefer ha-Ikkarim,* I.2 (p. 55).

23. See Esther 9:27 for this expression and *Sefer ha-Ikkarim,* I.14 (p. 128) for the source of this argument.

24. Abravanel's comment here is very interesting, reflecting back as it does on his defense of Maimonides in chapter 18. There he had strenuously defended Maimonides' claim that Exodus 20:2 was a commandment, ordaining belief in God's (necessary) existence. This corresponds to the first principle. Exodus 20:3, prohibiting belief in more than one God, corresponds to the second principle, that of unity. As was noted above (*Rosh Amanah* 18, note 22 and Introduction, p. 49), Abravanel in his commentary to the Decalogue rejects Maimonides' view notwithstanding his defense of him here in the *Rosh Amanah.* But here in chapter 23 he hints at his ultimate disagreement with Maimonides by saying that of the thirteen principles, "only one—or two, according to the opinion of Maimonides—is included in the Decalogue." That is, according to the opinion of Maimonides but not, as we know from the *Commentary,* according to the opinion of Abravanel. This supports my contention in the Introduction (p. 50) that Abravanel, having embarked upon a defense of Maimonides, pursued it even at the expense of masking his own opinions.

25. Exodus 20:3.

26. Sanhedrin, 99a.

27. Bava Mezia, 59a; Avot, III.12.

28. Bava Mezia, 59b. Abravanel does not follow the text exactly as we have it today. In this he follows Maimonides. See below, note 30.

29. T. J. Ḥagiga, II.1. See also Megillah, 28a.

30. Maimonides makes this statement just before the principles. In J. Kafaḥ's edition of the *Commentary on the Mishnah* (Jerusalem, 1964) it is on p. 210 (it is not in Wolf's translation).

31. I.e., Avot.

Chapter 24

1. I.e., that Judaism has no principles of faith.
2. Sanhedrin, X.1.
3. Sanhedrin, 90a.
4. I.e., appropriately.
5. I.e., that the mishnah listed principles of faith.
6. This expression is actually used at Moed Katan, 9a.
7. I.e., the beliefs listed in the mishnah.
8. Sanhedrin, 99a.
9. P. 285. *Editio princeps* has "II.14."
10. Literally: "from their mouths."
11. Avodah Zarah, 18a.
12. Literally: "as it is brought in their tradition."
13. This might be a reference to Eruvin 19a, where it is stated that only those Jews who hide the mark of their circumcision will go to Gehinnom, the implication being that no circumcised Jew will go to Gehinnom.
14. Literally: "life of the soul."
15. Shabbat 152a. Abravanel's text, which I follow, varies slightly from the standard version.
16. Berakhot, 18b.
17. This expression is derived from Habakkuk 2:4, which is quoted below.
18. The Hebrew reads *"li-olam ha-ba"* (*to* or *of* the world to come) as opposed to *"bi-olam ha-ba"* (*in* the world to come).
19. I.e., at the cost of their eternal lives.
20. *Ḥok.*
21. Abravanel divides the principles in this way above in *Rosh Amanah* 10:98–100.
22. A play on the Talmudic principle that, with respect to matters of evidence, "every man is considered a relative [close] to himself." See, for example, Sanhedrin, 9b and 10a and Yevamot, 25b.
23. Sanhedrin, 100b.
24. Sanhedrin, 101a.
25. I.e., for his own benefit. Such a person, Hillel says (Avot I.13), "passes away."
26. Abravanel has apparently conflated two independent texts here. At Ta'anit, 2b, we read: "R. Johanan said: Three keys the Holy One blessed be He has retained in His own hands and not entrusted to the hand of any messenger, namely, the Key of Rain, the Key of Childbirth, and the Key of the Resurrection of the Dead. . . . The Key of the Resurrection of the Dead, for it is written, *And ye shall know that I am the Lord, when I have opened your graves* [Ezekiel 37:13]." Deuteronomy 32:39 is used to prove the resurrection, however, at Sanhedrin, 91b.

27. Sanhedrin, 101b. See Rashi, *ad. loc., s.v. "U-vi-lashon agah."*

28. *Tanna Kamma.* I.e., by the author of our mishnah.

29. See above, *Rosh Amanah* 3, sixth objection (p. 69) and *Rosh Amanah* 15:140.

30. Sanhedrin, 90a.

31. This book (*Eternal Justice* in English) is not extant. See Netanyahu, p. 65.

32. Rosh ha-Shanah, 17a. Abravanel's text, which I follow, differs slightly from the standard version.

33. I.e., denial of resurrection, etc.

34. Hebrew dates are often indicated by quoting biblical verses in which certain letters (equivalent in letter value to the desired date) are marked off. Psalms 118:15 contains the Hebrew word *rinah* ("rejoicing"), the numerical equivalent of which is 255. Marḥeshvan, 5255 would be the fall of 1494. (The *resh* of *rinah* is marked twice, the *heh* once, and the *nun* not at all. This must have been a printer's error, for reading the date this way, one gets 1645 CE.) According to Netanyahu (pp. 62–68), Abravanel was indeed in Naples from 1492 through January 21, 1495. I do not know why he maintains (p. 73) that the book was written in Corfu in 1495.

Bibliography

In the following bibliography are listed all the works cited in the text, introduction, and notes. Works cited by Abravanel himself are marked with an asterisk. All page references to various works in the text, introduction, and notes, are to the specific editions listed here.

*Abraham ben David of Posquières. *Hasagot al ha-Mishneh Torah*.

*Abravanel, Isaac. *Ateret Zekenim*. Warsaw, 1894. Reprint: Jerusalem, 1968.

————. *Commentary on the Torah*. 3 vols. Jerusalem, 1964.

*————. *Maḥaze Shaddai* (lost).

*————. *Mashmia Yeshua*. Offenbach, 1767.

————. *Mifalot Elohim*. Venice, 1592. Reprint: Gregg International, London, 1972 (in Don Isaac Abravanel, *Opera Minora*).

————. [*Rosh Amanah*] *The Book on the Cardinal Points of Religion*. Translated by Isaac Mayer Wise. *The Israelite*, vol. 8. Cincinnati, 1862, pp. 212, 220–21, 228–29, 236–37, and 244–45.

————. [*Rosh Amanah*] *Liber de Capite Fidei*. Translated by Guilielmum Vorstium. Amsterdam, 1638 and 1684.

————. [*Rosh Amanah*] *Le principe de la foi*. Translated by B. Mossé. Avignon, 1884. Microfiche reprint: Zug, Switzerland: Inter Documentation Company, n.d.

————. *Shamayim Hadashim*. Roedelheim, 1829. Reprint: London: Gregg International, 1972 (in Don Isaac Abravanel, *Opera Minora*).

————. *Yeshuot Meshiḥo*. Koenigsberg, 1860. Reprint: Jerusalem, 1967.

*————. *Ẓedek Olamim* (lost).

*Albo, Joseph. *Sefer ha-Ikkarim*. Edited and Translated by Isaac Husik. 5 vols. Philadelphia: Jewish Publication Society of America, 1946.

Arieli, Naḥum. "Mishnato ha-Philosophit shel R. Shimon ben Ẓemaḥ Duran." Ph.D. Diss., Hebrew University, 1976.

Aristotle. *Nicomachean Ethics.*

——. *Physics.* Translated by P. H. Wickstead and F. M. Cornford. 2 vols. Cambridge: Harvard University Press, 1929.

Aristotle. *Posterior Analytics.*

Benihu, Meir. *Ha-Defus ha-Ivri bi-Cremona.* Jerusalem: Makhon Ben Zvi and Mossad ha-Rav Kook, 1970/71.

Bibago, Abraham. *Derekh Emunah.* Constantinople, 1522. Reprint editions: London: Gregg International, 1969 and Jerusalem: Makor, 1970. Selections, edited with introduction and notes by Chava Fraenkel-Goldschmidt, Jerusalem: Mossad Bialik, 1978.

Birnbaum, Philip. *Daily Prayer Book.* New York: Hebrew Publishing Company, 1949.

——. *High Holiday Prayer Book.* New York: Hebrew Publishing Company, 1951.

Blumberg, Zvi [Harry]. "*Ha-Sekhalim ha-Nivdalim bi-Mishnato shel ha-Rambam.*" In *Tarbiẓ* 40 (1971): 216–45.

Blumenthal, David R. "Maimonides' Intellectualist Mysticism and the Superiority of the Prophecy of Moses." In *Studies in Medieval Culture* 10 (1977): 51–67.

Carmoly, Eliakim. "Annalecten 8: Plagiate." In *Israelitische Annalen* 1 (1839): 101.

——. "Toledot Don Yiṣḥak Abravanel." In *Ozar Neḥmad* 2 (1857): 47–65.

*Crescas, Ḥasdai. *Or ha-Shem.* Vienna, 1859. Reprint: Tel Aviv: Offset Esther, 1963.

Duran, Shimon ben Ẓemaḥ. *Magen Avot.* Leghorn (Livorno), 1785. Reprint: Jerusalem: Makor, n.d.

——. *Ohev Mishpat.* Venice, 1590. Reprint: Tel Aviv: Zion, 1971.

Enzyclopedia Talmudit. Vol. 8. Jerusalem, 1957.

Epstein, Isidore. *The Responsa of R. Simon ben Zemah Duran as a Source of the History of the Jews in North Africa.* London: Oxford University Press, 1930. Reprint: New York: Hermon, 1968.

Fox, Marvin. "Prolegomenon" to the reprint edition of A. Cohen, *The Teachings of Maimonides.* New York: Ktav, 1968.

Friedberg, C. B. and B. *Bet Eked Sefarim.* 2nd ed. Tel Aviv: Friedberg, 1954.

Friedlaender, Michael. *Essays in the Writings of Abraham ibn Ezra.* London: Trübner, 1877. Reprint: Jerusalem, 1964.

Gersonides [Levi ben Gerson]. *Perush al ha-Torah.* Venice, 1547. Reprint: 2 vols., n.p., n.d.

Ghazzali, Abu Hamid al-. *Makasid al Falsifa.* Latin text edited by J. T. Muckle under the title *Algazel's Metaphysics.* Toronto: Institute of Medieval Studies, 1933.

Goldschmidt, E. D., ed. *The Passover Haggadah.* Jerusalem: Mossad Bialik, 1960.

Goodman, Lenn Evan, transl. *Ibn Tufayl's Hayy ibn Yaqzan.* New York: Twayne, 1972.

Goren, Shlomo. *Torat ha-Mo'adim.* Tel Aviv: A. Zioni, 1963/4.

Guttmann, Jacob. "Die Stellung des Simon ben Zemach Duran in der jüdischen Religionsphilosophie." In *MGWJ* 52 (1908): 641–72 and 53 (1909): 46–79 and 199–228.

———. *Die Religionsphilosophischen Lehren des Isaak Abravanel.* Breslau: M. and H. Marcus. 1916.

Hartman, David. *Maimonides: Torah and Philosophic Quest.* Philadelphia: Jewish Publication Society, 1976.

Harvey, Warren. "Hasdai Crescas." In *Encyclopaedia Judaica,* vol. 8, cols. 1080–85. Jerusalem: Keter, 1971.

———. "Hasdai Crescas' Critique of the Theory of the Acquired Intellect." Ph.D. diss., Columbia University, 1973.

Heller, Joseph. "Mahuto vi-Tafkido shel ha-Sekhel ha-Po'el lifi Torat ha-Rambam." In S. Bernstein and G. Churgin, ed. *Sefer ha-Yovel Likhvod S. K. Mirsky.* New York, 1958, pp. 26–42.

Heller-Wilensky, Sara. "Isaac Arama on the Creation and Structure of the World." In *PAAJR* 22 (1953): 131–49.

———. *Mishnato ha-Philosophit shel R. Yizhak Arama.* Jerusalem: Mossad Bialik, 1956.

Herst, Roger E. "Where God and Man Touch: An Inquiry into Maimonides' Doctrine of Divine Overflow." In *CCAR Journal* 23 (1976): 16–21.

Horowitz, Yehoshua. "Halakhot Gedolot." In *Encyclopaedia Judaica,* vol. 7, cols. 1167–70. Jerusalem: Keter, 1971.

Hyman, Arthur. "Maimonides' Thirteen Principles." In Alexander

Altmann, ed. *Jewish Medieval and Renaissance Studies,* Cambridge: Harvard University Press, 1967, pp. 119–44.

*Ibn Ezra, Abraham. *Perush al ha-Torah.*

Idelson, A. Z. *Jewish Liturgy and Its Development.* New York: Schocken, 1972.

*Isaac ben Joseph of Corbeil. *Amudei Golah* [*Sefer Mizvot Katan*]. Jerusalem, 1960.

Jacobs, Louis. *Principles of the Jewish Faith.* New York: Basic Books, 1964.

———. *Studies in Talmudic Logic and Methodology.* London: Valentine, Mitchell, 1961.

Jaulus, Heinrich. "Simon ben Zemach Duran." In *MGWJ* 23 (1874): 241–59, 308–17, 355–66, 398–412, 447–63, and 499–514.

Judah Halevy. *Kuzari.*

Karo, Joseph. *Kesef Mishnah.*

*[Kayyera, Simeon?]. *Halakhot Gedolot.*

Kellner, Menachem Marc. "Gersonides and His Cultured Despisers: Arama and Abravanel." In *Journal of Medieval and Renaissance Studies* 6 (1976): 269–96.

———. "Maimonides and Gersonides on Mosaic Prophecy." *Speculum* 52 (1977): 62–79.

———. "R. Isaac Abravanel on the Principles of Judaism." In *Journal of the American Academy of Religion (Supplement)* 45 (1977): 1183–1200.

———. "R. Levi ben Gerson: A Bibliographical Essay." In *Studies in Bibliography in Booklore* 12 (1979): 13–23.

Lazaroff Allan. "The Theology of Abraham Bibago." Ph.D. diss., Brandeis University, 1973.

Lerner, Ralph. "Natural Law in Albo's Book of Roots." In Joseph Cropsey, ed. *Ancients and Moderns.* New York: Basic Books, 1964, pp. 132–47.

*Maimonides. *Commentary on the Mishnah, Seder Zeraim, Introduction.* Translated by Fred Rosner as *Moses Maimonides' Commentary on the Mishnah: Introduction to Seder Zeraim and Commentary on Tractate Berachoth,* New York: Feldheim, 1975.

*———. *Commentary on the Mishnah.* Tractate Sanhedrin, Chapter Ten *(Perek Ḥelek).* Editions and translations cited: Abelson,

Joshua, "Maimonides on the Jewish Creed." In *Jewish Quarterly Review* (O.S.) 19 (1907): 24–58;

Friedlaender, Israel. *Selections from the Arabic Writings of Maimonides*, Leiden: Brill, 1909, reprint edition: Leiden: Brill, 1951.

Gottlieb, M. *Perush ha-Mishnah la-Rambam, Masseket Sanhedrin.* Hanover, 1906.

Holzer, J. *Zur Geschichte der Dogmenlehre in der jüdischen Religionsphilosophie des Mittelalters: Mose Maimûni's Einleitung zu Chelek.* Berlin: M. Poppelauer, 1901.

Kafaḥ, Joseph. *Mishnah im Perush Rabbenu Moshe ben Maimon*, vol. 4. Jerusalem: Mossad ha-Rav Kook, 1964.

Rabinovitch, Mordecai Dov. *Rabbenu Moshe ben Maimon: Hakdamot li-Perush ha-Mishnah.* Mossad ha-Rav Kook, 1961.

Wolf, Arnold Jacob. "Maimonides on Human Immortality." In *Judaism* (15) 1966: 95–101, 211–16, and 337–42. Reprinted in Isadore Twersky, ed. *A Maimonides Reader.* New York: Behrman House, 1972, pp. 401–23.

*———. *Guide of the Perplexed.* Translated by Shlomo Pines. Chicago: University of Chicago Press, 1963.

*———. *Sefer ha-Madda.* Translated by Moses Hyamson. New York: Feldheim, 1974.

*———. *Sefer ha-Miẓvot.* Translated by Charles B. Chavel. 2 vols. London: Soncino Press, 1967.

*———. *Treatise on Resurrection.* Edited by Joshua Finkel. New York: American Academy for Jewish Research, 1939.

Malter, Henry, ed. *The Tractate Ta'anit of the Babylonian Talmud.* Philadelphia: Jewish Publication Society, 1928.

**Mekhilta de Rabbi Ishmael.* Translated by Jacob Z. Lauterbach. 3 vols. Philadelphia: Jewish Publication Society, 1933.

**Midrash Rabbah.* Translated under the editorship of H. Freedman and M. Simon. London: Soncino, 1933.

**Midrash Tanḥuma (Yelamdenu).* Edited by Solomon Buber. Vilna: Romm, 1885.

Midrash Tehilim.

Mihaly, Eugene, "Isaac Abravanel on the Principles of Faith." In *HUCA* 26 (1955): 481–502.

Minkin, Jacob. *Abarbanel and the Expulsion of the Jews from Spain.* New York: Behrman House, 1938.

*Moses ben Jacob of Coucy. *Sefer Miẓvot Gadol.* Kopys, 1807.

*Naḥmanides [Moses ben Nahman]. *Perush ha-Ramban al ha-Torah.* Edited by Charles B. Chavel. 2 vols. Jerusalem: Mossad ha-Rav Kook, 1977. English translation by Charles B. Chavel *(Commentary on the Torah).* 5 vols. New York: Shiloh, 1971–76.

———. *Hasagot al Sefer ha-Mizvot.*

Netanyahu, Benzion. *Don Isaac Abravanel: Statesman and Philosopher.* 3rd ed. Philadelphia: Jewish Publication Society, 1972.

Neumark, David. *The Principles of Judaism,* Appendix to Volume I, numbers 3 and 4, of *Journal of Jewish Lore and Philosophy.* Cincinnati, 1919. Reprint: New York, 1920.

———. *Toledot ha-Ikkarim bi-Yisrael.* 2 vols. Odessa: Moriah, 1912 and 1919.

Nissim ben Reuben Gerondi. *Perush al Bereshit.* Edited by Leon Feldman. Jerusalem: Makhon Shalem, 1968.

Nuriel, Abraham. "Mishnato ha-Philosophit shel R. Abraham ben Shem Tov Bibago." Ph.D. diss., Hebrew University, 1975.

Pirkei de Rabbi Eliezer. Translated by Gerald Friedlander. London, 1916.

Plato. *Timaeus.*

Rabinowitz, Abraham Hirsch. *Taryag.* Jerusalem: Boys Town, 1967.

*Rashi. *Commentary on Sanhedrin.*

Rawidowicz, Simon. "On Maimonides' Sefer ha-Madda." In his *Studies in Jewish Thought.* Philadelphia: Jewish Publication Society, 1974, pp. 317–23.

Reines, Alvin. *Maimonides and Abarbanel on Prophecy.* Cincinnati: Hebrew Union College Press, 1970.

Rosenberg, Shalom. "Torat ha-Shemot bi-Philosophia ha-Yehudit bimei ha-Benayim." *Iyyun* 27 (1976–77): 105–44.

*Sa'adia ben Joseph al Fayyumi. *Book of Beliefs and Opinions.* Translated by Samuel Rosenblatt. New Haven: Yale University Press, 1948.

Sarachek, Joseph. *Don Isaac Abarbanel.* New York: Bloch, 1938.

Schechter, Solomon. "The Dogmas of Judaism." In *Studies in*

Judaism (First Series). Philadelphia: Jewish Publication Society, 1905, pp. 147–81.

Scholem, Gershom. *Major Trends in Jewish Mysticism.* New York: Schocken, 1954.

Schweid, Eliezer. "Bein Mishnat ha-Ikkarim shel R. Joseph Albo li-Mishnat ha-Ikkarim shel ha-Rambam." In *Tarbiz* 33 (1963–64): 74–84.

Schweid, Eliezer. *Ha-Philosophia ha-Datit shel Rabbi Hasdai Crescas.* Jerusalem: Makor, 1970.

Sifra.

Sifri.

Sever, Moshe. *Mikhlol ha-Ma'amarim veha-Pitgamim.* 3 vols. Jerusalem: Mossad ha-Rav Kook, 1961.

Steinschneider, Moritz. "Abraham Bibago's Schriften." In *MGWJ* 32 (1883): 79–96 and 125–44.

Stieglitz, Ya'akov. "Yod-Gimmel ha-Ikkarim shel ha Rambam." In *Sinai* 58 (1965): 58–61.

Trend, J. B. and Loewe, R., eds. *Isaac Abarbanel: Six Lectures.* Cambridge: Cambridge University Press, 1937.

Twersky, Isadore, ed. *A Maimonides Reader.* New York: Behrman House, 1972.

―――. *Rabad of Posquières.* Cambridge: Harvard University Press, 1962.

Urbach, Symcha Bunim. *Mishnato ha-Philosophit shel Rabbi Hasdai Crescas* (volume 3 of his *Amudei ha-Mahshava ha-Yisraelit*). Jerusalem: World Zionist Organization, 1960.

Waxman, Meyer. "Maimonides as Dogmatist." In *CCAR Yearbook* 45 (1935): 397–418.

Werblowsky, R. J. Zvi. *Joseph Karo: Lawyer and Mystic.* Philadelphia: Jewish Publication Society, 1977.

Wolfson, Harry Austryn. *Crescas' Critique of Aristotle.* Cambridge: Harvard University Press, 1929.

―――. "The Plurality of Immovable Movers in Aristotle and Averroës." In *Harvard Studies in Classical Philology* 63 (1958): 233–53.

Ya'ari, Abraham. *Ha-Defus ha-Ivri bi-Kushta.* Jerusalem: Magnes Press, 1967.

Yalkut Shim'oni.

Biblical Passages Appearing in the Text

Rabbinic Passages Appearing in or Referred to in the Text

Index